THE CONQUERING INDIAN

Romans 8:37

"...We are more than conquerors through Him who loved us."

Compiled by Mark Ward, Sr.

Indian Life Books

Intertribal Christian Communications (Canada) Inc.
PO Box 3765 RPO Redwood Centre
Winnipeg Manitoba R2W 3R6 Canada

THE
CONQUERING
INDIAN

Compiled by Mark Ward, Sr.

Copyright © 1994 by
Indian Life Ministries

Unless otherwise marked, all scripture quotations are from *The
Holy Bible, New Life Version,* published by Christian Literature
International, Canby, Oregon, and are used by permission.

Cover art and design by Don Monkman.

ISBN 0-920379-13-3

Printed in Canada

DEDICATION

This book is dedicated by the board and staff of Indian Life Ministries to the following men who, over the years, have made *Indian Life Magazine* an effective tool of ministry among Native North Americans. It is through their ministry of writing, that many Aboriginal people have found Jesus as their Saviour. It is because of their effort that this book has been made possible.

Raymond L. Gowan: Founder of *Indian Life Newspaper* and editor from 1967- 1976, and from 1978 - 1979. He also edited 11 issues of the *Native Times Newspaper* from 1986-1987. With the publication of this book, Mr. Gowan celebrates his 80th birthday and 60 years of ministry, of which 45 years have been in Aboriginal work.

Tom Claus: Editor of the *Indian Life Newspaper* with Mr. Gowan as contributing editor from 1976-1978.

Chuck Fiero: Founder of *The Indian Christian* and editor from 1968-1972.

Dan Wetzel: Editor of *The Indian Christian* from 1972-1974

George McPeek: Founder of Intertribal Christian Communications and editor of *The Indian Christian* from 1974-1980 when the two publications merged to create *Indian Life Magazine*. Mr. McPeek continued in the role of editor until 1988.

Jim Uttley: Editor of *Indian Life* from 1988-1992

Mark Ward, Sr.: Interim editor from 1992-1993

Ed Hughes: Interim editor 1993-1994

Don Monkman: Graphic Artist of *Indian Life Magazine* from 1986 till present. Don has brought a consistant artistic quaility to the magazine over the years.

PREFACE

Hello, friend. My name is Ray Gowan. I'm happy to introduce you to *The Conquering Indian*.

As a boy, I got started down the wrong track. Before long I had a number of thefts charged up against me. But, before I was 17, I found a wonderful Friend. He wiped my record clean. He changed my life. He gave me great peace. He kept me out of jail and our State prison. He didn't care that I was dirt poor, part Indian and a nobody in other people's eyes. That's right! He loved me with a deep love like I had never known before. I think you've already guessed my Friend's Name. His Name is Jesus!

No, I didn't meet my Friend in church. People can meet Him anywhere for He is everywhere in the Person of the Holy Spirit. Yes, He is right where you are just now. You may think that Jesus has no interest in you. But no matter who you are or what you have done...just remember that the Bible tells us about a great sinner who simply cried out, "God, be merciful to me, a sinner..." God heard that man's prayer and changed his life. God has power to change the worst of sinners.

This book, *The Conquering Indian*, has many stories of people just like you, just like me. When they met Jesus, these people's lives were changed for good, as mine was, as yours can be today.

My friend, *The Conquering Indian* has been made possible because concerned Christians have given their dollars so you could have this book. Jesus, the Friend of all sinners, gave more. He gave His life on the Cross so you could become, through faith in Him, a Conquering Indian.

To find Christ, you may want to use the suggested helps and prayer at the end of this book. If you are in an institution and you need a Bible, please write to me at the following address:

Ray Gowan

Indian Life Ministries

PO Box 3765 RPO Redwood Centre

Winnipeg MB R2W 3R6

I may never see you face to face here on earth. "But whoever puts his trust in the Son has life that lasts forever." (John 3:36)

So, go for it! Confess and forsake your sins. Dare to believe and trust the Son (Jesus) for your salvation. You will be glad you did! And in heaven we will meet!

Covenant to meet me there.

Ray Gowan

Ray Gowan
June 30, 1994

FOREWORD

You are holding in your hands a very special book. Why is this book so special? Let me explain.

When Jesus helped people, the Bible says they often told others. Once a blind man was healed and the people gathered around and asked, "What do you say about Him since He opened your eyes?" The man simply replied, "One thing I know. I was blind, but now I can see. If this Man were not from God, He would not be able to do anything like this" (John 9:25, 33 NLB). His statement was so powerful that the proud religious law-keepers forced him out of the place of worship. Today the church calls this "sharing your testimony."

When a person tells how Christ changed his life, such true stories give hope that He can do the same for you and me. Preachers can talk for hours about salvation from sin. But when a Native person tells how Christ changed his life, it can give hope to other Natives who struggle with life's problems.

Now for the first time in one book, The Conquering Indian lets readers appreciate the richness and scope of Native Christian testimonies and faith experiences. Since 1967, when the predecessor of Indian Life Magazine first appeared as a newspaper, each issue has featured stories of First Nations people who have come to know Christ as their Saviour. From these pages, seventy of the best stories have been selected and then grouped into ten chapters according to the problems Aboriginal people often face in life. You will read how Christ has helped Native people overcome destructive habits and attitudes, broken families and relationships, and much more.

All the stories in this book are true. However, if you try to look them up in past issues of Indian Life Magazine, that will only hinder your enjoyment of the book. Several factors made it necessary to edit the text of the original articles: (1) Some testimonies have been shortened and others expanded so that all stories are comparable in length. (2) To help the book flow smoothly, testimonies have been edited for consistent style and first-person narration. (3) In giving the book an overall purpose and organization, testimonies have been edited to emphasize chapter topics and strengthen explanations of Biblical principles. (4) With so many stories, which often happened many years ago, it was not possible to see how these people are doing today. No effort has been made to "update" any of the stories. Some individuals are now home with the Lord, and others may have fallen into new problems. For that reason, and because the circumstances of some people may have changed so they would now prefer to avoid publicity, the names and home reservations in each testimony have been deleted. We believe it is enough that all stories were true when first published, and trust they are still a blessing today.

This new book, The Conquering Indian, can be used in different ways to meet your individual needs, or the stories can be read simply for enjoyment and encouragement. They are also excellent to read with children and other family members who do not know who Jesus Christ is and what He can do for them. Since testimonies are arranged in chapters according to various life problems, you or your church can use copies to counsel people who are experiencing these troubles. Finally, each chapter concludes with a brief "Things to Think About" section so the book can be used for personal or group Bible study.

Mark Ward, Sr.
Montclair, Virginia
June 30, 1994

ABOUT THE AUTHOR

Mark Ward, Sr., is a professional writer who has authored more than 300 articles in numerous national publications. He is editor of the Directory of Religious Media, published annually by National Religious Broadcasters, and has edited six national magazines with more than half a million circulation. His interest in Native American ministries led him in 1992 to serve as interim editor of Indian Life Magazine and to supervise introduction of its new design. Mark lives in Montclair, Virginia, with his wife and two children.

CONTENTS

Chapter 9
Conquering Pride and Self

Chapter 10
Conquering Apathy and Indifference

CHAPTER ONE

Conquering Alcohol and Drugs

1. The Shock Treatment That Healed My Soul

Key Verse - Romans 3:23

"For all men have sinned and have missed the shining greatness of God."

As a shy teenager, alcohol seemed to help her courage. That's how she ended up living with a man she met at graduation. Soon she was pregnant and the two were married. Then his real personality came out, and it wasn't very pleasant. His drunken rages eventually drove her to the same kind of behavior she hated.

THE BACK DOOR creaked open and banged shut. It was one o'clock in the morning. My husband was back. He had been away for days. By the way he entered, I could tell it would be another one of those nights. "How come everyone's asleep?" he demanded. "Because it's one o'clock in the morning, and keep your voice down because the children are sleeping," I answered nervously. But he wasn't satisfied and shot back, "Why are they sleeping?

Shouldn't they be getting ready for school?" Then he slid into a kitchen chair and slumped over on the table.

I asked where he had been and how much he drank. But I was interrupted by his loud and angry voice. "It's none of your business where I've been! And you wouldn't fool me if you said you've been here with the kids all this time. I know better than that! Don't try to tell me you're so pure." I shook my head. Almost from the day we met, he had always been a wanderer. He didn't travel that much, he just didn't stay around home that much. And he didn't just stick to me. There were other women.

That was hard for me to take. I came from a strict religious family and grew up in a rural community in northern Manitoba. Marriage and family were supposed to be sacred. But it didn't seem that way now. My husband was right, I wasn't that pure myself. As a lonely teenager I had used alcohol to fill my emptiness, but it only made me more lonely. When I met my husband at my high school graduation, he seemed to be the special friend I always wanted. We hit it right off and soon we were living together. When I got pregnant several months later, we decided to get married.

After my child was born, I was so happy. But the contentment only lasted for a while. Though I didn't know it then, people cannot take the place of God. The loneliness returned, especially when I started having problems with my husband. Either he had changed, or I was just now beginning to see how he really was. As our fighting got worse, he drank more heavily and spent more time away from home. It was very hard, because he would leave me with our little baby and go off for days. He never told me where he was going or when he'd be back. He'd just walk out the door. I wouldn't see him for several days and then he would come drunk and often in a rage.

During my difficult times I sometimes turned to church. But more often I turned to what I used to do in school—go out drinking with my friends. After eights years with my husband, I didn't want to be married anymore. He had often walked out on me and was unfaithful almost from the start. To tell the truth, I wasn't always faithful either. But we only hurt ourselves by trying to take revenge through other relationships. I knew it was wrong for marriages to be destroyed, but felt that separation was my only choice.

Deep down the separation bothered me. So I started drinking more than ever. I hurt a lot of people, especially my children, but I just didn't care. Then at my lowest point, God brought a special friend into my life. She told me about Jesus but at first I didn't want to listen. I wanted nothing to do with another religion, when the faith of my family wasn't doing me any good. Yet one day she said something that made me stop and think. I had told her my belief, that people were at peace when they died and done forever with pain and sorrow. "Only if they are born again," she replied. I remembered a Bible verse she once told me, "For all men have sinned and have missed the shining greatness of God" (Romans 3:23, NLB). After two months more of wrestling with Jesus, I surrendered my life to Him and asked Him to change me.

Still, my old habits were hard to break. I was glad He forgave my past sins, but hadn't really let Jesus take control of the things I was doing now. In time I was back to drinking and fooling around, so you couldn't tell any difference between my life now and my life before trusting Christ. I was doing the things I accused my husband of doing—leaving my kids for long periods and, worst of all, getting involved with another man. That's when God allowed something to happen that brought me back to Himself. The correction was so difficult I never want to go through it again. I found myself pregnant with another man's child.

It was almost more than I could bear. I knew then that it was totally wrong to live this way. Now God had to "shock" me back to my senses. Yet he brought good from a bad situation, for this unwanted child brought me back to the Lord. This time I gave Him total control of my life—and I meant it. I began to have a real burden for my husband and asked God to restore our marriage and the love I once had for him. But that was not to be, because eight months later he was killed in a car accident while out drinking with some friends.

With my husband gone forever out of my life, I am now responsible for three children. It's a privilege and I enjoy them very much, as I try to bring them up in God's way. The Lord has been faithful in providing for our needs, often through special Christian friends who help us. Today I am attending Bible college to learn more about God, for my desire is to live for Him and serve Him. I really believe a Christian who lives for himself, and does not practice what he believes, is the most miserable person on earth. He knows better! And its a tragedy if alcohol keeps him from knowing the Lord and living for Him.

2. God Found Me in a Cardboard Box

Key Verse - Philippians 2:13

"He is working in you. God is helping you obey Him. God is doing what He wants done in you."

From the beginning he was a misfit, an unwanted and illegitimate Indian. He tried being good to earn praise. Then people expected him to be good, and as a teenager he went bad to get their attention. Soon the alcohol and drugs started. His wife gave this Chippewa man a clear choice, and he made it!

NO SOONER HAD I walked in the door, when my wife said to me, "I want you to make a decision." Putting a quart of whiskey on the table, she gave me an order demanding that I make a choice. "This bottle or our marriage!" she demanded. "That's easy," I replied. I picked up the bottle and told my wife, "See you later!" By now my two daughters, four and five years old, had come into the room. "Daddy, please don't go!" they cried. I walked to the front door, picking them up in my arms. "Honey, I love you very much, but I have to leave." That's all I said. With that I walked out the door, never to see them again for seventeen years.

For some, this experience would have seemed like the end. But for me, it was just more of the same. My life had been a downer from the start. I was born to an unwed Chippewa mother and left at birth in a Wisconsin orphanage. At age two I was placed in a foster home and lived there for the next fifteen years. Even before I started school I felt "different," an unwanted misfit who did not belong. Growing up, these feelings plagued me every day—rejection, hate, loneliness, fear. Because I was always getting beaten up by older kids, I learned to fight first and speak later. That's how I released my feelings.

In high school I was a star athlete and a good student. These accomplishments brought me praise and acceptance, so I worked hard. But after a while people thought it was normal for me to do these things, and the praise stopped. When I was fifteen, I started hanging around with a bad crowd. I did terrible things so the gang would praise me. That year I began drinking, and was arrested and put in jail for stealing a car.

At seventeen, I received a scholarship to play football at the University of California. There I earned two college degrees. But I also got involved in the drug scene, using heroin and morphine. Before long my habit was costing $250 to $300 a day. To get the money, I began making deliveries for drug dealers. It paid very well and I made a lot of money doing it.

During my college days I met and married my wife, and soon we had two daughters. It was after six years of marriage that she demanded I chose between her and the bottle. I chose the bottle, and kept on delivering drugs. Not long after our marriage broke up, I got busted and ended up in prison for seven years. By the time I was released, my wife had divorced me and I had no idea where she and my daughters were. So I went right back to what I did best, drinking alcohol and using drugs. In the years ahead I drifted all across the country—Los Angeles, Chicago, Minneapolis and everywhere in between.

My string ran out in St. Paul, Minnesota. I was picked up 104 times by the police for drunkenness. They sent me to the drying-out unit more than 100 times. I was placed in fifteen different treatment centers. Finally they said there was no hope and told me not to come back. Then one night, it was December and very cold. I was sleeping in a cardboard box. In a dream I saw myself dying and woke up terrified! "God, if You're real," I cried out, "then I ask that You take my life. I don't want to live anymore. I've made a mess of my life. I've hurt a lot of people and I'm sorry for what I've done. If You're for real, then please take my life!"

After a while, I got up from the snow and walked over to the rescue mission. A man there was talking about how Jesus died on the cross for our sins. He said I no longer had to walk in the guilt of judgment over the things of the past, that Jesus could set me free. The man asked if anyone wanted to make a decision and let Christ take control of his life. My hand shot up automatically. Then he asked us to come to the front of the chapel, but I got scared. So I bullied two other drunks into coming down the aisle with me, and all three of us gave our lives to Jesus that night!

In my case, God delivered me instantly from the

desire to drink and do drugs. I stayed and worked at the mission for a year, as they helped me study the Bible and grow in my faith. There I met and married a godly Christian woman. For five years we ministered to people on the streets, before I returned to the rescue mission as chaplain. Today I still serve there, and after becoming an ordained minister I have also begun a ministry to the homeless and addicted. Each day I am thankful that, "God is working in you. God is helping you obey Him. God is doing what He wants done in you. For God did not give us a spirit of fear. He gave us a spirit of power [discipline] and of love and of a good mind" (Philippians 2:13, 2 Timothy 1:7).

After becoming a Christian, I began faithfully praying that the Lord would get me back together with my children. I drove to northern Wisconsin and found out where they lived. When we met, both my daughters cried with tears of joy and welcomed me back with open arms! They were both married, and one of them had a son. But for all those years they saved the things I had bought them as little girls, hoping someday I would be back.

Then I got up the nerve to call my foster mother. I was the last of thirteen foster children she had raised, and she had always prayed for me. We had not seen each other for many years, and until now I did not even know if she was still alive. For her part, she had prayed for me all those years, not knowing what had become of me. When she met me at the door, tears were streaming down her cheeks. Then I told her how Jesus had saved me, and we cried together.

A year later I got a call telling me she was very ill.

She was on her deathbed when I saw her, but had a great big smile. "All my dreams and prayers have been answered," she told me. We visited for a while and had a wonderful talk. Then I had to leave. But as I turned to go, the last thing I ever heard her say was, "God really does answer prayer!"

3. Up the Creek in Downtown Denver
Key Verse - 2 Timothy 2:20-21

"In a big house there are not only things made of gold and silver but also of wood and clay. Some are of more use than others. Some are used every day. If a man lives a clean life , he will be like a dish made of gold. He will be respected and set apart for good use by the owner of the house."

How does a Christian live by faith? After years of wondering, he found the answer and began serving God faithfully in his church. Then it came time for a big decision in his life, and this Creek man left God out of his thinking. Things went down hill from there, and he ended up drunk and homeless on a city sidewalk.

IT WAS APRIL Fool's Day. I had just gotten off a big drinking binge and was wandering around downtown Denver. People were staring at me. I must have looked really out of place. It was the financial district and all around me were executives in expensive suits, while I was wearing an old coat with a hood and carrying a scuffed-up suitcase. My face had not seen a razor in a long time, and I was dirty and smelly and looked bad. I had hit bottom and I knew it—and so did everyone else who saw me. I was running. Running from the Lord. For eleven years I had traded everything I had for alcohol. Now He was closing in on me.

I am a Creek Indian from Oklahoma, where my grandfather was a medicine man and our family was deeply into the old ways of doing things. When I was fourteen, my family moved to far western Oklahoma where no other native people lived. Because I was accustomed to Indians ways, I became a loner and had few friends. However, there was a small gospel church near our house and some white people from there would visit us. They invited me to Vacation Bible School and that's when I first heard about Jesus. That name stuck in my mind and I started going to the church on Sundays to learn more. After a while, though I don't remember the exact date, I trusted Christ as my Savior. I was serious and really meant it, but still had many questions about how I should live my life as a Christian believer.

In high school I drifted away from the church. I really didn't do anything bad, not even drinking or fooling around with friends or girls. After graduation I went to college and there I met my wife. She belonged to a Christian students group and got me going to church again. It was fun, but I still had questions about how to live as a Christian. We graduated after two years and moved to California, where we attended a native church. My questions became more urgent as I felt God calling me to live for Him. But how? I had a talk with the pastor and, with his help, made a real commitment to giving the Lord control of my life. For the next seven years my wife and I served God faithfully in that church.

Then we moved back to Oklahoma. I think that is where my problems began. We really did not pray about whether to move, but just went ahead without seeking to know if this was God's will. From the beginning, His blessing did not seem to be with us. Things just did not go right with our move and our new life in Oklahoma. Before long I fell away from God and got caught up in alcohol and drugs. But God kept after me. All the time, it seemed, I would hear His name or see it in print. Then I would feel really guilty inside. However, I did not stop what I was doing.

After a while, I got so sick of the booze and the guilt, I tried to commit suicide—twice. When it did not work I was in a bad spot. I did not want to live and yet I could not die. This is when I began to sense there was no getting away from God. I left like He was chasing me, so I ran. But His Spirit followed me through Texas, Arizona and finally to Colorado. The more I ran, the more I felt His call. It seemed like He was saying, "It's about time you stopped doing all of this. You're not getting any younger, and I need you to do something for Me."

Things came to a head that day as I was walking through the financial district of Denver. I suddenly got a big lump in my throat. I tried to swallow but could not. I felt like I was going to pass out, and at last in desperation I sat down on my suitcase in the middle of the busy sidewalk. Then I cried like a baby. Tears were running down my face. It started to snow and I looked up at the sky. A patch of clear blue was framed between two tall glass skyscrapers, and I felt like I was looking at a cathedral. At that moment it seemed the Lord had caught up with me!

I knew my problems would not go away unless I asked God to help. And that is what I did. In a choked-up voice I cried out, "Lord, I give up. I'm tired of running away from You. I've gone as far as I can go. I've hit bottom and the only way I can go is up. Lord, forgive me for what I have done." The choking lump in my throat went away, and I felt like a brand new person. My first thought was to call my wife. It was months since I had seen her, and over the years I would only drop in once in a while. I hardly knew my children. But at that moment, I had to tell her what had happened and ask her forgiveness too.

There was only one problem. I had no money for the telephone. Now this old coat I was wearing had maybe a dozen small pockets all over the place. I had been through all the pockets hundreds of times during the last month, searching for money to buy booze. Suddenly my stiff, cold fingers felt something. It was a quarter! I walked to the bus station and called my wife. It was hard to talk because I had started crying again. But when she heard my story, it was her turn to cry. "I don't have any money," I told her, "but if you can send me a bus ticket, I want to come home."

Those were some of the hardest words I have ever had to say. But since then, the Lord has begun to bless my life again. That very day, God took away my desire for alcohol. Before I could not go a day without it and now I was set free! After I got my life back in order, and found God told me the truth—there was some work He wanted me to do. He wanted me to serve Him, and today I am a church pastor ministering to the Chosen and Arapaho people of Wyoming.

I guess that I was like a clean glass that was taken outside and dropped in the dirt (2 Timothy 2:20-21). But once I let the Lord pick me up and wash me off, I was a vessel ready to be used again. And I am so glad I don't have to run anymore. Life is so much better when you walk with the Lord instead of running away from Him!

4. God's Wine Now Fills My Cup

Key Verse - Proverbs 23:31,32

"Do not look at wine when it is red, when it shines in the cup, when it is smooth in going down. In the end it bites like a snake. It stings like the bite of a snake with poison."

Alcohol was everywhere. Her parents drank, so she ran away and joined her own drinking crowd. When her boyfriend left their home and children for a binge, this Cheyenne-Pawnee-Ute woman would retaliate by doing the same. The child welfare agency was ready to end the cycle, until she found a different way.

I WAS LOOKING for friends and thought I would find them through drinking. All I wanted was to be with people, to feel like I belonged. But I soon found alcohol was a thief, not a friend. It stole my parents from me, and now alcohol was robbing me of every hope I had for happiness. "In the end," as I at last discovered, "it bites like a snake" (Proverbs 23:32).

Alcohol first affected my life at the age of four. My parents were both alcoholics and felt they could not look after my younger brother and I anymore. So they sent us away to live with my grandmother in the country, where our family are members of the Cheyenne, Pawnee and Southern Ute tribes. We lived with her for eleven years. Grandma was kind, but kept a spotless house. Being the oldest child and only girl, I had to work very hard. By the time I was five, I had learned to cook, do dishes and wash clothes. And I had to look after my brother and two little cousins who also lived with us. But Grandma took us to Sunday School and I liked that very much. I enjoyed the singing and Bible stories. I also learned about Jesus, but did not come to know Him as my Savior. My mind was too full of questions about why I had to live without my parents.

When I was fifteen, my mother took us back. She had been living with my father off and on over the years, and now I had two sisters and another brother. Mom had a good job at the time, but she still drank. Sometimes she would disappear and, because I was the oldest, I had to look after the family. I was so disappointed with my mother that I started rebelling to get attention. I sniffed glue, then tried killing myself, but none of it worked. Finally, after high school I just decided to run away.

I spent a year in Salt Lake City with a rough crowd. Then I met a guy from Canada and spent six months living in Alberta. However, I got word that one of my cousins had hung himself in jail and was dead. I had lived with him for so many years, I considered him my brother. So I came home to Colorado and found a job as a teacher's aide. That made me want to attend college, and after a while I left for school in Albuquerque. That's when I really started running with the drinking crowd. I did not enjoy the booze, but the kids were friendly and I wanted people to like me.

Through all the parties, I met the man who would become my husband. We got to know each other and moved in together. Before long I was pregnant and we moved to my mom's place in Colorado. I agreed to care for his two-year-old daughter from a previous marriage, and then there were three of us. By the time our baby was born, my boyfriend's drinking was out of control. He would "go to the store" and not return for a couple of days. Then he came home in a drunken rage, accusing me of running around on him and not loving his daughter.

The Bible is sure right when it says, "Wine makes people act in a foolish way. Strong drink starts fights. Whoever is fooled by it is not wise" (Proverbs 20:1). That described my boyfriend, and it wasn't too long before it described me. After a while of being mistreated, I decided to get even. When my boyfriend was sober I would run off and leave him with the children. Let him see how it felt! Then maybe he would stop beating me.

But things got so bad, the social services agency had to step in and take our children away. A few months went by, and after a big fight we decided getting married might turn our relationship around.

Then maybe his daughter would then respect my authority. Yet things never got better, just worse. He would party, come home and beat me, and I would call the police. When he wasn't running from the police, I was pounding my fist on the table and begging him to stop drinking.

Since my childhood I had drifted away from church. I still prayed for my husband on occasion, but I also wanted to pay him back. As the months went by, we lost our children to social services three or four times. Then we would get them back by promising to straighten up. We tried marriage counseling and alcohol treatment centers, but after a brief improvement the drinking would start again. And each time social services would come again and take the children. At last they said our children would be put up for adoption. I was really frightened and didn't know what I would do if I lost them for good.

A few months before, we had started going to church. I read my Bible a little and felt a bit closer to God, but I knew something was still missing. Then one night at a revival service, I came to a decision. I called the pastor and told him I was troubled and wanted to give my life to Jesus. I had tried to make deals with God before, but now I really meant it. The pastor prayed with me over the telephone, and I trusted Christ as my personal Savior. From that point on my behavior began to change. There was no more drinking and running away. My bitterness and hate toward the way people had treated me began to be replaced by the love of God. If God could forgive me, then I could forgive them.

After I decided to live my life as a Christian, my problems no longer seemed so heavy. Now I could pray about them and know the Lord would take care of them. This took away my need to worry, because God was in charge and He loved me. Later He answered my prayers and restored my children. He has given me many Christian friends who encourage me to remain faithful. My husband still goes off drinking sometimes, but even when I am crying God seems to say, "You can cry but there is nothing to worry about." He has become the Friend I was always looking for, the one I never found in alcohol.

5. Rocked to Sleep by Satan

Key Verse - 2 Thessalonians 1:8-9

"He will punish those who do not know God and those who do not obey the Good News of our Lord Jesus Christ. They will be punished forever and taken away from the Lord and from the shining greatness of his power."

Maybe it was the potent mix of drugs, alcohol and rock music. But suddenly this native woman was face to face with the reality of her life, and she could not stand it! Frantic for help against the evil that was claiming her, she found God was only a phone call away.

SEPTEMBER 16 WAS the most horrible, most wonderful and most important day of my life. It was about four in the afternoon. I had come home, the house was empty and so I turned on the radio. A rock band was playing one of my favorite songs. The words were, "For those who like to rock we salute you." Well, you know how wrong words can sometimes get in your head? You swear you heard them. It was like that now. Maybe it was the alcohol or dope in my system. I think it was God. But the words I heard were, "Satan we salute you," repeated over and over. It hit me with full force. I fell on my face and started to cry. Because the words were true. I had dedicated my life to Satan.

That realization shocked me. I was raised in a Christian home and taught to live in a respectful Christian manner. But my rebellion started early. I thought home was a prison where the jailers, my parents, regulated everything I did. I thought their religion was for old people and wanted nothing to do with it. Mom and dad had to drag me to church services, which I considered the ultimate boredom. As I became older, I discovered a whole world was out there waiting for me. Day by day I got more entangled with its pleasures. I yearned for excitement and adventure and satisfaction. That desire got me into drinking and then the drug scene.

When my parents moved us to Winnipeg, I took full advantage and began selling drugs and hanging around with rock bands. I rejected my family and rejected God. I could not even stand the thought of Him. But inside, though I would not admit it, I was lonely and empty and unhappy. Maybe that's why I let my parents drag me off once in a while to their new church in Winnipeg. It was different than all the others I had gone to. The people were sincerely friendly and genuinely happy. I could actually feel

God's presence in that church.

Then came September 16. I really came face to face with myself, and with the ultimate evil I had come to serve. To me the horror was indescribable. I became frantic and could not control myself. A voice kept telling me to overdose on a large amount of LSD that I had in my possession. I nearly did, and it took all my strength to resist. Finally I ran downstairs and threw myself on the kitchen table. I had to get out of the house! Then I saw the phone book lying on the table. Incredibly, someone had left it already open to the church listings!

I just called a number and was put in touch with a pastor's wife. She could not come over, but just then my father came home and agreed to drive me to her house. When I got to her home, I explained what I had just experienced. She asked if I knew what would have happened to me if I had died. I had to admit I did not know. Then she showed me from the Bible (Matthew 25:41; Revelation 14:10-11, 20:15) about a real place called hell. She made me understand that God is a holy God who cannot, by His very perfect nature, tolerate sin. It must be punished. Man is sinful—I know that from looking at my own life. Man's sins must be punished. This is the everlasting torment of hell, where man is separated from God forever (2 Thessalonians 1:8-9).

I realized that I did not want to go to hell. But then the pastor's wife gave me the Good News. The Lord loved me so much, He did not want me to be punished and forever separated from Him. So He did the only thing that could save me. He paid the punishment Himself! When Jesus died on the cross,

He suffered the punishment for all my sin, so that I would not have to take that punishment if I put my trust in His sacrifice to save me. When I understood this, I got down on my knees with the pastor's wife and prayed to God. I admitted to Him that I was a sinner and asked Jesus to be the Savior I needed.

Then I was about to ask Him to take control of my life, when the words would not come out. I thought about all my alcohol and drugs and rock music and parties. Did I really want to give them up? Then it hit me like a ton of bricks! No way did I want anything to stand between me and God. I gave up my fight against God. He won. I surrendered my life to His complete control. Then an indescribable feeling swept over me of joy and peace, of being clean. What a day! The greatest horror of my life had been turned into the most wonderful thing I will ever experience.

6. Angel Learns How to Fly Higher

Key Verse - 1 Thessalonians 5:22

"Keep away from everything that even looks like sin."

This Muskokee man was still a teenage Navy recruit when a service accident left him with a fractured skull. Only pills could dull the pain. Soon he was hooked, locked into a pattern. When the guilt was too much, he took an overdose. And when he passed out, his wife called the medics. Over and over again.

I DIDN'T TRUST anybody, not even my wife. The white in me hated the Indian. The Indian in me hated the white. And the combination of the two hated everybody else. I'd been a bouncer, a bounty hunter, a professional wrestler. But I couldn't break the hold of pain and pills and alcohol that had brought me down for the count.

I was born in Florida, half Muskokee Indian and half Scot. When I was eleven, I said some words about Jesus I didn't really understand and tried to act like a Christian. But it didn't stick. Three years later I left Florida and the church behind, and got work in Texas as a bar room musician. Three more years and I joined the United States Navy. However, I was only in the service a short time before I was seriously injured. I lost half my right lung and fractured my skull, which caused brain damage. They discharged me, a frightened teenager, as 100 percent disabled.

For a while I just knocked around, not doing much of anything. My injury gave me a lot of pain, and that's how I got on dope. Pain became my excuse for doing my own thing. Before long I was taking from 28 to 56 pills a day, and chasing these down with booze. This kept me real high all the time. I followed this pattern for eighteen years. For a while I wrestled professionally—under the name of "Angel," though I was anything but a good guy. After that I worked as a bounty hunter, then a bar room musician and bouncer. I also took back cars when people fell behind in their payments. All the while I chased one woman after another.

It was during a wrestling match that I first met the woman who was to be my wife. We fell for each other and were later married. Neither of us were

Christians, but we stayed together. I still took my pills and alcohol, and she took care of me. Sometimes I would say, "I'm going to quit this stuff because it's not doing me any good." But within 24 hours I would start going through withdrawal and end up in really bad shape. Then I would go back to the pills.

This went on for many years. At times I would get so depressed about my life, I would purposely take an overdose of pills. My wife would wait until I got too weak to do anything, and then she would call the police. They would rush me to the hospital, pump my stomach and then lock me up for a couple weeks while I dried out. It never did any good. In three or four months the same thing would happen all over again. During this time I began having nightmares about being trapped in sewage and filth, while evil creatures came to get me. Though I figured the dreams were caused by the pills and booze, they frightened and bothered me.

Then I met someone who made a difference in my life. I was going to a mental health clinic at the veteran's hospital in New Orleans. Every other Wednesday, a young lieutenant from the Salvation Army would take us patients on an outing. I didn't trust him anymore than I trusted anybody else. But as time went by, there was something about him that seemed to get through to me. We talked quite a lot, though I was full of pills and alcohol. After a while he invited me to his church. Right away my defenses went up. So I gave him what I thought was a cute brush-off, "Maybe someday I'll surprise you and come."

But his invitation stuck in my mind. A month or so later I asked my wife and three sons if they wanted to go to church the next day. They all said yes. I was impressed how the Christians welcomed us with open arms. It didn't seem to matter that I was all boozed up and high on pills. They just took us right in and accepted us. So we came back for the Sunday evening service, and after that we started going every week.

After several weeks like this, our day of decision arrived. I can't remember what the sermon was about, but I can remember the date. It was July 12. That day our whole family, my wife and I along with our three sons, all went to the altar and trusted Jesus Christ as our Savior. But after the service I felt there was one more thing the Lord wanted me to do. In my bedroom that night, I got down on my knees and prayed, "Jesus, I gave you my heart this morning. Now I want to give you my body, for what it's worth. I know it's not much, but it's all I've got. If You want me to serve You, then take away all this booze and all these pills from me."

Then I picked up the liquor and the pills and flushed them down then toilet. I was determined to "keep away from everything that even looks like sin" (1 Thessalonians 5:22). My wife was scared because she had seen me quit before. In about 24 hours she expected the withdrawal pains to begin, and then I would be back on the pills. This was always a rough time for both of us, and she was afraid. But the Lord answered my prayer. When I poured those pills and the booze down the toilet, and asked God to take them away from me, He did just that! I had no withdrawal symptoms at all. And the great thing is when He took away the pills and alcohol, He also took the hatred that filled my life for so long.

I know God was behind this change, because later some things happened to me that proved it. If I had not been a Christian, these things would have made me wild and dangerous. I would have hurt someone. And because I was a 260-pound professional wrestler, and had studied martial arts in Japan, I could do a lot of damage. But God had truly taken my hate away, and I was no longer capable of hating and hurting. For the next several years I played music in church instead of in bars, and helped with the preaching and things like that. Then I got a problem with my lungs and the doctor said the air in Arizona might be good for me. So we packed everything up and moved west.

About three years later I was invited to some evangelistic meetings at the Cocopah Indian reservation in southwestern Arizona. When I got there and saw the mission church, I knew it was the place the Lord wanted me to be. I've been there ever since, and God has been doing a great work among our people. And He's been doing it one person at a time, the same way He did it with me. God keeps calling to us, and when we come of our own free will He changes our lives, cleans them up and makes them worth living. Today my wife and I have a great burden for the Indian people, and we pray every day that God will be the difference in your life too.

7. Baby's Cry Melts Stoned Heart
Key Verse - John 14:27

"I give you my peace and leave it with you. I do not give peace to you as the world gives. Do not let your hearts be troubled or afraid."

His parents let him down by divorcing. His school let him down by unfairly kicking him out. So this Cree teenager went to the city and found the drug scene. Later he found Jesus, but had nobody to keep him reading the Bible. Drugs were nearly strong enough to reclaim him, but God was there when it counted.

"DON'T TELL ME what to do," I yelled. "I can do whatever I want!" "But you're only thinking of yourself," my wife said. "What about me and the baby?" I couldn't care less, I thought, as we continued to argue. Then suddenly, I lost complete control of myself. All the anger that was building up inside let loose. In a few seconds, my wife was on the floor and I had a grip on her throat. Sure, I could do whatever I wanted! But in reality I was a slave, controlled by anger and hate and dope.

I learned to be independent the hard way. It was tough enough to leave my Cree reservation in northern Manitoba and go away to residential school. I never dreamed my home would be broken up by the time I returned the next summer. But it was. My mother had left and only dad was there to greet us four kids. That was my pattern for the next ten years. Off to boarding school for ten months, then two months at home with my dad each summer. Gradually I began to feel that the school was my home, and so I got to like it there.

Trouble began when I passed eighth grade with a low mark that I felt was undeserved. To show my resentment, the next fall I started stepping over the boundary lines and challenging the rules. This did not last long. I soon found myself facing the principal. He gave me the choice of obeying the rules or leaving. I chose to leave. Being sixteen, the city lights held a great attraction for me, more than the reservation. So that's where I headed. Many of my relatives already lived in Winnipeg, so I drifted from one to another until I got in trouble with the law.

After several weeks in a juvenile detention center, I was placed in a foster home. It was during this time that I was introduced to the drug world. Having heard so much about it, I was curious to learn more. I never hesitated when I had a chance to try some LSD. There were other kinds of drugs too, and I wanted to try them all! It was a strange new world, but I liked it. When I turned eighteen, I left the foster home to live on my own. I was soon drinking heavily, bumming around the main drag with my friends. We did anything for excitement.

Car theft and an attempted breaking-and-entering got me four months in jail camp. I did not enjoy that experience, but I had a lot of time to think about my life. And it was there I had my first real contact with Jesus. A preacher came and talked about "being saved." I had been brought up to believe in God, but I had never heard such words before. I tried to reason out what the preacher meant, but I could not. Yet a seed had been planted, and the notion of "being saved" stuck with me even after I was released.

Then I ran into a different kind of trouble. My girlfriend and I broke up. I was broken-hearted and needed something to fill my emptiness. One evening my sister invited me to a Bible study where I saw young people like myself talking about Jesus. It troubled me and at first I thought it was pretty weird. But that same night I trusted the Lord Jesus Christ as my personal Savior. This time I understood what was meant by "being saved." Yet I had no experience with other Christians or with the Bible, and didn't know how I should live for God.

My life was pretty messed up, and Satan began putting great bitterness in my heart. I hated the world and blamed society for my condition. My own heritage meant nothing, for I thought it was degrading to be an Indian. Everything seemed hopeless. There was no future for myself. I considered suicide but the thought of death terrified me, so I began to create my own little world.

Drinking and partying gave some good times, but gradually I turned more and more to dope. The effects it produced were beautiful to me. When I was stoned, all my problems would disappear. There was no death, no life, no worries, just colors and music. I loved it! Being high became natural to me. I smoked joints everywhere. Nothing mattered except my happiness. Dope cost big money, but I gladly worked overtime to support my habit. This was the drug scene and I made every effort to count myself in.

Girls never took the place of dope in my life, but I

did get involved with a few. That was when I met my wife. She had run away from home and together we found a place to live by ourselves. I soon ushered her into my far-out world of drugs and immorality. Everything was going fine, until one day she told me she was pregnant. It was bound to happen, but the situation became confusing and I was mainly concerned about myself. As she got bigger, I began to feel like an idiot when I took her out. So I would just leave her at home, sometimes for days, because I was unwilling to face reality.

When our baby girl was born, I was proud. But I knew a lot of changes were going to take place, and that made me angry. I wanted to meet my new responsibilities, but I didn't want to give up my dope and drinking. I was still a boy trying to have my unlimited dreams. That's why we got into that terrible argument. Nobody was going to mess up my life! But our baby's cries finally brought me to my senses. I let go of my wife and slowly got to my feet. She and the baby were both deeply hurt and crying, and it was all my fault. I fell on my knees and hugged my wife, and we cried together. "I'm sorry," I pleaded, "I love you and I do want to take care of you and the baby."

I never wanted such violence to happen again. My wife loved me and had put up with a lot, and I did not want to hurt her anymore. And I wanted something lasting in my life. But I realized now I could not do it by myself. That's when Jesus came into my mind. I remembered how I had become His child, and suddenly I had a desire to get rid of anything that stood between me and my Savior. In desperation I threw all my drugs and dope things into the garbage. Other things that had value I sold, like my records.

Having cut myself off from the past, I turned instead to Jesus. I found out that, even though I had given up on Him, He had not given up on me. I had fallen, and Christ was there to pick me up. And I had the joy of telling my wife about Jesus and seeing her become a brand new Christian! Since then we have gotten married and been blessed with another wonderful daughter. Today the words of Jesus have become very special to us, "I give you My peace and leave it with You. I do not give peace to you as the world gives. Do not let your hearts be troubled or afraid" (John 14:27). Now I am proud to be an Indian, but I am prouder still to be His Indian.

THINGS TO THINK ABOUT

1. The Shock Treatment That Healed My Soul

Alcohol and drugs may provide a short lift. But finally they end the way of all sin. Perhaps you, like the native woman in this story, are asking questions about that end. Read Romans 3:19-26. Why are all people guilty before God? What solution has God provided to make you right with Himself? How can you claim that solution?

2. God Found Me In a Cardboard Box

In your own strength, you cannot truly conquer sin—and it is sin that is the root cause of alcohol and drug abuse. Read Philippians 2:13 and 2 Timothy 1:7. In Whose strength can you overcome sin? In what ways does this help come to you?

3. Up the Creek in Downtown Denver

As a Christian, you have God's Spirit living within you, to help you obey Him. You need that help because you still have the "sin nature" with which all people are born. With His help you must fight that sin nature, or God cannot use you for His service. Read 2 Timothy 2:20-22. If you live a clean life, in what way will God use you? What attitudes are to be found in the person who desires to live cleanly?

4. God's Wine Now Fills My Cup

Ever wonder why alcohol is so closely tied to violence? Read Proverbs 20:1 and 23:29-35. Can you put in your own words what can happen, as described in these Bible verses, to a person who abuses alcohol? According to Proverbs 23:30-31, is the alcohol to blame or are you responsible?

5. Rocked to Sleep by Satan

During Bible times, as in native peyote religions, people who worshiped false gods often used drugs to open themselves to control by the spirit world. People who abuse drugs today also leave their minds open to Satan. The native woman in this story was shocked to find where this was leading her. Read Matthew 25:41, Revelation 20:15 and 2 Thessalonians 1:8-9. Is hell a real place? How do you know? According to 2 Thessalonians, what is the ultimate punishment?

6. Angel Learns How to Fly Higher

If you have struggled with a temptation, whether it is alcohol or drugs or pornography or gambling or rock music—anything that leads you away from God—then put it away from you. Don't have it around where it can be a temptation to you. Get rid of it! Read 1 Thessalonians 5:22-24. In staying away from sinful situations, what should you be striving for instead? Why would having sinful things nearby prevent you from reaching your spiritual goal? Why will God help you?

7. Baby' s Cry Melts Stoned Heart

Drugs and alcohol bring violence and grief and pain, while Jesus offers peace. Read John 14:25-27. Why is the peace Jesus offers different from the "peace" offered anywhere else in the world? How is God able to make this peace real and practical in your life?

CHAPTER TWO

Conquering Sexual Sins and AIDS

1. Labor Pains That Won't Stop

Key Verse - 1 Peter 2:16

"Obey as men who are free but do not use this to cover up sin. Live as servants owned by God at all times."

She was abused, deceived, and poorly advised—first by her family, then by her boyfriend, and now by people who said abortion was her only option. When it was all over, and even after she became a Christian the awful pain stayed with her. Today the sorrow lingers, but she has found the way to peace.

AT SEVENTEEN, unmarried and pregnant, I was the perfect victim. Though I had been misused all my life, I was about to experience the worst abuse a woman can ever suffer. I didn't know it at the time, but my doctors had already decided to abort my baby—whether I wished it or not.

My life was always rough. Both my parents were alcoholics and, since the age of nine, I had to become both mom and dad to my younger brother and sister. I don't remember the first time I was sexually abused. It was just a way of life. Everyone seemed to be involved—family friends, baby-sitters and relatives. At school I was always a failure, since looking after my brother and sister didn't leave much time for studying. My teachers figured I was just a lazy Indian and put me through a lot of embarrassment and discrimination.

My first boyfriend was white, so we had to sneak around to see each other. If I didn't give in to him, he didn't want me anymore. So for three years I went along with it, thinking this was the only love I could get. I didn't think I was worthy of a decent relationship. Then at age seventeen I got serious with another boy and we moved in together. I went to a clinic for birth control pills and also some vaccinations I needed. About six weeks later I discovered that I was pregnant, and we were both happy.

Then I read something about the pills and vaccines I had gotten, how they could damage an unborn child. The doctor said the only way to find if my baby had a problem was to wait until it was large enough for an ultrasound test. So my boyfriend and I prepared to wait. We were going to have a baby, and abortion wasn't even considered.

A short while later, we moved to another town. I went for a checkup and told my new doctor about my concerns for the baby. Right away, she sent me to a specialist in the city. Unknown to me, she had already decided my baby should be aborted. The specialist agreed and told me there was a 40 percent chance my baby was severely deformed. Abortion was the only option, he said.

Since I was under age, my mother had to sign a consent form. She refused, but the clinic scheduled an operation anyway for the next day. My mom found out and contacted a national pro-life organization, which sent a lawyer to help fight the system. The next day when I came for the operation, I found it was cancelled. I accepted that and determined to live with the consequences.

The day before I flew home, I told my aunt how my abortion was cancelled. She got angry. "It's a woman's right to choose an abortion. Your mother can't stop you!" Before I knew it, my aunt started directing my life. First she took me to the child welfare agency, where she did all the talking. They didn't even ask me what I thought or wanted. By the time my aunt was done, I was a ward of the province. My mother was charged with child abuse for withholding medical services.

As I listened to all they said, I began to believe them. But I was deceived. They talked about a "blob of tissue" and a "fetus." They didn't want me to think about a "baby." Once my aunt got custody of me, she signed the consent form for the abortion. I was 23 weeks pregnant, so the doctor described how he was going to give me a "saline" injection. But again I was deceived. He said there was a 50 percent chance of me dying if I waited for normal childbirth. Later I learned that in a modern hospital, this just doesn't happen anymore. He also didn't tell me I would give birth anyway, but to a dead child.

Nor did the doctor tell me the saline solution was a concentrated salt mixture that would literally eat away at my baby, inside and out, causing it to bleed to death. They even forgot to mention that if the solution got into my bloodstream it could harm me permanently. So I really did not give an informed consent. They didn't give me enough information to make a proper decision. Everybody just kept saying abortion was my only option.

What followed was 18 hours of excruciating labor, induced by the saline injection. My boyfriend thought I would be done in about an hour. When he saw I was in labor and understood what was happening, he started crying uncontrollably and had to leave. After it was over, I saw a man in a white coat with a towel over both his hands. The nurses tried to stop me from looking, but I saw the man was taking something away. He needed two hands to carry it. That was when I realized it wasn't just a "blob of tissue." It was my baby. I learned later from a friendly nurse that it was a perfect baby boy with no deformities.

After the abortion, the child welfare agency placed me in an "independent living" program. Since 83 percent of couples who have an abortion end up separating, they figured my common-law relationship would end as well. But my boyfriend and I beat the odds. In the years ahead we had three children. This in itself is a miracle, for after an abortion there is a 40 percent chance the woman will never have another child. Some methods of abortion make it impossible to have children at all.

While I was pregnant with our third child, my boyfriend and I had a big fight. I decided to leave him and go home. I caught a ride with two guys who had been drinking and there was a terrible accident. As the car went out of control, I cried to God for help. I flew threw the windshield and the car rolled over, nearly landing on me. By a miracle, neither myself nor my unborn child were harmed.

The day this baby was born, I asked the pastor's wife from a local church to come and pray for me and the baby. As she began praying, I started to cry. I knew there was a God and my children were a blessing He had given me. I was really touched. Three weeks later I trusted Jesus as my Savior and became a Christian. Later my boyfriend also received Christ. In time we realized our common-law relationship did not please the Lord and we were married.

Though God has forgiven our sins, we have had to live with their consequences. The abortion left us both deeply wounded. When we could finally discuss it, my husband said he had nightmares for two years. I tried to ignore the hurt for five years, and only with God's help have I started to heal the scars. The pain of being an abused and neglected child is behind me, but the sadness from my abortion lingers. When you steal or fight or drink, you can apologize to the people you hurt and make up with them. With abortion, you cannot do that. The one you have wronged is forever out of reach.

Some experts say there is no "post-abortion syndrome," but I know they are wrong because I am living with it today. Friends tell me, "The Lord has forgiven you. You have three beautiful children now and have to get on with your life." That is true. But it is so hard. I am involved in an organization for women abused by abortion and find consolation in sharing my story as a warning to others. And to those who are seduced by the arguments for "choice," I tell them from the Word of God, "Live as free men, but do not use your freedom as a cover-up for evil; live as servants of God" (1 Peter 2:16, NIV).

God chose to put a life in my womb, and I went against His choice. God had a plan for my life, and I went against His plan. For all that, I am no less loved by God and no less saved by Christ. And He has a wonderful plan for my life today. But my life will always be different than it would have been. They don't tell you that when you get an abortion.

2. Aids Can't Destroy My Soul

Key Verse - 1 Corinthians 6:18

"Have nothing to do with sex sins! Any other sin that a man does, does not hurt his own body. But the man who does a sex sin sins against his own body."

Abandoned in a strange city by a false friend, this Cree man lived on the streets and became a male prostitute to survive. When the HIV test came back positive, he wasn't surprised. And he was too busy snorting cocaine to take any medicine. At last he came down with AIDS and had to face the terrifying truth.

I WAS ABOUT TO enter Grade 11, when my roommate invited me to go to Los Angeles. Since I was away from my Cree reservation in northern Manitoba, and attending high school in Winnipeg, he was about the only friend I had. When I met him at the bus station, he said the bus was leaving in fifteen minutes. He asked if I really wanted to go. I said yes, because he was my only friend.

I was just seventeen when we arrived in Los Angeles, and excited about discovering a big new city. But that didn't last long. One day my friend left for work but didn't come home to our apartment. Three days later he called and said he had skipped out and gone back to live in Canada. I was devastated. Because of this, I lost my apartment and eventually ended up on the streets.

Desperate for money, I became a male prostitute. Many street people do this, including many native people. It's called "survival prostitution," selling our bodies to other men in order to survive. For nearly three years I was a "gay for pay." Life on "the strip" was my only social life. Santa Monica Boulevard is a long stretch, and there were a fair amount of native people doing prostitution. So we would get together and talk. The other place I went to regularly was jail. Sometimes it would be a prostitution charge, and sometimes petty things like obstructing pedestrian traffic.

I was in jail when my life took a sudden turn for the worse. I became ill and was released to a nearby general hospital. They told me I had tuberculosis. But after some more tests, they discovered I had the AIDS virus. At first I was upset, but later it didn't bother me. There was a part of me that expected it. Most people on the streets are aware of the risk. We just don't talk about it and pretend it doesn't exist.

My life on the streets ended after a man picked me up and we started living with his mother. It turned out he was a habitual criminal and drug addict. Eventually he got me to shoot up too. We would steal his mother's money to buy cocaine. This went on for two years. I was so hooked on cocaine that I didn't bother to take the medicines I was given for AIDS.

Finally I returned to Winnipeg. I made a brief trip home to the reservation, to visit with my family, but soon I was back in a Winnipeg hospital with a full-blown case of AIDS. The terrible truth finally hit me, but I did not curse God. My aunts and uncles had gone to Bible school, and they had often told me about God's love.

I knew the Lord wasn't to blame for what was happening to me. A lot of it was my own choosing. "Have nothing to do with sex sins! Any other sin that a man does, does not hurt his own body. But the man who does a sex sin sins against his own body" (1 Corinthians 6:18). Though I was a "survival prostitute," deep down I knew that I had a choice. I knew what I was doing was wrong and would carry a price. Yet I went ahead anyhow, because it seemed like the easiest road.

Soon after I was hospitalized, the hospital chaplain came to visit me. He talked to me about my need to get right with God, and I trusted Jesus as my Savior right there in my bed. My curse turned out to be a blessing! I don't know how much more time the Lord will give me, but for now I am strong enough to travel and share what I have learned with other young people. I tell them Hollywood makes street life seem exciting, but Satan is deceiving them. I also tell them no matter what I did in the past, all my sins have been forgiven. God is powerful and He loves me, and that's what keeps me going.

3. Love Sick Heart Finds Perfect Lover

Key Verse - Leviticus 18:22

"Do not lie with a man as one lies with a woman. It is a sinful thing."

The test came back on his birthday and it was positive. What a present! Yet it was his own fault. It began in school with sex magazines and "fast" friends, and led to a homosexual lifestyle and years of promiscuity. But though he didn't know it, AIDS was the birthday present he needed most.

THE LIGHTS WERE flashing. The music was loud and vibrant, a disco beat. A lot of people were talking and dancing and having a good time. I had never been in that kind of place before. I was under age, so the idea of just being there was great. This was the party scene, and that's where I wanted to be!

I was there with an old friend from high school. He had invited me to go with him to this night club. It was a gay bar. This place was very exciting! It was just the kind of thing that puts you in a mood of letting loose, setting aside your morals. As we left the bar, my friend invited me to spend the night. I accepted, and that night I had my first sexual experience—a homosexual one.

I came from a strong family. My dad was in the

military and we travelled around quite a bit. When I was ten, we moved to Texas and began attending a local church. When my sister trusted Jesus as her Savior, the Lord began dealing next with me. I understood heaven and hell were real places, and the only way to heaven was to be saved through Christ. A few weeks later I too put my faith in Jesus.

A year went by, then dad told us he had been transferred to Alaska. It sounded exciting, and I was anxious to make new friends. Since I wanted to fit in, I went along when the guys on my school bus started passing around sex magazines. I began to think if I could have sex, then I would be somebody. During junior and senior high school I got more involved in pornography and masturbation, as well as alcohol and drugs. They made me feel more accepted, and that was important to me because I had always been a loner. And I had a strong desire to become sexually active and show the guys I was a man.

By the time our family moved to Virginia in my junior year, I was constantly arguing with my parents. Finally I decided to leave. I went back to Alaska, got odd jobs and finished my last year of high school. I also became close to an older guy who had gone to my school. He was a good dancer, someone who had it all together. He was sexually active, so I really looked up to him. And he's the one who took me to the gay bar. When I had sex with him that night, it wasn't really the actual sex that I enjoyed. What seemed important was having finally reached my goal of having sex, and of being "loved" and accepted.

The years went by and I became involved in many relationships. I ended up going back to Virginia to attend college. That's when my parents found out about my homosexuality. They were pretty upset and made it clear that they loved me but could not accept my lifestyle. While in Virginia I began my first serious homosexual relationship. We moved in together and at first it was exciting. But soon our relationships fell apart. The sexual part got boring because I was used to the thrill of having different partners.

One day during this time, I came across a gospel music station on the radio dial. As I listened, the Lord touched my heart. Deep down I knew the homosexual lifestyle was wrong. Later I picked up a Bible and read, "Do not lie with a man as one lies with a woman. It is a sinful thing" (Leviticus 18:22). I began to question the commitment I made to Jesus when I was ten years old. "What did that really mean?" I asked myself. "If living the life of a homosexual is against God's will, what does that say about my commitment to Christ?" I began to feel uncomfortable, and that was one reason I walked away from my partner.

Shortly afterward I moved to Washington, D.C. I had never been in a big city before and it was exciting! I was determined to end my homosexual lifestyle, but I soon found it would not be easy. Washington has the fourth largest homosexual population in the United States. And without knowing it, I moved into a homosexual neighborhood. Also, I never read my Bible or went to church. And I was still smoking marijuana.

After three months, I was mad at God for not taking away my homosexual desires. In my frustration I just decided to "give in" and go back to "having fun." I started another relationship, and a year later we moved to Alaska with big plans to open a gay nightclub in Anchorage. We ran out of money, but still managed to find good jobs and even built a house of our own. Things were going well. In the back of my mind I wanted to get right with God someday. But not when I was having such a good time.

After about three years, things started falling apart. We piled up some huge credit card bills. My partner was stressed out at work. I was bored and secretly having sex with other men, a lot of one-night stands or going to gay theaters to have sex with people I did not know. Then I began waking up in the middle of the night soaked with sweat. I never connected it with AIDS until I went to see my doctor. The tests came back on my birthday, and I was HIV positive. What a birthday present!

My partner noticed I was unresponsive during sex. He tried to reach out and save our relationship, but I didn't want to tell him I had the AIDS virus. Our relationship broke down, and finally my partner walked away from his job and left me to pay all our overdue bills. For the next several months I was in shock and just stopped paying bills. Before long I had to declare bankruptcy. All I could do was continue to have sex with many people, not even caring enough to tell them I had the AIDS virus.

Just when I decided my life must change, God stepped in. I had a special project at the office and was assigned work with a woman who was a Christian. She enjoyed Christian radio and we began listening together. One day I heard that a gospel singer I liked was coming to town. I went to the concert, and through his music the Lord seemed to say, "You are My child. I love you. I am here for you. Come home." The next Sunday I went back to the church and told the pastor my story. "I have decided to leave the homosexual lifestyle and I want help."

He arranged for me to meet regularly with someone who helped me study the Bible and learn to live for God. It was hard to walk away from my old lifestyle because all my friends were homosexuals. But the Lord has been faithful to give me godly friends whose goal is to seek Him in everything they do. They helped me learn that everyone is born with a broken relationship. We're all seeking love, affirmation and security. God never intended us to find that in other human beings. He always intended that we find it in Him. Apart from Christ's death on the cross, allowing me to catch the AIDS virus is the single most loving thing my Father could have done for me. He knew what it would take to turn me back to Himself.

4. Preacher's Kid Loosed From Gay Lifestyle
Key Verse - Luke 9:23

Then Jesus said to them all,"If anyone wants to fol-
low Me, he must give up himself and his own desires.
He must take up his cross every day and follow Me."

His father was distant, his older brothers were
at school, and he lived in a white neighborhood
with no boys his own age. Then he was exposed
to homosexual pornography, and his yearning for
male approval took a new direction. This Navajo
man struggled for many years, until he found
something more powerful than emotion.

IT WAS ALL SET. We had planned it well. My cousin
and I were set to steal some porno magazines from
the corner bookstore. On Saturdays we went to the
local movie theater. Next door was a bookstore.
When we were in junior high school, porno magazines were displayed on the front counter where
anyone could pick them up. So one Saturday we
decided to each grab a copy and run down the alley.

It worked! But when we stopped to look at our stolen prizes, I realized I'd picked up the wrong magazine. I opened my magazine to find pictures of naked men. I had never seen any magazines showing
nudity before. Sex was never talked about in my
Navajo family. I was rather shocked, but found myself almost immediately aroused. I threw away my
magazine, but later that evening I went back to the
dumpster and snuck it home.

My father was a minister for a very strict church, so my home life was strict too. Dad was well known on the reservation, so we were expected to be a "perfect" family. I was the youngest of six children, and none of us were allowed to have friends outside our church. If we did not live by my father's rules, he taught us God would punish us. Rules were my life, since dad was very busy with his church work. He preached all over the Navajo reservation and did not have much time for our family.

Since we lived off the reservation in New Mexico, most of my friends were white. As a little boy, about the only children my age were girls. We played dolls together. Dressing up and playing with these girls was a big secret. A few times I was caught and scolded by my sister or brothers. But I had nothing else to do. My brothers and sister were at boarding school, and dad was away preaching. I wanted male companionship—just a friendly slap on the back. But my father never gave me that. The only bonding I had was with my mother, and we were very close.

About the time I started junior high school, I began to feel my interests were more towards guys than girls. Stealing that first magazine began a habit that lasted for many years. I would take them from stores all across town, then look at the pictures and get excited. In junior high we also began undressing for gym, and I would fantasize about the adult teachers who came in with their shirts off. I knew deep down this was all wrong, but I did not stop.

In high school I dated a few girls, but preferred looking at men. I was introduced to alcohol, but didn't drink much until I went to college. My brothers were all getting married and wanted to know why I never even dated. My dad was having problems in his church and his marriage, and treated mom in ways I did not like. This all put a lot of stress on me, and I began drinking heavily. Then I got into a homosexual relationship, but kept it secret. Finally I quit school, received vocational training and got a job in Albuquerque.

In the city, I attended church for a while but stopped going. I was heavily into drugs and alcohol, and twice was charged with drunk driving. At the office, however, there was a Christian man who befriended me. The first Sunday I attended his church I really felt at home. Later I went to a weekend retreat and shared my story with our speaker. I was crying as I told him I wanted to know Jesus personally. We prayed together and that night I trusted Christ as my Savior.

After that I became very involved in the church, was baptized, taught Sunday School and joined the choir. My homosexual desires faded away. In the thrill of becoming a new Christian, everything seemed to be going so well. But living for Jesus can't be based upon emotions. You must decide to obey Him each day for a lifetime. "If anyone wants to follow Me [Jesus], he must give up himself and his own desires. He must take up His cross every day and follow Me" (Luke 9:23). The initial excitement can only carry you so far. Then you must decide, day by day, to give up yourself and take up your cross.

That is a challenge, because it requires an act of the will. As the initial thrill settled down, Satan began to attack my weak point. I discovered there were gay bookstores where I could see and hear men having sex with other men. I started going to these places, and very soon I became utterly defeated as a Christian.

"What's wrong with me?" I thought to myself. "I'm a Christian, so why is this happening?" I started blaming other believers. "They accept alcoholics," I said, "but homosexuality they won't even talk about." At last I blamed God and decided He didn't love homosexuals. I was really struggling and didn't know who to talk to. This wasn't a topic I could share with just anyone. Finally I wrote to a popular Christian musician whose songs I admired. In my letter I told him, "I need to find some comfort, but just don't know what to do."

Two weeks later, a package came for me. I ripped it open and inside was a Christian book for people struggling with homosexual desires. One section listed Christian organizations that help people who want to leave the homosexual lifestyle. I contacted a group in Denver, and later moved there to finish my college education. The ministry helped me study the Bible and base my Christian life not upon changing emotions but upon God's unchanging Word. I learned God really does love me, and I cannot blame others for my own sinful choices.

Sorry to say, I did lose some friends when I told them I was struggling with homosexual desires. But my mom was supportive, and even my dad was understanding. Now I have many Christian friends I can talk with, who encourage me to stay focused on God's Word. These are all recent developments in my life, so I still have struggles. But I also thank God for many positive changes. He has been with me from the start, and He will carry me through to the end.

5. Power of Porn Conquered at Last

Key Verse - Matthew 5: 28

"But I tell you, anyone who even looks at a woman with sinful desire of wanting her has already sinned in his heart."

It began with magazines, until all he could think about at school was having sex with every girl he saw. Then he graduated to videos and porn theaters, and began having affairs when his wife wasn't enough to satisfy him. Yet he did admire something about her, the way she stuck by him with a love he didn't deserve.

FOR MORE THAN sixteen years I was obsessed. Not with alcohol or drugs. Sniffing glue wasn't my thing. I was obsessed with pornography. It started when I was ten years old and saw a magazine at my uncle's house. Sixteen years later, pornography had such a powerful death grip on my life that only God's intervention kept me from destruction.

I grew up on a reservation in northern Manitoba. Twice a year my parents took the family to Winnipeg. The trip was 600 miles by train, and we were always excited. When I was ten, I had no reason to think our trip that year would be any different. But it was. Times were bad and my folks couldn't afford to raise five children. My uncle in the city offered to take us, and we were being sent to live with him. It would be five long years until I saw my house and my dog again.

My uncle was a wild fellow and lived with his third wife. Things happened in his house I can't repeat. And he was obsessed with dirty magazines. It didn't take long for my brothers and I to find them. My uncle did not mind. He and my aunt used to laugh. I was the youngest, and I guess they enjoyed watching me stare wide-eyed at the photographs of naked women.

It was fun for a while, but after I had looked at everything I wanted more. When I was twelve, I discovered that I could do some of the things I saw in the pictures. My uncle thought that was natural, to go from dirty pictures to playing around with myself. By junior high school, sexual fantasies and girls were all I could think about. I began looking at the magazine articles, and not just the pictures, so I could dream up even more fantasies.

When I was sixteen, I met a girl who would later become my wife. Though she was only fourteen, she was the most beautiful girl I had ever known. She had the kind of body I had come to love through the pages of those magazines. We started having sex right away. Two years later we got married so we could have sex whenever we wanted. After a couple of years, though, our marriage didn't satisfy my sexual desires anymore. I wanted more of what I saw in my pornography.

On a trip to Vancouver, a friend introduced me to

adult video stores. I hadn't seen these before. Soon I was ordering videos about once a week from British Columbia. And I was watching those videos almost every day. After a store opened in Winnipeg, I would go and use the private viewing booths. While looking at the movies I would act out what I saw. Before long, I was no longer sexually satisfied at home. I wanted my wife to be like those models in the movies. But with two children and another one on the way, she just didn't quite fit the part.

I threatened to walk out on my wife if she didn't satisfy me. But she knew I was in trouble and wanted to help me. Though she didn't do the things I wanted, she stuck by me. She put up with my dirty magazines and all-night trips to the video store. I also had another girl or two, but my wife didn't give up. About a year after we were married, she started going to church with her mother. My wife didn't have to hear very many Bible stories before she asked the teacher how she could become a child of God. Now that she was a Christian, my wife wanted to keep us together so I could find Jesus too.

My obsession with pornography continued until the year our oldest child began school. My wife had continued to live for the Lord, and deep down I was impressed by her spirit. When she asked me to take her to a big gospel crusade in Winnipeg, I said okay. After the sermon the preacher invited people to come to the front of the auditorium, if they wanted to trust Jesus as their personal Savior. I went forward and a man showed me from the Bible that I must admit to God I was a sinner, and that I wanted to turn away from my sin. Then if I asked Jesus to save me, He would give me forgiveness and eternal life.

All this I prayed, and that night I felt a joy I had never known. Here was the answer to my problem! In the days ahead, I wanted to really live for Jesus. First I got rid of the magazines and videos around my house. But let me tell you, the hardest thing to get rid of were all the dirty thoughts. As long as these thoughts ran through my mind every day, it was always a temptation to masturbate or visit bookstores or see my lady friends.

"From the inside, out of the heart of men come bad thoughts [and] sex sins" (Mark 7:21). That means my thoughts and actions grew out of a heart that I had filled with pornography for sixteen years. I wanted to get rid of those chains and knew I was not strong enough to do it myself. But God gave me a new heart, along with His power to conquer my old obsession. It took almost three years to break completely free, but with God it was possible.

Today I satisfy my desires by "drinking water from my own pool." That means being with my wife. God gave me a wife to "be happy...[and] be filled with great joy always because of her love" (Proverbs 5:18-19). It's so much better than anything pornography offers! The Bible warns, "Keep far away from [street women and sex pictures]. Do not go near the door of her house. If you do, you would give your strength to others and your years to those without loving-kindness. You would cry inside yourself when [through VD or AIDS] your flesh is wasted away" (Proverbs 5:8-11). I wish I had read this years ago. Then I might not have wasted sixteen years of my life bound by the chains of pornography.

6. Family Turns Heartache Into Happiness
Key Verse - Proverbs 6:28-29

"Can a man walk on hot coals, and his feet not be burned? So is he who goes into his neighbors wife. Whoever touches her will be punished."

Her family traveled throughout Indian country sharing the Gospel through music. She met many people and one day, in pity, gave herself to a troubled boy who needed a friend. Would Jesus forgive her? She learned He already had on the cross. Then she discovered that she was pregnant, and it seemed her life was over.

I WAS SIXTEEN at the time it happened, and it left me with so much shame and guilt that I felt God would never be able to forgive me. What made it worse is that I knew better. My sisters and I had traveled all our lives with our parents in a Christian preaching and singing ministry to native people. I knew what the Bible said, but it still happened. Afterwards, when our family would go into churches for concerts, I could hardly sing because my guilt was so strong.

All my life I had known about Jesus. I loved Him for dying for me, and could hardly believe someone could love me so much. It often made me cry to think of Him bleeding and dying on the cross for me. But in spite of all this, I did not know Jesus personally until I faced this crisis.

My parents brought me up in a loving but firm way. I was taught to respect them, and was taught about the things of the Lord. And I was certainly not one of those kids who got away with whatever she wanted to do. I really love my parents for teaching me the way they did. In our travels across the United States and Canada, we met a lot of people. One of them was a guy who became a friend of mine. When our family was in his area, the two of us would spend a lot of time talking together.

One time he told me some personal things about himself. He figured nobody liked him or nobody wanted to be around him, and that is why he had hardly any friends. As he shared this with me, I felt sorry for him. The way he talked really worked on my feelings. I ended up giving him something that was very special to me—I gave myself to him as a woman. I felt really bad afterward, and kept feeling that way each time it happened. I did not know how to handle it, and thought Jesus would never be able to forgive me for what I had done.

Things got so bad, I had to talk with someone. I telephoned a girlfriend and told her what had happened, and how hurt and angry and guilty I felt inside. And what hurt most, I told her, was that the Lord could never forgive me. "But He already did," she said. "He forgave you when He died for you. He's just waiting for you to accept His forgiveness." Those were the words I needed to hear! Then I realized Jesus was not just "the" Savior. He was "my" Savior, and I placed my trust and my life in Him. Once I knew my sins were forgiven, I had a new and joyful feeling of peace inside that is still with me today.

My girlfriend urged me to speak with my parents.

"The thing you did," she explained, "went against what your parents think and stand for. You should tell them what you told me." That would not be easy, but I knew she was right. I thought my parents would be angry with me, but they put their arms around me and forgave me. That really cleared the air and I felt so good.

Then a month later, I discovered that I was pregnant. At that moment, it was just like everything crashed in on me. I felt really horrible, like I was being punished. Why did this happen? For weeks, somebody in our family was always crying. Yet as we comforted each other, the crisis brought us even closer together as a family. Sometimes I felt no hope, but then my father would quote from the Bible, "All things work together for the good of those who love Him and are chosen to be part of His plan" (Romans 8:28). This kept me going, because I knew God loved me.

But it was a difficult time. The Bible says sex sins have lasting consequences. "Can a man [or woman who does a sexual sin] carry fire in his arms and not be burned? Can a man walk on hot coals, and his feet not be burned?...[He] does not think well. He who does it is destroying himself. He will be hurt and ashamed, and his shame will not be taken away" (Proverbs 6:27-28,32-33). Many thoughts ran through my mind as I tried to figure out what to do. Some people said I should get an abortion. Others suggested adoption, and we even had families in mind to take the baby and raise it. But the day I felt the baby move inside me, I realized this was a human being. I could not simply kill it or give it away.

I was already in love with it.

To help me think, dad invited me to go with him on a ministry trip to Canada. Another Indian gospel singing group was also in town, and I went to hear them. After the concert I introduced myself. One of the singers was a boy my age, and over the next two days we became friends. It was so much fun, I completely forgot I was pregnant. The last night when he kissed me goodbye, I knew I was in love. Afterward I told a friend and he said, "That's great, but does he know you're going to have a baby?"

At that moment I felt awful. I loved him and did not want to lose him, but he had a right to know. The next day I told him everything. At first he did not really know what to think or say. He just cried with me. In the weeks ahead he really struggled with his feelings. He knew marriage would be unfair to everyone, if he could not see my child as his own. But he loved me, and asked God to give him the ability and courage to also love the unborn child I was carrying. The Lord answered his prayer and, about a month before I was due, he told me, "I realize God wants the best for me, and that both you and the baby are gifts from Him."

We gave my baby girl an Indian name that means "a miracle of God." The summer after she was born, we became engaged and were married in the fall. Through all this, the Lord taught us something very special. Despite all the wrong things we have done, God loved us and gave us His Son. Through Jesus, we can be adopted as a child of God. My husband says when he understood this, it was only natural for him to love my daughter. "She is not mine naturally," he explains, "but is mine because I have chosen her, just as God chose me. When I look at her, I am reminded all over again that God loved me enough to adopt me into His family. That makes our little girl a double blessing."

We are so glad God brought us together. As husband and wife our talents have combined, so that we can serve the Lord more effectively together through our music. Now we travel and sing and tell native people about Jesus. As I look back at the pain I suffered, I know also that I caused much pain for others. But God took a bad situation and turned it around for His glory. That took a miracle. And He can make a miracle happen in your life too, if you let Him.

7. Walking the Lonely Trail of Obedience

Key Verse - James 3:11

"Does a well of water give good water and bad water from the same place?"

They had lived together for years without being married, had two sons and were happy. Then he became a Christian and saw this relationship was not pleasing to God. What should he do? He did not want to lose his common-law wife, and she was threatening to leave because of his new faith.

WHEN I BECAME a Christian, I did not know I would face such big decisions. Though I was not married at the time, I had a common-law wife and two sons. After I trusted Jesus as my personal Savior, I kept on living with her in hopes she would also become a Christian. Then we could get married. But I was very young in the Lord and my thinking was still patterned after the ways of the world. I thought it was okay to keep on living together, for I was "married" in a sense and I loved my "wife."

As time went by, I read the Bible and learned more about how to live for the Lord. Other Christians encouraged me. After a while I did not feel right about living with a woman to whom I was not married. Yet I kept excusing it and figured God would understand my situation. At first this seemed true for I was so happy being a Christian, doing the Lord's work and growing stronger in my faith. But my common-law wife was a different matter. It seemed harder for us to get along together. We began to argue more and I could not understand why.

I became discouraged and talked to a Christian friend who gave me some advice. He read a passage from the Bible, "How can that which is good get along with that which is bad? How can light be in the same place with darkness? How can Christ get along with the devil? How can one who has put his trust in Christ get along with one who has not put his trust in Christ? (2 Corinthians 6:14-15). Jesus is the Light of the world (John 8:12) while Satan is darkness," he explained, "and light and darkness don't mix." The reason my common-law wife and I did not get along is because we served different masters.

Later I attended a Bible conference for native people. I prayed with a group of men and we asked God to either save my common-law wife or else show me what to do. I really wanted her to become a Christian so our family could stay together. Our relationship was almost ready to break up. So I went home after the Bible conference and tried to make things work.

The Lord was still working on me, however. When I tried to share my Christian faith with others who needed Jesus, the Lord showed me I had to take care of the problems in my own life. If I did not, then my testimony would not be very effective. "A well does not give both good water and bad water" (James 3:11). As I had prayed at the Bible conference, God was now convicting me of what I needed to do. When I read my Bible, I came across the word "fornication" (sex sins) so often that the word really burned in my heart.

God was telling me I was a bad example for Jesus and for my church. Slowly He opened my eyes to understand the situation, and at last my stubborn will was broken. I saw my life the way God saw it. One verse from the Bible made it plain, "You [believers] should not keep on being with a person who calls himself a Christian if he does any kind of sex sins" (1 Corinthians 5:11). I knew what I had to do. Three months after the Bible conference, my common-law wife and I broke up our relationship.

It has been hard living alone without her. But I get much comfort from another verse in the Bible, "Do not fear, for I am with you. Do not be afraid, for I am your God. I will give you strength, and for sure I will help you. Yes, I will hold you up with My right hand that is right and good" (Isaiah 41:10). I feel much closer to the Lord, now that the wall of sin between us has been removed. Two months after my relationship broke up, I was baptized and later began teaching Sunday School for children. This is a great blessing to me. I am also attending Bible school to learn more about God. "Teach me Your way, O Lord. I will walk in Your truth. May my heart fear your name" (Psalm 86:11).

I continue to ask the Lord to save my former common-law wife, and we stay in contact because of our two sons. The Bible says, "Put your trust in the Lord Jesus Christ and you and your family will be saved from the punishment of sin" (Acts 16:31). This does not mean that since I am a Christian, God is obligated to save my wife. Each person must decide for themselves to trust Jesus as their own Savior. But because of my faith in Christ, the Lord promises to work in a special way in the lives of my wife and sons, to convict them of their sins and need for Jesus.

In the meantime I am waiting patiently for God's will to be worked out in my own life. I take hope in a Bible promise that has become very special to me. "Do not throw away your trust, for your pay will be great. You must be willing to wait without giving up. After you have done what God wants you to do, God will give you what He promised you" (Hebrews 10:35-36).

THINGS TO THINK ABOUT

1. Labor Pains That Won't Stop

Supporters of abortion say they believe in "choice." But not all choices are the same. Some choices are good and some are wrong. You should choose to do right. Read 1 Peter 2:13-17. What is your duty as a citizen of your reservation and your country? Why is this your duty? How should you respond to a wrong law or situation?

2. Aids Can't Destroy My Soul

You can try to justify sexual sin by blaming it on the circumstances. But you always have a choice, and with God you always have a Helper. Read 1 Corinthians 6:15-20. Why should you keep your body pure? If you are a Christian, why does your body not belong to you?

3. Love Sick Heart Finds Perfect Lover

The Bible describes homosexuality as sinful and unnatural in many places. Read Leviticus 18:22 and

1 Corinthians 6:9. Then spend some time to read and study Romans 1:18-32. According to that passage, what attitudes (verses 18-23) lead to homosexual sins (verses 24-27), and what other behaviors (verses 28-32) result from these attitudes?

4. Preacher's Kid Loosed From Gay Lifestyle

If you struggle with wrong sexual desires, then you cannot overcome them by mere feelings. Emotions change, so you must anchor yourself to something that does not change. That something is Jesus. Read Luke 9:23. Learn to take every thought captive in obedience to Him. Read 2 Corinthians 10:5. Do you "take up your cross" according to your feelings or through a conscious act of your will? What does this act involve? How often must you decide to do this?

5. Power of Porn Conquered at Last

Pornography entices you with thoughts of meeting your sexual desires in ways that God does not intend. These thoughts lead to attitudes and actions

that are harmful and lead you away from God. Read
Proverbs 5:1-23 and Mark 7:21. What are the dangers of sex sins? Why is marital love better? Do immoral thoughts lead to actions?

6. Family Turns Heartache Into Happiness

Sexual sins have longlasting consequences. Nothing may happen to you the next day, but eventually your sin will overtake you. Read Proverbs 6:24-35. Why are sex sins so serious? Why do the consequences last so long? Why is the harm so difficult to repair?

7. Walking the Lonely Trail of Obedience

Like the native man in this story, you may be faced with a choice. To obey God and live for Him, you must give up a relationship or sexual practice that gives you certain pleasures—perhaps something you became involved with before trusting Christ. Read 1 Corinthians 5:11, and James 3:11-12 and 4:4. Can a believer, who does not give up sex sins, function properly as a Christian? Why not?

CHAPTER THREE

Conquering Broken Families and Relationships

1. I Sang, Sewed and Swam for Jesus

Key Verse - John 6:37

"All whom my father has given to Me will come to Me. I will never turn away anyone who comes to Me."

Orphaned by a tragic accident, this native girl became an unwanted burden. A kindly couple took her and showed her the way of salvation through Christ. Then she was forced to leave and forbidden to speak the name of Jesus. Yet she kept the knowledge in her heart, little knowing how God would use it!

FOR A MOMENT, I forgot that I was sitting just outside the door. I was stitching a new pair of moccasins, but my thoughts were on a Cree hymn I had learned to sing. Suddenly my uncle, who was visiting, came bursting outside. Grabbing me by the hair, he knocked the moccasins out of my hands. Then he pounded my ten-year-old body until I fell sense-less to the ground. "Let me hear sounds like that again," he screamed, "and it will be the last sounds you ever make!"

My life was filled with problems. It all started four years earlier, when I was six and my parents drowned in a terrible accident. Since nobody else would care for me, I was taken in by relatives who really did not want me. For months I was treated meanly and given little to eat. They had a hard enough time car-ing for their own family, without having an extra mouth to feed.

Several months after the accident, a white mission-ary passed through our village. When he saw how frightened and hungry I was, he offered to take me. His home was several hundred miles away in Nor-way House, at the top of Lake Winnipeg in north-ern Manitoba. There I became part of his family and attended at the mission school with his children. I memorized many Bible verses and hymns, because this new music delighted me. But most of all, I came to know Jesus Christ as my Savior.

Then a stranger came to Norway House. He was my younger uncle who had come from far away to sell his furs. When he saw his brother's child was here—and since he and his wife had no children of their own—he insisted on taking me with him. They treated me kindly enough, though I was kept very busy with chores. I worked hard and it was comfort-ing to sing the hymns and say the Bible verses I had memorized.

After two years with my new family, my other uncle

moved into our village. As a young man he had been robbed by some white traders who first got him drunk and then stole all his furs. He became filled with hate and cruelty, and did everything to keep Indian people from having anything to do with white men. Over the years he learned much about poisons and spells, and used this knowledge to make people obey him. The first time he heard me singing, he flew into a rage and beat me senseless. When I awoke, my aunt said I must never sing those words again or my older uncle would poison us. So I had to be satisfied with singing to God in my heart.

One summer the three of us moved to a small island in a large lake. Here we found plenty of birds and fish, and were free from the power of my cruel older uncle. It was perfect, for I could slip into the quiet woods to do my sewing and sing hymns. I did not know my uncle was curious and often followed me. Hiding in the bushes, he would listen to my songs and try to understand their meaning.

Towards autumn we knew it was time to store as many birds as possible for winter food. My uncle took his canoe to shoot some geese, when the rifle backfired in his hands. He was knocked overboard and so badly wounded that he could not swim. Hearing his cries, I dove into the water and brought my uncle back to shore. He was already quite elderly, and now he was dying. My aunt and I knew we could not help him much—when suddenly he whispered, "Sing!"

I was startled but obeyed. After a few verses my uncle asked, "Who is this Jesus?" I told him Jesus was the Son of the Creator God, who died to rescue us from the bad things we have done. Then I remembered one of my verses: "For God so loved the world that He gave His only Son. Whoever puts his trust in God's Son will not be lost, but will have life that lasts forever" (John 3:16).

My uncle was thrilled. "Say it again and again," he whispered. When I had repeated the verse several times he asked, "Can you remember any more?" Then I recalled how my teacher at the mission school used to tell us something Jesus once said, "I will never turn away anyone who comes to Me" (John 6:37). At that my uncle asked, "Did He say this was for Indians, too? Can we go to Him the same way the white man goes?" "Oh, yes" I said excitedly, "the missionaries told us that everyone could come, Indians as well as whites. Jesus said, `Everyone who calls on the name of the Lord will be saved'" (Romans 10:13).

"Sing again to me," my uncle said, and so I sang. "What did you say was His name?" he asked again. "Jesus," I replied with a sob. And with that name on his lips, he was gone. Someday I will see my uncle again in heaven. Then I can thank him for showing me a great lesson. For years I went from home to home, but I was never separated from God. I can always come to Him and, wherever I am, He can use me.

2. Abandoned by Parents, Adopted by God

Key Verse - Psalm 100:5

"For the Lord is good. His loving-kindness lasts forever. And He is faithful to all people and to all their children-to-come."

Runaway children sometimes leave notes, but this time it was runaway parents. Ever since that day he came home to an abandoned house, this native teenager was determined never to love again so nobody could hurt him. He got a degree and a job, and it seemed he wouldn't need anybody. But he was wrong.

NO ONE WAS HOME. Everything was gone, each room was bare. I had just come home from a weekend trip with my buddies—and now all that remained of my world were my meager belongings, set in a pile on the living room floor. There was a note on top.

"Dear Son," it read, "your dad and I have split up. I can't afford to keep you. You're on your own. Love, Mom." Love? Was it love to leave your fourteen-year-old child out in the cold? I struggled with the meaning of love for years following. I was totally unprepared for the shock of being abandoned, and so I became afraid to love people and let them love me. That way I wouldn't be hurt or rejected again.

My parents raised me, along with six brothers and a sister, in the state of Oregon. We lived a poor life, often going without food for almost a week at a time.

By age twelve I was already drinking and smoking pot to escape the turmoil in our home. The problems reached their peak that day I was fourteen, and from that point my mind has memories of blackness, scenes hardly worth thinking about.

To find the sense of "family" that was missing in my life, I joined a violent street gang. We were dangerous and the townspeople feared us. But our violent lifestyle was also a danger to ourselves. Soon after my parents split, I was hit by a car. At age seventeen my heart stopped beating for three minutes after making a hit during a football game. Two years later a truck tire blew up in my face, throwing me thirty feet and shattering my wrist. That same year I had an accident while using a chain saw that nearly cut off my right hand.

It wasn't long after the chainsaw accident that I learned one of my brothers, who also was a gang member, had been killed. In a drunken stupor, he decided to rob the house of an elderly couple who were supposed to have a lot of money. He barged into the home and, while he attacked the woman with a knife, the husband ran for his gun and put a bullet through his heart. Then eleven months later my older brother, who was just 22, was electrocuted and killed while trying to steal some high-power line.

These tragedies really shook me up, but didn't change me. It was a big blow to lose my two brothers, yet my heart only got harder. Ever since that day my parents split, I was determined not to let anything hurt me again. Even my own brushes with death did nothing to change my proud outlook. The fact that I lived through my accidents should have shown that Someone was watching out for me. But I never admitted that, because I could not believe Anyone could love me so faithfully.

What a messed up life I had! Things had gotten a little better during my last years in high school, when a foster couple gave me a comfortable home and some discipline. After graduation I even spent two years in the armed forces, then went to college for three years and earned a degree in criminology. Life seemed okay for a while, but my basic problem had never been faced.

Drugs and alcohol crept back into my life. I told so many lies that soon I didn't know who I really was. Confused and alone, my drug habit got worse, sometimes costing me $400 a day. At this rate I would soon be dead, so I fled to Montana and began a new life there. For a time I worked as a farmhand and a fireman, kicked my drug habit, and thought my life was set. Then I made a foolish mistake that made me more hopeless and wretched than ever.

I was 27, at my lowest point and looking for a way out, when someone invited me to church. During the service the pastor seemed to be speaking right to me. He spoke about pain and hurt and rejection, and I sure knew what those were! At the end when he said, "Who wants Jesus?" I shot my hand into the air. I wanted Him! The pastor and I prayed together and I asked Jesus Christ to be my Savior.

Why did I do it? Since losing my parents I was afraid of love. Now I was giving my life to the God of love. Wasn't I worried that He might let me down too? Yet I learned, "The Lord is good [and] His loving-kindness lasts forever" (Psalm 100:5). By now I realized that nothing else worked. God allowed me to try my own way—and though things sometimes got better for a while, in the end my hard heart brought me down. Then when I was at my lowest point, God showed me the way out.

I loved my two brothers who died, but there's nothing I can do for them now. They made their choice, as far as I know, not to serve God and now their eternal place is in hell. This breaks my heart, yet spurs me to tell others they don't have to end up there. I was also heading to hell until Jesus came into my life. Today He has given me forgiveness and freedom, love and fulfillment, and a reason to live. Though I lost my family, the Heavenly Father has adopted me into His own family and made me His child.

3. Nightmare Turns Into Blessing

Key Verse - 1 Samuel 1:28

"So I have given him to the Lord. He is given to the Lord as long as he lives."

It was a terrible decision. She could give up her oldest son so the other two would have a father, or keep all three and raise them alone. The decision was even harder because she herself was given up as a child. Yet she also knew the hardship of being without a father. How could God get her through this?

TO ASK A MOTHER to give up her child is almost like asking her to die. I know what it's like. My mother gave me up when I was a little girl. Never would I have dreamed that I would do the same when I became a mother.

My mother had me when she was only fifteen. When my grandfather found out she was pregnant, he forced my dad to marry her. But he did not accept me. "This is not my daughter," he said when I was born. So a year later I was given to my grandparents. They showed me love and taught me many things, until my mother took me back when I was nine.

During these years I really didn't feel loved, though I realize now that my parents just didn't know how to show it. To me it seemed I was just there to work for them. I washed clothes, fetched water and chopped wood. If there was no water in the house I had to get it, even in winter temperatures down to 60 degrees below zero. I would go out barefoot, break the ice and bring back the water.

While I learned to work, I didn't learn to read or write until I was fourteen. Because my father's ancestry is only part native, the boarding school would not accept me. Our family was treated as white people, so we weren't accepted even on our reservation. But the white community didn't accept us either, so we just became drifters.

When we moved to the city I wasn't allowed in the public school because I couldn't read or write. They put me in a school for kids who were mentally slow. All I did was build little boxes and things like that. For a girl of fourteen that made me very angry! And since people stared at me, I walked to school instead of taking the bus. After a while I dropped out because my dad said girls didn't need school, they just needed to get married.

I got engaged to a boy I had met when I was fourteen. But soon after we started dating, he began beating me when other boys so much as looked at me. Soon I was expecting his baby, but I couldn't take any more abuse and left him. By the time our son was born, he found another girl who was carrying his child. So I took off with my baby and struck out on my own.

At eighteen I met the man who would become my husband. My son was eight months old and he accepted both of us. We lived together almost right from the start. He bought me a new place and many brand new things—everything I ever wanted. Then he left for another province where he had a job in the bush. Because he came home only every other week, my new life soon became very lonely. I had left my family behind in Manitoba and moved to Alberta, where I didn't know anybody.

One day at a restaurant I met a couple of native women who were my own age. One of them was really nice and right away I knew there was something different about her. I told her how lonely I was, and we became good friends. She went everywhere I dragged her, even to bars. My friend never smoked or drank, but would just sit and talk with me. She never preached to me, and at first I didn't even know she was a Christian.

Then she invited me to a Teen Challenge coffee house. Despite my skepticism I went for the sake of our friendship. I never met so many friendly people! Young men and women, all my age, were standing up and sharing stories of what Jesus Christ had done for them. It really amazed me. From then on I would go every Saturday night with my friend. "This is what I want," I thought to myself.

When our group was planning a special program at the church, I was reluctant to go. As a favor to my girlfriend I agreed, thinking that it wasn't really a "church" service. During the meeting she would get so excited that I laughed at her. But she was also praying for me the whole time. At the end of the program, the speaker invited anyone who wanted to come forward and "accept Jesus Christ." I had not heard that expression before, but somehow I knew that I needed to go. My friend went with me, and she led me in prayer as I asked Jesus to be my Savior.

I started going to a Bible study, and soon there was a definite change in my life. For one thing, I no longer argued with my common-law husband when he came home late from the bar. He called me a "Jesus freak" and one day he smashed all my Christian teaching tapes. However I knew the Bible teaches, "By obeying your husbands, they may become Christians by the life you live without you saying anything. They will see how you love God and how your lives are pure" (1 Peter 3:1-2). He could see I was different, and I could tell he was thinking about it.

Then God began to convict me about my relationship. My common-law husband had never made any plans to marry me and I didn't want to live like that.

I knew the situation did not please the Lord, yet I did not want to lose my husband either, for by then we had a baby together. My husband had told me if I ever left him, "Don't expect me to come running after you. Once you leave, that's it." I was willing to marry him, but felt I could not continue living common-law.

In deciding to leave, I also prayed, "Lord, if you want me to marry him, send him to me." Two weeks later he telephoned and said he would marry me. But I insisted, "If you want me, you'll have to come here." That is what I had prayed, and I had to stick with it. In three days he was at my door to take me back.

Soon we were married in the church where I had become a Christian. Not too long after this we had another boy together. Now that my husband had two sons of his own, he turned against my firstborn. He would only play with his own two boys. When my own four-year-old son wanted a dad to play with, my husband would yell, "Get out of here! I'm not your dad! Stop staring!" It hurt me so bad. I started fighting with my husband all over again. But I also started praying again.

At first I wanted to blame God. Then one night I was reading to my boys from a Bible picture book, how Hannah said of her firstborn son Samuel, "I have given him to the Lord...as long as he lives" (1 Samuel 1:28). Hannah believed her son belonged to God, even when that meant giving young Samuel up to go work in the temple. Was I willing to give my own son to God, no matter where He might lead him?

At home our problems were getting worse. My son would hide behind the couch when my husband came into the room. For a long time, until he was four, my son would not speak. Eventually I sent him to our church pastor's home whenever my husband was back from the bush. During those times my son got to know a young couple who worked with the teens in our church, and who often took him horseback riding. The three of them became very close.

All this time I began to think more about Hannah and Samuel. I could have left my husband, but then all three of my boys would grow up without a father. I didn't want that! After much prayer I phoned the young couple who had grown so close to my son, so we could talk. They would love to take my son, if that's what I wanted. Suddenly I was filled with relief and knew that God had provided His answer.

God has been good to me, and He has been good to my son also. Today he is a confident young adult, and a Christian who really loves the Lord and desires to serve Him among our native people. He has told me, "Mom, being taken from you was like a nightmare. But now I love you for what you did. Even though it was hard, I know you did what was best for me." It was hard for both of us, but God has taken that pain and turned it into something beautiful. My other two sons have also grown into young men, and looking back I can say the Lord provided what was best for them, too.

4. The Rage of a Bull and The Rage of a Child

Key Verse - Philippians 3:13-14

*"No, Christian brothers, I do not have that life
yet. But I do one thing. I forget everything that
is behind me and look forward to that which is
ahead of me. My eyes are on the prize. I want to
win the race and get the prize of God's call from
heaven through Jesus Christ."*

**Her parents weren't ready for a baby and so,
after much pain and abuse, this Cree girl was
given to a foster family. There she learned about
Christian love, but could not practice that love
or be used by God until she could forgive her past.**

I WAS A FOSTER CHILD. My birth parents were
Cree, from a reserve in central Manitoba, but they
didn't live there. They were very sick with tuberculosis and spent a lot of time in a special hospital for
people with this illness. The hospital let my mother
out when I was about to be born, but because of my
parents' disease they were not allowed to keep me.
Within six days of my birth the Children's Aid Society took me away to a foster home.

The authorities placed me with a kindly white couple who were Christians and lived in a German farm-
ing community in our province. As an infant I became very attached to them. When I was thirteen
months old, however, my parents were released from
the sanitarium and wanted me back. It was very hard
when my foster parents took me to the bus station
to meet my birth mother. I screamed when they gave

me to this "strange" woman and walked away. They too were crying.

I spent quite a while with my birth parents, but it wasn't a happy time. They couldn't really take care of children because they had a drinking problem. And being very young, I guess I got on their nerves at times. When this happened they got angry and were very rough with me. One time I was abandoned in the woods. It was very cold and I nearly froze to death. This affected my young body and I got a disease that caused tumors to grow inside the bones of my legs. The doctors had to do several operations and keep me on a lot of painkillers. I didn't have a say in what was happening to me, and this thought tormented me greatly.

Finally, after a lot of abuse and suffering, the Children's Aid Society took me from my birth parents and placed me back in my old foster home. At first it was very disturbing, for I had become fearful of people and scared of being left alone. My foster mother had to hold me all the time or I would scream. The only way she could do any work was to have her husband hold me. I had many nightmares. But each time I woke up screaming, my foster parents would comfort me. They would say how much they loved me and that everything was alright.

One day my foster dad took me out to the barnyard where I could watch the farm animals and get some fresh air. I had just come home from the hospital in a full body cast. Suddenly I saw a bull charging straight at me. I couldn't move, but just closed my eyes and waited to die. Then I felt someone lift me up, and it was my dad. From that time I had a very real sense of love and loyalty for him, for I knew then my foster parents would never abandon me.

As a native girl in a small German community, I looked different than the white children. But for the most part we fit in well. Only as I grew older did I begin to see how some people treated Indians differently. Sometimes I would be blamed for things in school by people who thought being different made me a troublemaker. With the guidance of my foster parents, I learned not to let this bother me. I did very well in music, played the piano in public, and found I could get jobs at the grocery store and other places around town.

It was in fourth grade that I came to know Jesus in a personal way. My foster mother was talking to me about the special times in my life, and that made me think about the day my dad saved me from the charging bull. "You know dad really does love and care for you," she explained to me, "but your Heavenly Father loves you even more than dad ever could." With that my mom told me how Jesus died on the cross for my sins, and prayed with me as I trusted Christ to be my Savior. From then on I knew He would never leave me.

When I was eighteen the law said I could visit my birth parents whenever I wanted. But I wasn't ready to face them. My foster parents helped me with my bitter feelings. They never condemned my birth parents, but didn't agree with them either. "Yes, there were problems," they said, "but sometimes that happens when parents have a lot of children. They can't handle the stress. Some people end up drinking and doing different things because they don't know what else to do."

My foster parents helped me learn it's good to talk about these things when others who love God can give you advice and encouragement. The Bible says, "In a multitude of counselors there is safety" (Proverbs 11:14, KJV). At times I felt really angry about my birth parents and hurt about the things that happened when I was younger. When I began feeling this way, my foster parents talked with me about learning to love as Jesus did.

At age eighteen I went to Bible school. My foster parents arranged for me to visit my birth parents, and I felt a real battle inside. But a week before, God stepped in when a preacher came to my school to speak. I had a front-row seat and somehow we made eye contact. After the meeting he introduced himself and sensed I was worried about something. "If you keep your eyes on the Lord and learn to forgive those who have wronged you," he told me, "then God can use you. But that forgiveness has to take place. God can't use you when there is bitterness in your heart."

A few days later I went to visit my birth parents. I'm so glad God showed me the need to put bitter and resentful thoughts out of my heart! Now I see my birth parents quite often, and they like to call me on the telephone. They have both become Christians and are serving the Lord. And God has been able to use me too. I serve Him as a wife and mother, and have also taken courses at a Christian seminary to help me counsel others who hurt.

In counseling I tell them what I learned, that as a Christian I must "forget everything that is behind me and look forward to what is ahead of me. My eyes are on the prize. I want to win the race and get the prize [of serving God]" (Philippians 3:13-14). God does not want us to dwell on past wrongs, but press ahead in His service. As Jesus taught us in The Lord's Prayer, we forgive others because He first forgave us (Matthew 6:12).

5. Ten Year Old's World Falls Apart

Key Verse - Philippians 4:13

"I can do all things because Christ gives me the strength."

Eventually the alcohol, drugs, sexual abuse and abandonment split the family apart. Since the authorities took her brothers and sisters away, this Salteaux woman was never able to see some of them again. As a girl she trusted Christ and, though sometimes she did not live right, she could always count on Him.

MOM HAD LEFT US before, but this time it seemed longer. My sisters and I took turns looking after the babies, while the rest went to school. For food we raided gardens or borrowed bread from different people on the block. When there was a knock at the door, we hid until the people went away. Then one day some people knocked and did not go away. They said they would break down the door, so we let them in. It was the child welfare authorities, and they had come to take us away.

I was born in western Manitoba and lived on my dad's reservation until the age of five. We are members of the Salteaux tribe, related to the Ojibwes. My parents married when they were about eighteen and I was born very soon after. Then came two more girls, each of us about a year apart. My mom took care of us really well in spite of her young age. But dad had a real problem with alcohol. When my second sister died at six months old, neither my father nor his family came to the funeral. They were all out drinking. His family was very rough and many of them died violent deaths because of their drinking.

My dad worked for several farmers but his jobs never lasted. Finally he and mom decided to move to the city. By this time I had another little sister. It was exciting to live in the city, though we had a simple home. When dad was sober he was kind and loving and good to us. But even with our new life in the city, he kept on drinking. My father was always jealous of mom when he got drunk, and would slap us kids around to get the answers he wanted. Once he threw my sister against the wall, so that she needed medical attention afterwards.

With all these pressures, my mother began to drink too. Then sickness became a problem. She would be in the hospital for treatment, sometimes without us knowing where she was. Other times my mom would go off drinking, and once she was gone for a whole summer. Different people would look after us, some good and some very bad. Or we were left by ourselves.

When dad came home and found mom was gone, he would find her and beat her. Then mom would call the police and they would take my father away. Over the years, my mom went to the hospital a lot because of the beatings dad gave her. By this time, our parents were hardly ever together. Mom started having other relationships and after a while I had two more brothers, each from a different father.

Many strange people began coming and going in our house. They started coming after us kids so that we had to lock ourselves in a bedroom or bathroom for protection. Sometimes, however, we could not escape. Strange men would take me or one of my sisters off to some room, and we would just give up. We did not tell anyone because we were ashamed and scared, and nobody would believe us. Only now that we are adults can we talk to each other about these things.

Then came the day we were all so afraid of. Mom had been away for a week or more, and there was no sitter. We knew mom would come back sooner or later, but the children welfare agency got there first. They put my three brothers in different foster homes, while the three girls stayed in our home with a woman from the agency. Later a judge said our brothers had been put up for adoption and asked if we wanted the same. We said no, and spent the next seven years or more in foster homes. Because my youngest brother was a baby, he was adopted right away and I never saw him again. I did see my other two brothers about a year later, just once before their adoptions were final. My sisters and I stayed together for a while, then we were separated and never saw each other again for many years.

All this was very hard on me, because I was only about ten. In the following years I was moved from place to place, never settling down. But one thing helped keep me going. When we were together as a family, mom took us to church if she wasn't drinking. The people there showed us a lot of love, and brought us food and Christmas presents. Once a lady told us, "Wherever you go, Jesus is always there. You can always depend on Jesus if you ask Him into your hearts." One Sunday my mother prayed at church to receive Christ as her Savior. I also wanted Jesus in my life, so I prayed and received Him too.

Now that I was in foster homes, I really started to depend on prayer. Everything else was gone, but Jesus was there to comfort me. Some of the foster homes were good, but in others the people came after me like those strangers who used to come into our home. Nobody would believe my story, so I just put up with it and hoped it would soon end. At last some friends of our family tracked me down and got permission for me to live with them. They were good to me and taught me some solid lessons in life.

When I was fifteen my rebellious years began. I quit school and ran away, then got my own job and apartment. I also got in touch with my mom and two sisters. Out of this difficult time, something very positive happened. I met a boyfriend whose family was involved with an Indian church. Through them I started going too, and learned it wasn't enough just to know Jesus. I must make a commitment to living the way God wants. Since then my life has really changed. After seven years, when I was 22, my boyfriend and I got married. Now we have a loving home and two children of our own.

I stay in touch with my two sisters, and recently made contact with the oldest of my three brothers. He has been in serious trouble and will be in prison for a long time. For a time it seemed he might receive a capital sentence. I was so concerned that I sent him some Indian Christian magazines and books. Since then, through the letters he writes, I believe he has put his faith in Jesus Christ and begun a new life.

Over the years I have seen and experienced a lot of pain. But I have learned that, through the strength I find in the Lord and His Word, I can make my own choices. Just because my family fell to pieces does not mean I have to do the same. I have chosen to be different, for "I can do all things because Christ gives me the strength" (Philippians 4:13).

6. Elder Explores Childhood Pain
Key Verse - Colossians 3:13-15

"Try to understand other people. Forgive each other. If you have something against someone, forgive him. That is the way the Lord forgave you. And to all these things, you must add love. Love holds everything and everybody together and makes all these good things perfect. Let the peace of Christ have power over your hearts. You were chosen as a part of His body. Always be thankful."

It was supposed to be a picnic, but turned out to be six long years at boarding school. His mother

**divorced and remarried, and when this Ojibwe
boy finally came home his stepfather kicked him
out. The anger led to a lifetime of resentment,
and a lifetime of problems, until at last he made
a choice.**

ONE DAY WHEN I was six years old, my mother
packed several of us children up, took us to the rail-
road station and put us on the train. Mom gave us a
basket of food and said we were going on a picnic.
After talking to the conductor and telling us to be-
have, she waved goodbye. It sounded like fun, so
we left in high spirits. We rode for a very long time
until the conductor opened our basket and told us
to eat. After a while we came to a large city and were
moved to another train. By this time I was tired of
our adventure and hoped this train would take us
home. Instead it took us to an Indian boarding
school.

We were there for three years without seeing our
parents. Then after a brief time at home one summer, we spent another three years at the school. For
me the timing of this separation could not have been
worse. From the ages of six to twelve, when I was
shaping my values and conscience, my parents were
not there to give me support. When we returned
home to stay after six years at school, we found my
mother had divorced my father and was already remarried. It was a shattering experience that soon
got worse.

From the start, we could not get along with our
stepfather and were soon sent to our grandmother.
This meant not only was our real dad gone, but so

was our home. We were never to live with our mother again, except for brief visits. We had no communication with our dad, not even knowing where he was or what he was doing. Grandmother met our basic needs, but could not take the place of parents. This made us double losers. We missed our parents' input as children, and we missed out again during the difficult teenage years. Between living with our grandmother, and spending our summers working on farms, we were raised without any kind of parental guidance. As a result, my brothers and I became the biggest thieves in two counties.

Though I was not aware of it at the time, there was great anger building up inside me. I resented my mother for divorcing my dad and also for remarrying. I resented the two stepfathers that followed. I was also very bitter about being sent away to school and the way mother did it. I resented the school, the teachers and the government.

World War II brought further separation to our family. I was drafted in 1943 and chose to join the Army Air Corps. I wanted to be a bombardier, and today I am sure the idea of dropping bombs was a reflection of the rage inside me. It was one way I could get back at the world for all the hurts I had suffered. However, I was too tall and heavy for flight service and was assigned instead as a radio control operator. For 28 months I served in the Mediterranean theater, and as the war progressed we lost a lot of bombardiers. When a call went out for volunteers, I applied and was assigned to a bomber crew.

On about our twenty-fifth bombing mission, our plane was badly shot up. I was wounded, but we made it back to the airstrip. I felt luck had finally deserted me and became terrified of being shot down on every mission. Then came a really difficult mission and, to get my courage, I went out drinking beforehand with a vengeance. I had been introduced to alcohol at an early age, because my mother made home brew to earn extra money and my father stashed illegal moonshine. Now I spent all my time on the ground drinking, and would sober up just enough to fly the next day. It was the only way I could handle my fear, and resulted in my becoming a confirmed alcoholic.

There were a lot of desperation prayers during those days. I did not know for sure if God existed but, in case He did, I pleaded with Him to bring me back safely from my bombing raids. If He held up His end of the bargain, then I promised to give Him my life and be anything He wanted. This was my prayer each time as we headed toward our targets. By the time the war was over, these promises were very real to me—but so was the hold of alcohol on my life.

When I was released from the army, I returned to Wisconsin where my mother was living. She did not live on a reservation since our people, Ojibwes of the St. Croix Band, did not have one. With time on my hands I did what I knew best—drinking. For the next year I went from one party to another, celebrating with friends and relatives who were just returning from the service. I remembered my promises to God, but for the moment I was marching to the orders of alcohol.

One day toward the end of my first year back from the war, a brother of mine came to visit. He was a minister and, when he invited me to spend a week with him, I was not too excited. There were a lot of parties I did not want to miss. But my brother kept after me until I agreed. He brought me to a prayer meeting at his church, and at last I came face to face with the promises I made to God during the war. My brother asked if I had ever considered giving my heart to Jesus. When he said that, I knew God was coming to collect! And so I made my decision to become a Christian that night.

This was not an instant solution to my problems, but it was the most important decision I ever made. At last I was in touch with Someone Who would never leave me or turn His back on me. Things went well for a number of years after that, then alcohol dragged me down and nearly killed me. I think a big part of that was my failure for many years to deal with all the bitterness and resentment I had built up since childhood. But God was faithful and gave me a second chance. Today my wife and I have the privilege of telling Indian people that God can deliver them from the grief and turmoil of childhood separation, alcohol and other social ills that native people face.

I regret it was only late in life that I dealt with the hurt and anger from my childhood. Over the years I had developed a ministry of counseling Indian people with alcohol problems. In talking to hundreds of native people, I became aware of the problems faced by children who lived apart from their parents. My own life fit that description to a tee! I knew that with God's help these feelings must be rooted out if I wanted to live completely for Him.

By this time my mother had passed away, so I went out to her grave and asked God to forgive the way I had resented her all those years. Then I decided to love my mother, and with that decision the root of my anger was removed. There is no longer a reason to be upset. To my thinking, that's a lot better than finding ways to "control" my rage for the rest of my life. I would much rather be rid of it once and for all, and get on with the joy of living for Christ! "Try to understand other people. Forgive each other. If you have something against someone, forgive him. That is the way the Lord forgave you. And to all these things, you must add love. Love holds everything and everybody together and makes all these good things perfect. Let the peace of Christ have power over your hearts" (Colossians 3:13-15).

7. My Defensive Walls Fell Down

Key Verse - Psalm 50:15

"Call on me in the day of trouble. I will take you out of trouble, and you will honor Me."

With her marriage broken, this Micmac woman just wanted to be left alone. Before long, however, the volcano of hurt, pain and anger began to erupt. Her children were deeply affected, and at last she felt completely cornered. Only then was she ready to reach for the one thing that could save her.

I KNEW IT was the end of our marriage. After ten years I could not take it anymore. I just gave up. "I don't need anybody," I said to myself. "I can do it alone." So I stopped talking and visiting with my friends and relatives. When the phone rang I would not answer. I locked the doors after the children went to school, and again after I let them in when they came home. I did not allow them to play outside. My curtains were closed all the time. That was how I lived my life.

I am a Micmac Indian. All my life I have lived on our reserve in southeastern Quebec. Unlike most children on the reserve, I grew up with many rules because my parents were of a different religion and very strict. It kept me from getting into bad habits, but as a teenager I was inwardly rebellious. Then some boys made a bet with the man who would later become my husband. They said he would not be able to get me to go out with him. He won the bet, and I surprised myself and everybody else by later marrying him. He was a good provider, but our marriage had a rocky foundation. Neither his parents nor grandparents had been married, so his home had not been very stable. By contrast, I was overprotected as a child.

We had two children, and then a set of twins. But the twins died a few after hours after they were born. This was hard to take, but there were many more hard knocks to follow before the Lord got my attention. My husband and I argued all the time, and he began to run around on me. By now we had another child, and I watched the three of them while he partied all night. Slowly our paths began to separate. We stopped talking to each other because there was nothing to talk about. When I found out he had been unfaithful, I could not handle it and decided to leave.

My husband didn't want me to leave. "I'll make it up to you," he said, telling me that we could still make a go of it. So I stayed and things seemed to improve for about a year. Then the problems started all over again. That's when I felt the walls were closing in on me. I cut myself off from everybody and filed for divorce. Our nine-year-old daughter took it very hard. She knew we would never be a family again and blamed herself. Her grades dropped in school. She stopped caring and did not trust anyone. All she did was cry all day long for about a year. I took her to every doctor in the area but they could do nothing.

Inside I was like a volcano, ready to blow up over anything. It is a miracle I did not seriously hurt anyone. I was crying constantly and asking how these things could happen. Sometimes my sister-in-law came to visit, but I would not talk to her either. Several times she asked me to go to church, but I said no. If only I could be left alone, I thought, then I could make it on my own. Yet at last there came a day when I felt really cornered. I realized that I could not go on anymore and desperately needed help.

Right about that time, my sister-in-law invited me to hear a special speaker who was coming to her church. I finally agreed to go because I knew she would not leave me alone unless I went. I sat there during the meeting but would not speak to anybody. However, the more that preacher talked about what Jesus had done for me, the more I knew Jesus was what I needed. I had tried to manage my own life but it had not worked. Near the end of the service, the pastor said, "Does anyone want to ask Jesus to forgive his sins and take over his life?" Then he said those people should come to the front of the church.

I was standing in the back row, trying to get enough courage to go down the aisle. As I went forward, the pastor met me about halfway. He knew about my marriage problems. With his hand on my shoulder, we prayed together. I cried out, "Lord, I've made a mess of my life. Now it's Your turn. Handle it for me." In that moment when I confessed my sins and asked Jesus to take control, the walls I had built around myself fell down. Christ had set me free! And with great joy, I saw my three young children also receive Christ that same day. We have been serving Him ever since.

Now we are praying for my ex-husband and his two children to be saved. He comes to visit once in a while, and I don't hate him or his girlfriend. The Lord took away all the hate and replaced it with His love. He has also helped my daughter with her problems, and I have seen her grow spiritually as a Christian. God has graciously provided all three of my children the opportunity to attend a Christian school where they can get a good education and learn His Word. Today I would never go back to my old life, where I tried to run things my own way. I thought that I could make it alone, but it's so much to know that God says, "Call on Me in the time of trouble and I will deliver you" (Psalm 50:11).

THINGS TO THINK ABOUT

1. I Sang, Sewed and Swam for Jesus

Like the native woman in this story, you may not find out for many years why God allowed a broken home to put you in the place where you needed to be. Meanwhile He promises to supply your needs. Read John 6:35-40. What must you do to satisfy your spiritual hunger and thirst? Is this promise given by Jesus available to anyone?

2. Abandoned by Parents, Adopted by God

When you are abandoned by those you loved and trusted, you may decide never to love again. Maybe that way you'll never be hurt again. But there is Someone whose love you can count on. Read Psalm 100:5, then go back and read verses 1-4. According to verse 5, what are three things you can say about God? Because you can count on Him, what difference (according to verses 1-4) should it make in your life?

3. Nightmare Turns Into Blessing

Sometimes a separation between parent and child, or among family members, cannot be avoided. Read 1 Samuel 1:28. Even when a child or loved one must depart, there is one thing you can do to help assure their protection. What is that? How can it help?

4. The Rage of a Bull and the Rage of a Child

Separation can lead to bitterness and anger toward the parents or guardians who seemingly betrayed and abandoned you. Read Matthew 6:12 and Philippians 3:13-14. What does Philippians 3:13-14 call you to do? How would failure to obey Matthew 6:12 prevent you from fulfilling that call?

5. Ten Year Old's World Falls Apart

Few people will ever share such deep devastation as the Salteaux woman in this story. But as she found out, no situation is so bad that God cannot overcome it. Read Philippians 4:11-14. You can learn to face any circumstance. What makes that possible? If you claim such strength, how will it change the way you live?

6. Elder Explores Childhood Pain

The bitterness of a broken family can sink deep in your heart, so deep you don't even realize it. But because the things you say and do are governed by what is in your heart (Mark 7:20-23), a bitter spirit will affect the way you live. Read Colossians 3:13-15. What attitude is necessary for true forgiveness? When this attitude is present, what are the resulting benefits?

7. My Defensive Walls Fell Down

When a marriage falls apart, your first reaction may be to shut out the world. But that's like trying to dam the ocean. Cutting yourself off does nothing to relieve the hurt and pain. Read Psalm 50:15, then go back and read verses 10-14. Why is God able to fulfill His promise to help you in times of trouble? What is required of you to receive this help?

CHAPTER FOUR

Conquering Loneliness and Suicide

1. Self Hatred Replaced By New Identity

Key Verse - Proverbs 14:12

"There is a way which looks right to a man, but its end is the way of death."

The downward spiral seemed to have no end. She moved from one town to another, hoping for a new start. Yet the story was always the same. She hated herself and had no hope of ever changing. Then she met someone whose life had been turned around, and wondered if it could happen to her.

THE ALCOHOL AND DRUGS were starting to have their effect on me. I had visions of going insane, of people coming to take me away. This is when I began thinking of ways to kill myself, so I could get away from it all. I had no hope. Even the drugs and alcohol were unable to help me forget anymore. At this point in my life I didn't care about anything. I hated what I was, but did not have much hope of changing. At times I figured even my baby son would be much better off dead.

I was very bitter, very angry—and very mean. Nobody loved me, and I wanted to keep it that way. To protect myself I turned off my feelings. If nobody could get close to me, then I would not get hurt. At the same time, I didn't care how much pain I caused others. I hurt a lot of people that way, some of them very badly. But it didn't matter to me what I did or to whom I did it. The more people were scared of me, the better I liked it.

I come from a large family. There were nine boys and five girls. By the time I was born, many of my brothers had already moved away. My growing years were pretty miserable, and I grew up with a very bitter attitude toward everybody, even myself. When I was a teenager I rebelled against my parents' authority for I wanted to live my own way. I didn't answer to anyone—and as for God, He was Someone totally foreign to me. I felt that I could never reach Him, so why bother?

At age fifteen I left home, began to drink, and drifted from one relationship to another, always searching and never finding. After two years I was worn down and went back home to attend high school. Soon I got involved with an Indian guy from a nearby reservation. When I got pregnant we both quit school and began living together at his parents' home. I tried so hard to make it work, but it was a losing battle. My son was four months old when I left his father.

One of my older brothers helped me find a job and an apartment at Slave Lake in Canada's Northwest Territories. It was a new start. But before long I was drinking again. After that I was introduced to drugs and began doing a lot of heavy stuff. All I lived for was myself and drugs. Nothing else mattered. Eventually I had no friends left at all, and lost both my job and my apartment.

Luckily I had sent my son back home to Alberta, and later my mother convinced me to come back too. My sister and I got an apartment together. But when I got a job in a tavern, the destructive cycle started all over again. Sometimes I didn't get off work until two or three in the morning, and then I would go partying until daybreak. While I was sleeping it off, my sister often had to break into the apartment and take my my son because I could not care for him.

The crowd I was running with was pretty tough. Today I'm amazed how the Lord must have been protecting me. I used to carry drugs with me and sell them at the tavern, but was never caught. Other times the parties would get out of hand and turn violent. Often I didn't even know how to get home, but would wake up at my apartment somehow in one piece and unhurt. But inside I was hurting badly, and my thoughts of suicide became stronger and stronger.

Desperate for a change, I decided to try another new start. I quit my job, moved to Edmonton and stayed at my brother's house. His wife also had a brother who was staying there, and this brother had just become a Christian. He talked about religious stuff all the time, but I paid no attention. In fact, I thought something had snapped in his mind from the drugs he'd been taking, and I felt sorry for him. If his Jesus-talk bothered me too much, I told him to shut up and leave me alone. God was okay for him, but not for me.

The Bible says, "There is a way which looks right to a man, but its end is the way of death" (Proverbs 14:12). That sure describes my situation! I was following my own way, but whether by suicide or by some other means, I was sure to end up dead. Yet if "the way of a fool is right in his own eyes," he can find wisdom by "listening to good teaching" (Proverbs 12:15). Perhaps I was so desperate that I was ready for some sense. Because as the weeks went by I became more interested in the "Jesus talk" I was hearing.

I noticed a definite change in the life of my sister-in-law's brother. Smoking and drinking were left behind, and he had a kind of peace about him. He looked so happy, but I figured there was no way it could ever happen to me. Suicide was a much more practical answer for my troubles. Yet he kept inviting me to church and finally I agreed, just to shut him up for awhile.

When we got there I began to get a funny feeling. I wanted to turn and run, but something made me stay. I don't remember what the preacher said, but I do remember the love that was evident all around me. Being at that church gave me a "happy fluttery" sensation, like you get on a date. I went back again the next night, and this time when the preacher asked if anyone wanted to accept Christ, right away I responded. I prayed and asked Jesus to forgive me and be the Lord and Savior of my life. At that moment, all thoughts of suicide were gone forever! Inside I felt new and clean, and knew that Jesus was real and that He loved me.

After awhile I moved back to the reservation. I learned one of my girlfriends had also become a Christian, and she told me about a native church that was being started in our town. Once I started going, and attending a Bible study for women, I really began growing in my newfound faith. My life was changing—and my family could not understand it. They thought I was crazy, that it would never last. When I was baptized at the church, my mother disowned me. That hurt a lot. But as I honored God, He gave me peace. My self-hatred was gone, for now I found my identity in Him Who made me the way I am.

Since then, God has even restored the relationship with my mother. From going to Bible school I had learned a lot about God and His Word. But when my parents divorced, I had to learn even more about how to forgive and how to love as Jesus did. Now my mother and I are closer than we've ever been, and she respects my Christian beliefs. Today I am praying Jesus will save her too, just as He saved me from a life so bad I wanted to end it. He cared enough to come into my life in the nick of time, and turn me around when nobody else could. I probably wouldn't be around today if it weren't for Him. When the Bible says He died in my place, for me that's very literally true!

2. The Big Black Hole in My Life

Key Verse - Romans 10:9-10

"If you say with your mouth that Jesus is Lord and believe in your heart that God raised Him from the dead, you will be saved from the punishment of sin. When we believe in our hearts, we are made right with God. We tell with our mouth how we were saved from the punishment of sin."

More parties and more drinking. Her life was going nowhere, and she didn't care. After all, her father was dead and God was to blame. The tragedy drove her mother to alcohol, and she soon followed. Then she met some native young people who were different, who seemed to have what she lacked. What was it?

WHEN DAD DIED, my whole life seemed to fall apart. I hated him for leaving me. And I bitterly resented God for taking him away. I hated life, too, and wanted to die. I thought this would get rid of my loneliness and the aching in my soul. And that is when I noticed the bottles of pills on my dresser.

But my life was not always like this. I have many good memories of my father from my early childhood. He was always there to help me when problems came up. Being the only daughter and the youngest child, his love for me was very apparent. My father was also a Christian, and this made life better for all of us. When I was eight years old, I too made a profession of faith in Christ.

Two years later, however, when I was ten, my father died of a heart attack. It was then that problems began to grow in our family. My mother, who had made a profession of Christian faith shortly before I was born, began now to have doubts. Soon she turned herself to the power of alcohol. I changed, too, for I was filled with resentment and could not bring myself to talk about it. Within two years after my father died, I knew what an alcoholic was; I had become one of them.

My life at this point was very miserable. My mother and I still talked to each other a bit, but there was a big black hole in our lives. It seemed like I was not really living; I was only existing. The word "suicide" was beginning to take shape in my mind. The more I thought about ending my life, the more it seemed the only answer. Then one weekend when my family was gone, I had a plan.

As usual, I was home by myself. I wanted to take my life, but was afraid so I decided to go out for the evening and get drunk. That way I could work up the courage to do the deed. When I got back home that night the house was very still. Being alone, it felt all the more empty, just like my life. I was filled with so much bitterness and loneliness that I just wanted to end it all. That is when I headed for the pills on the dresser. Pill bottles seemed to be everywhere. The invitation was open. Quickly I opened one bottle after another until I had swallowed nearly four bottles of pills.

I can't remember what happened at this point. I must have called a friend to see if she wanted to see me one last time before I died. She came right away, and walked into an awful sight. I was drunk, alone and bloody. Blood was scattered all over the room because I had slashed my arms with a razor blade. The next thing I remember is being surrounded by four walls, and from the smell I could tell this place was a hospital. My life was spared but I didn't know why. I could only feel like a failure because I wasn't dead.

For another four years my life went on as before—parties, getting drunk, more parties, and getting drunk again. The cycle was vicious. By age seventeen my life was going nowhere, and to me it just didn't matter anymore.

Then one weekend I was invited to go along to a Christian conference for native people. At first I was resentful because the white people seemed to control everything and that made me mad. I hated white people for all the past and present wrongs that had happened to the Indian people. However, I was soon impressed by the friendliness of the many native Christians I met. They seemed different and happy. So I decided to stop being mad and to start listening.

Someone came up to me and explained how I could have salvation by trusting Jesus as my Savior. Right away I was flooded with memories of my father, who was a Christian, and the profession of faith I had made as a girl. But to be truly born again, a person must not only "profess" Christ with words; he must also "possess" Him in his heart. The Bible says, "If you say with your mouth that Jesus is Lord, and believe in your heart that God raised Him from the dead, you will be saved from the punishment of sin.

When we believe in our hearts, we are made right with God" (Romans 10:9-10).

Perhaps as a girl I had only spoken words. Because right now I did not feel that I was God's child. I couldn't bring myself to God because I was too sinful, and figured God probably hated me anyway. Then someone told me how God loves people just the way they are. I thought about this all throughout the conference. God could forgive me, but did I really want to give up my drugs and alcohol? I left the conference without making up my mind.

Words still echoed in my mind as we travelled home, words that wouldn't leave me alone. After six hours in the car, I reached home and went right to bed. Yet exhausted as I was, before shutting my eyes and going to sleep I somehow managed to mumble a prayer in the darkness. "Jesus, can you come into my heart tonight? I want You to be there, okay? In Jesus' name, Amen." With that I drifted into a deep and restful sleep. I felt so happy and so different in the morning! And so I prayed again to confirm my decision and thank Jesus for making me His child.

Soon I was convicted about my need to stop smoking. At that time I was smoking a pack of cigarettes every day. However, when I prayed and asked Jesus for help, almost at once I couldn't stand the smell of tobacco smoke anymore. Later I had a desire to begin serving the Lord and sharing my faith with other Indian people. God led me to a native Bible school in Ontario, and there I began to use my talent for singing. Before, I would only sing to the Lord privately. At Bible school I began to go out with student gospel teams to sing and give my testimony. Since then I have shared my faith as much as possible, giving all the credit to the One who made it possible.

And God has touched my mother too. Soon after I finished Bible school, my mother reconfirmed her commitment to Christ by giving herself in baptism. Ever since that time she has changed. The two of us no longer have a big black hole in our lives. Instead we have one very big, real God. And that's good enough for us!

3. I Lost My Son and Found God's Son

Key Verse - Romans 1:2-4

"The Good News was promised long ago by God's early preachers in His Holy Writings. It tells of His Son, our Lord Jesus Christ, Who was born as a person in the flesh through the family of King David. The Holy Spirit proved by a powerful act that Jesus our Lord is the Son of God because He was raised from the dead."

His son had always followed in his footsteps. So when the boy hung himself, this native father had to admit he hadn't been a very good example. In great anguish he searched his soul and realized he was headed down the same hopeless path. But unlike his son, at least he still had a choice.

IT WAS THE LAST day of March when I went to my trapline on Assinika Lake in northern Manitoba. I needed to check my traps. My son was to follow.

When I got there, I first set some beaver snares. Then I checked my fish net. Toward evening I went for firewood from the bush. As I was returning to the cabin, I met some men from my village. They came to tell me of my son's tragic death. He had locked himself in a closet and hung himself.

After I heard the message, I said to the men, "Go on ahead. I have dogs to go home with." As soon as they left, I too got on my way. Then as I crossed a portage and moved on to the next lake, I saw a plane flying low. It landed for me because I was wanted at home right away. I untied my dogs so they could return on their own, and then I boarded the plane. In a short time we were back in the village.

As I walked up to my home, I could see many people had gathered, some inside and some outside. Here I saw my son on the floor, partly in the closet where he had died. I felt a heavy wave of sorrow come over me, but I did not cry. I merely touched my son's body. Then at last tears began rolling down my face. My wife wept bitterly. I could hear her wailing. Soon the RCMP arrived to take the body out for investigation. We had to wait for it to be returned before we could have the funeral.

It was no longer easy to be at home. I was very depressed and my wife suffered much also. At times she would get up during the night and walk around weeping. This upset me very much, and I did not know what to do. Finally the day came for my son to be buried. After the funeral I decided not to go home for awhile, but go to my traplines on Assinika Lake. And so I walked about in the wilderness, but found no peace. I was constantly reminded of my son who used to trap with me. To ease my memory, I removed his belongings whenever I came upon them.

Then one night I picked up my Bible, which I always had with me at the cabin. I began reading from the first chapter of Romans. As I read the words written by the apostle Paul, I remembered how he actually met Jesus on the road to Damascus (Acts 9:1-7). Now in his letter to the Christians in Rome, Paul explained what he knew about Jesus—that His coming was promised by God, and we can know Jesus is God's Son because He was raised from the dead (Romans 1:2-4).

As I saw this in my Bible, I became fearful. Jesus is real, and I had just read the proof. Something came over me until my head throbbed with pressure. I put the Bible aside and laid down on my bed. As I lay there beside the crackling fire, my eyes closed, in my mind I had an image of a man walking. He was in darkness not knowing where to go. Then the man came again, this time walking in bright light. Suddenly I knew that man was me! Though it seemed only a dream, it made a big impression upon my heart. Either I could walk in darkness or in light.

I gave this a lot of thought. Early the next morning, as I got on my way, I was still thinking. I began to see the need for a change. For years I had lived a life of steady drinking, smoking, chewing and speaking evil. Every possible sin was committed. Even as I lived, I destroyed myself. I saw how my own child had followed my example and ended up taking his own life. That is why I now wanted to leave my old ways and never return to them again.

I decided to see the church leaders in the village and tell them about my desire for a new life. We prayed together and I confessed all my sins to God. Nothing was left unturned. But when I at last got up from my knees, I knew Jesus had forgiven it all and saved me from destruction. In the years since trusting Christ as my Savior, He has given me a new heart and helped me walk in the light. When I see people doing the things I once did, I am sad for they do not have the peace Jesus gives.

Walking in God's light is something I do step by step every day. When I get ready to leave every morning, I ask Him to help me do good all day, and that the Holy Spirit would guide me. When my work is done I thank Jesus for giving me strength and safety. At mealtime I thank Him for providing the needs of my body. At bedtime I pray that I might sleep well. This is how I live now, since I gave my life to Jesus.

When I see someone who has not found Jesus yet, I reach out to him. I know so many of them. When I get the chance I ask them, "Would you like to follow Jesus, Who has given His life for us? God will keep His promise and give us eternal life. And He will let us conquer the things that destroy us." Some have understood me and taken this new life, and I am so glad because of the pain they have been spared. For me, losing my son was hard, but God used it to bring me out of my darkness and into His light.

4. A Handful of Pills and a Razor Blade

Key Verse - Psalm 23:4

"Yes, even if I walk through the valley of the shadow of death, I will not be afraid of anything, because you are with me. You have a walking stick with which to guide and one with which to help. These comfort me."

This Salteaux Indian grew up without rules. His father was lawless and lived only for himself. When he died, the boy was never in a foster home long enough to learn any discipline. So he just took what he wanted. And when the authorities threw him in jail, he had nothing left to take but his own life.

WHEN I WALKED into the federal penitentiary I was a very mixed up person. The thought of spending eight lonely years behind bars was more than I could face. In desperation I swallowed a handful of pills I managed to get and waited until they took effect. Then while I felt numb, I slashed my arms open with a razor blade. Thanks to a friend who found me, I got immediate help and my life was saved. That gave me another chance at life, but also the opportunity to find a completely new life in Christ.

At the time, however, I had mixed emotions about still being alive. Ever since the judge said eight years, my head was still spinning at the very thought. "This can't be happening to me!" a voice screamed inside me. "There must be some mistake!" Laying now in the prison infirmary, I wondered what there was to live for? Up to that time my past was just one great echo of my father. Though he had died several years before, his lawless ways were still my patterns. As I suddenly came to realize where this road had led, all my boyhood dreams came crashing in on me.

I grew up as a Salteaux Indian in Manitoba, in a very undisciplined home. Neither my dad, nor anyone else, encouraged me to live a good life. My father just went out and spent what money he had on his own enjoyment. To feed us, my mother was forced to get food from our neighbors. And when it came to the law, dad felt they were always out to get him. The law had no benefits for Indians! Growing up with this attitude, we thought nothing of stealing from other people's vegetable gardens—or going out with my dad on Sundays to steal from yards and homes while people were in church.

Things got pretty lonely with a dad who only cared for himself and was often gone. Yet at least we had a family and a home. Then when I was about seven, my father died and us kids were placed in foster homes. Now it was lonelier than ever! Since foster homes are never permanent, I was always being moved around a lot. And each place had its own rules. That was frustrating for me, a boy who had never used knives and forks—much less learned to say, "Pass the salt, please." After being in about eight different homes, all with different standards, I still had no pattern to follow. All I had was the one I developed from watching my dad.

When I was old enough, I moved to the city of Winnipeg. City people were much harder than country people. Even the Indians were different. I had expected friends and excitement, but now I was lonely again. For me, fitting in meant bluffing my way around. As the months passed I grew harder inside. It didn't matter to me anymore whether a person was Indian or white—because I challenged them all! It was better that way, not trusting anybody so I wouldn't get hurt.

Liquor was a big problem for me, and it led to violence and crime. Since there was nobody but me, why not take what I wanted and fight anyone who stood in my way? Soon the juvenile authorities knew me like a book. They finally decided I was an "incorrigible person" and sent me to a reform school, where I learned and developed new ways to steal. When I finally got out, it did not take the authorities long to discover my new pattern of crime. Once again I was picked up by the police, whom my dad taught me were no good. With my past record working against me, the judge sentenced me to eight years in prison.

In the weeks and months after my suicide attempt, the loneliness of my life was like a crushing weight. There seemed no reason to live, because my old pattern had not worked. Yet I was open to finding a new pattern, and through a friend I learned about the Lord who "takes care of the children who have no father" (Psalm 146:9). My father had given me no guidance, but Jesus "gives Light to every man" who believes in Him (John 1:9). The more I learned about Christ, the more I wanted to follow Him— and one day I decided I would, and did.

As I look back now, my life reminds me of Psalm 23. As I came up from "the shadow of death," the

Lord like a shepherd used His stick "to guide and...to help" me (Psalm 23:4). Then I found the comfort these verses promise. In the years since then God has replaced my loneliness with fulfillment, and my lawless ways with His direction. I have been released from prison, married a beautiful Christian wife, and had the opportunity to attend Bible school. I am not sure where the Lord will lead me from here, but I am content to follow in His footsteps.

5. An Angel Brought Me Groceries

Key Verse - Isaiah 57:15

"For the high and honored One Who lives forever, Whose name is Holy, says ,'I live in the high and holy place. And I also live with those who are sorry for their sins and have turned from them and are not proud. I give new strength to the spirit of those without pride, and also to those whose hearts are sorry for their sins'."

She was only ninety miles from home, but it might as well have been ninety thousand! The wall that kept her away was solidly made of sin, guilt and shame. Yet in another sense this Navajo woman had come to the end of the road. And in so doing, she was able at last to make a new beginning.

THE LONELINESS NEARLY drove me crazy. On weekends I couldn't bear to stay home. I just had to be someplace to get my mind off the troublesome life I was living. I soon began to wander, leaving my kids again and again. Because I grew up in a Christian family, I had never thought my life would be like this. I guess that I just lost hope. My home just wasn't a "home" anymore. My husband was gone for good, and I was always out drinking and making the rounds at the bars. I had a miserable life—and twice during those days I had tried to end it.

Before then I tried to make a go of it. I was divorced, but had managed to get a decent job. Christmas was getting close. I wanted to make it a nice occasion for the kids. So I planned a trip to Albuquerque, about 200 miles away, to buy some Christmas presents. I arranged for the kids to stay with my uncle, since my sister and I would only be gone two or three days at the most. The car made the trip just fine and we bought the presents and headed for home. There were no problems until we got near Gallup, New Mexico. Actually, I was the one who made the problems.

"Why are you stopping? We're only ninety miles from home," my sister asked. "Well, we ought to put some gas in the car, and while we're here we can get something to eat," I answered. The place I chose to eat was a bar. It served food too. But we ordered a drink. Then another and another. Two days went by and we were still in Gallup and still spending most of our time in the bar. "I was supposed to be back to work two days ago," I told my sister. "I've got to call my supervisor." When I called, he said I didn't need to come back because I no longer had a job.

My sister asked what I was going to do. I didn't know. I was too ashamed to go home and face my family. What would I tell the children? So we just stayed in Gallup. Three months later my car was still in a Gallup parking lot. The Christmas presents were still in the trunk. One night while I was working in a bar, a man came from the finance company to take back my car, since I hadn't made my payments. When I asked if I could get the Christmas presents out of the trunk, he laughed. "You do your Christmas shopping early. This is only the end of February." I got the presents, but I never saw my car again.

Early in March I decided to go home. I was sick and ashamed of myself, and barely had enough for the bus fare. When I got to my house the children were gone. The house was open. The electricity had been turned off for not paying the bills. The water had frozen in the pipes and they had burst. The sink was broken. There I stood in the living room, knowing that my home was no longer a home.

Then I noticed the Christmas tree still in the corner of the living room. The tree was withered now, but there was a Christmas card on it. It was from my kids. They had made the card themselves, and at the bottom was written, "We love you." Tears began rolling down my cheeks. Here I was in my own house, yet so far from home! Somehow I managed to get my kids back together, but I still didn't have any peace. For the next three years I kept wandering, leaving my children again and again, anything to escape my loneliness. Before long I was back in Gallup. I ended up in the back alleys.

The road that brought me to this point was a long one. I was raised on the Navajo reservation in Arizona by loving parents who were dedicated Christians. But at the age of sixteen I met a boy. Mom was not too pleased about him, especially since we married before I finished high school. For the first three years we were very happy. Then the disagreements began. Over the next twelve years we had constant fighting, pain and bitterness. By then we had four children. But my husband was using alcohol and I couldn't take it any longer. So we decided to divorce.

After the divorce I moved the children to Cleveland, Ohio, where I took three years of business training. Then we went back to Arizona and I was able to get a good job. It didn't surprise me when my ex-husband turned up, asking to see the children. He didn't look good, had lost a lot of weight, and couldn't remember all the places he had been. I took him to see the kids, and began to feel compassion for him. The children needed a father, I thought. And since our emotions had a chance to cool off, perhaps now we could work it out.

We decided to get remarried. We even had another child and thought this would bring our marriage back together. But after the child was born, we were talking divorce again. Things had gone from bad to worse. When we argued, we brought up things that had happened while we lived apart. That same year we got another divorce. After that I just lost hope. I was crushed by loneliness because I thought my life would never work out again. Soon I began to live just like my ex-husband, leaving home to go off drinking—until finally I ended up, an utterly lonely and miserable woman, in the back alleys of Gallup.

One day as I walking down an alley, I thought about

the Navajo church where I had grown up. Then an old hymn we used to sing came into my mind, and with tears I cried out the words, "Pass me not, O Gentle Savior. Hear my humble cry." Then I told the Lord, "I'm a mess. I'm not the person I was meant to be. There's got to be a better way." The next evening I was sleeping off a hangover in the darkened corner of a dance hall. When I woke up, it seemed like a spotlight had been turned on me. Suddenly I realized what a sinner I was. I didn't want to be that drunken, lonely old woman anymore. In fact, the thought of alcohol now disgusted me. And most of all, I wanted to go home and be with my children.

Yet I had no transportation. The next day I was still listless from all the alcohol in my system. At this point, I believe the Lord stepped in. When I went back to the bar to collect my things, a woman noticed how desperate I looked. The Bible (Hebrews 13:2) says we sometimes meet angels without knowing it. Looking back, I know this woman was an angel God sent my way. She offered to take me, but I told her it was 90 miles. "I've got nothing else to do today," the woman answered, "and I'm not going to waste my time in this bar. It's a good day to look at the scenery. Let's go!" Along the way, she even stopped and bought some groceries for my kids.

That was the turning point in my life. I had come to the place where I was "sorry for my sins and had turned from them and was not proud." Only when a person is broken like I was, can the Lord "give new strength to the spirit of those without pride, and also to those whose hearts are sorry for their sins"

(Isaiah 57:15).

At the same time, my husband had also reached the end of his rope. He was sick and going blind, and the doctors said he had only six months to live. Since our second divorce, he had lived in alleys and gutters. He drank anything with alcohol in it, just to get drunk. Not knowing where to turn, he came back to his mother. Four days later I found him living there, when I brought my children to her house for a haircut.

My husband didn't want to see me. Like me, he had built up much bitterness over the years. He also thought I would be drinking and, in his condition, could not stand to be around it. But his mother spoke to him, "You should spend some time with your kids and take them out." So he came home with me, and after three weeks of silence my husband asked if I could find someone to pray with us. I thought prayers would help, but there was something deeper we both needed. We needed Jesus.

At the post office I ran into a man who was a preacher and asked him to pray with us. He told me about some meetings his church was having, and said he would talk to us there. My husband and I attended the next service. Toward the end, the preacher asked anyone to come to the front of the church who wanted to receive Christ as Savior. With tears flowing down our cheeks, my husband and I both went down the aisle, and asked Jesus to take control of our lives.

Today I know our relationship as husband and wife is like a triangle. We are the two bottom points and

God is the top. Before, when we did not look up to God, we remained apart at the bottom of the triangle. That's why we were so lonely. But when we started looking up to God, we met at the top where the sides of the triangle come together. Now the Lord has brought our whole family back together, and today we have four grandchildren. We are living proof that the only way to true fulfillment is Jesus, and you will always be lonely deep inside until you find Him.

6. God Interrupted My Hunger Strike

Key Verse - 2 Corinthians 5:17

"For if a man belongs to Christ, he is a new person. The old life is gone. The new life has begun."

No jail could hold this Apache teenager, except the jail of his own sin and hatred. When they finally locked him away for good, he had no reason to live. But as he lay near death from suicide, he overheard a voice outside his solitary cell. The voice spoke strangely, but the words penetrated his soul.

FOUR TIMES I TRIED to commit suicide by hanging. I had nothing to live for. As an Apache teenager in Arizona I was constantly in trouble with the law. It seemed I spent more time in jail than out of it. Ten times I broke loose, once by walking right through the office. But that was the last time. Seven mounted police caught me and took me off to jail again in handcuffs. Now they put me under maximum security and solitary confinement where I would eventually spend the next 223 days. My ankles were chained together. They took everything from me, leaving me to sleep on the cold cement floor without even a blanket. I was helpless, alone and without hope.

After 33 days in solitary I went on a hunger strike that I hoped would end my life. Food was given to me each day through a small hole in the door, but I refused it. This went on for thirteen days and it seemed my wish to die would soon come true. But on that day a Pima Indian missionary pastor came to the jail to hold a service. I could not see him from my cell but could hear his voice. The pastor sang a song, "Jesus Paid It All," and told how Jesus had found him in a Los Angeles prison cell and changed his life. He was awaiting trial for armed robbery, and at the time he thought his life was over and without any hope. "That's just like me," I thought. Despite my weakened condition, which sometimes made it hard for me to concentrate, I turned my full attention to what the pastor was saying. If he had an answer, I did not want to miss it!

This Indian pastor explained he admitted to God that he was a sinner, and asked Jesus to be his Savior. Then Jesus gave him a new heart and a new life, and made him a completely different person. "If a man belongs to Christ," the preacher explained, "he is a new person. The old life has gone. New life has begun" (2 Corinthians 5:17). That really hit my heart! More than anything else, I needed to become a new person. If it was true, then it was the best news I had ever heard. I wanted to know more about this Jesus. As I listened to the meeting outside my cell, the Holy

Spirit began showing me my past life—the cruel things I had done to my family. He made it clear that I was a sinner, and that Jesus alone had died on the cross for my sins. But then He conquered the grave, and by His power alone could I receive a new and eternal life.

When I heard this, especially how Christ had suffered and died on Calvary's cross for me, I got on my knees in that dark cell and did as the pastor outside—somewhere down the hall—was encouraging the other prisoners to do. He led us in a simple prayer, and I prayed, "Lord Jesus, I am a sinner. But I know You are alive today and able to change me. Wash me clean with Your blood and save me. Come into my heart today, and I will serve You." It is impossible to find words that describe the experience I had then with the Lord! After 46 days in solitary, I felt the joy of having the weight of my sin lifted. Another 177 days were to pass in solitary before I was released, but spiritually I had already been set free.

During my solitary confinement the police captain came to visit me several times. I told him that I had received Jesus Christ as my personal Savior. One day after my release from solitary, he told me a man was needed to watch the prisoners from 12:30 to 6:00 a.m. He asked me to be the jailer—but it seemed he wanted to test whether I really was a Christian. This time it was no temptation for me to try and escape. At six, the ladies' matron came into the jail and saw I really was a changed person. She went to the judge and returned within half an hour, saying the judge wanted to see me.

I appeared before the judge in his chambers and

he had my records in front of him. He said, "Young man, it seems your records are in such confusion that I am going to throw them in the wastebasket. I don't want to see you again in this court. You are free to leave." Six months earlier my record had been washed clean in heaven, and now my court record was cleared also! God had performed a miracle. I had put myself into a prison cell ready to die, but Jesus brought me out ready to live.

7. I Asked, I Looked and I Knocked

Key Verse - Matthew 7:7

"Ask, and what you are asking for will be given to you. Look, and what you are looking for you will find. Knock, and the door you are knocking on will be opened to you."

He was born a freak, rejected by his proud father and cruelly taunted by his classmates. Whether at home or at school, he was always lonely no matter how many people were around. Everyone gave up on him, until a kindly woman taught this native boy that God is always there for those who seek Him.

I WAS LONELY in my own home. During the first nine years of my life, as I grew up in the North Dakota hills, I wondered why my father never put his arms around me, never held me, never looked at me with pride. And I wondered why he and mother had such a hard time accepting me—why he blamed her and then she blamed him.

When I was born, people did not know much about severe cleft palate. My father took one look and saw I would never be the son he wanted—tall and strong, a proud hunter and fisherman just like him. His joy turned to anger. And so for the next nine years I lived with the pain of a deformed face; the pain of a severe heart condition and rheumatic fever in my legs; the pain of being unable to speak; the pain in my stomach from hunger and poverty; and the pain of being lonely in my own home and always wondering why.

One day I met the first friends I ever knew. They were the rats. I used to go down to the town dump to get the food and clothing other people threw away. Mostly I liked to run and jump and play with the rats, pretending they were my friends. They never laughed at me or pointed at me. But at night they went back to their holes, and once again I was left alone wishing somebody real would want me.

When I was nine, a man from the valley came to our home and said I must go to school. On the first day, the children came running to see me. They called "Flat Nose" and "Can't Talk," or "Smelly Injun" and "Donald Duck." Already school was teaching me something new—how to have people all around me and still be lonely. The next day one child grabbed my hair and threw me against the wall. Another child kicked me. One hit me and another spat all over my face. I ran back into the classroom and simply hung onto a desk. Then I overheard my teacher say to another teacher, "He can't learn. He can't talk. He's Indian. Why in my room?" But I hung on. What else could I do? I could not tell my parents, for they would only become more ashamed of me.

Finally one day, the teacher put me in a little room. Then I heard what sounded like a nail going into the hook on the outside of the door. As I spent time in that little room each day, I began living in two different worlds. In one world I wanted people to like me and teach me things; I could read and write quite well, but since I could not speak they assumed I could not learn. But in my other world I remember thinking, "If I have my father's knife, they won't laugh at me tomorrow or I'll hurt them. If that doesn't work, I'll get my father's rifle and then they'll never laugh at me again."

Walking home one day after school, some children asked me to go with them. As we went into the hills, they tied my hands behind my back and beat me until blood was running down my shirt. When I got home my father beat me again for being a weakling. From that day, I began to hate my father. Another time he hurt me in a way I cannot talk about, and I vowed someday I would kill him. In my hate I became one of the worst troublemakers my hometown will ever remember. Finally they just threw me in jail.

At that point, a woman from the valley heard my story and wanted to help. When I met her, I thought she would just laugh at me or hurt me. But all she wanted was for me to wash her car. She showed me how, then paid me a quarter when I was done. I couldn't believe it. A whole quarter! I didn't have to steal it or hide it. They wouldn't throw me in jail. My father wouldn't be angry. As I put that quarter in my pocket, something happened inside. I became motivated, filled with energy. When my friend asked me to visit her home, I was eager to go.

In the weeks that followed, the woman taught me how to chew and eat properly, by putting her hand in my mouth and showing me how to move my tongue. In the same way she taught me to speak by using her fingers to guide my tongue. Finally I made a proper sound all on my own. I could hardly wait to run home! My parents were there, and I showed them how I could chew my food and was learning to make sounds. That night my father heard, my mother understood, and they began changing. I began changing. And our community began changing. But the woman was not finished yet. She took her Bible, opened it to Matthew 7:7 and read the verse. Then she taught me about three little words— ask, look and knock. I couldn't understand it all, but she said one day I would.

With her help, the community saw I could succeed. When I was seventeen they sent me to a hospital where my deformed face and palate were surgically fixed. For six years the hospital also gave me speech therapy and I learned to speak clearly. When I graduated from high school, I became the first handicapped Indian to graduate at the top of his class! From there I went to the university and became a social worker. Later I went to another university and earned a doctor's degree, the highest degree anyone can get. But all the time I was still lonely, running from my family and my bad memories.

One day I met a woman at the university who,

like the woman in my childhood, was a dedicated Christian. We were married, but I could never talk to her about my past. After several years, she suggested we visit a small church in Minnesota. As I walked into that place, I felt like that woman in my youth had been changed into a hundred people. They greeted me, loved me, wanted me, believed in me. I began going every week, until one evening a man talked about a Bible verse found in Matthew. It was the same verse the woman had taught me years ago, that she said someday I would understand.

As the man read the verse (Matthew 7:7), the words came back to me, "Ask, and what you are asking for will be given to you. Look, and what you are looking for you will find. Knock, and the door you are knocking on will be opened to you." That night I could not sleep. My heart was still lonely and troubled by the past. But the Word of God promised that if I came to Him and asked for release, He would give it to me! The next morning on my way to work, I turned my car off the highway, stopped the motor, rolled down my window and looked up. Then I cried out, "God, I know you're up there. I'm a sinner and I want Jesus to come into my heart right now and save me."

In that moment I was "born again." The loneliness and bitterness left me, and I was filled instead with His love. Life changed for me. I began learning how to love others, and to love my wife and children as I should. And I learned how to love my father and pray for him. Today my wife and I have seven children, and we serve God by singing together as a family. I have traveled far and wide to tell what

Jesus did for me, and have seen many Indian people come to know Christ as their personal Savior. Looking back, I thank God for the woman in my childhood, and for the woman in my adulthood. But most of all I thank Jesus Christ who loved me, died for me, forgave my sins and taught me to love all men.

THINGS TO THINK ABOUT

1. Self-Hatred Replaced By New Identity

You'll go in circles for a while. But when you try to run your life without God, sooner or later you'll go down. Read Proverbs 14:12 and 12:15. How do these verses apply to your life? To what kind of "death" does rejecting God lead? How do you find the right way?

2. The Big Black Hole in My Life

The woman in this story depended upon her father, and when he was gone she had nothing. She tried to fill the void with drinking and parties, but that left her empty. Read Romans 10:9-10. Why must you believe Jesus in your heart, and not just say words? If you believe, how will that change your relation with God and fill your emptiness?

3. I Lost My Son and Found God's Son

Part of the grief in dealing with suicide is wondering how you might have stopped it from happening. Then there are questions about death and mortality. Read Romans 1:2-5. In what three ways do verses 2-4 prove that Jesus can be our Savior? According to verse 5, how can you use that proof to deal with desperate and needy people?

A Handful of Pills and a Razor Blade

The native man in this story became desperate and lonely, because he had nobody to guide him. Read Psalm 23:4 and 146:9. What do these verse suggests about the character of God? Now read John 1:9-12. How can you receive the Light that is promised by God to guide you?

4. An Angel Bought Me Groceries

When you reach the end of the road, either way you will be broken. Without the Lord you can give up, but with Him you can get up. Read Isaiah 57:15-21. What does God promise if you come to Him for help? What happens if you continue going your own way without Him?

5. God Interrupted My Hunger Strike

To escape the prison of sin and shame, and the cycle of despair and emptiness, you must become a completely new person. The old person won't do, because that's the problem in the first place. Read 2 Corinthians 5:15-21. What makes it possible for Jesus to give you a new life? When you receive this new life, what work should you desire to do?

7. I Asked, I Looked and I Knocked

Out of rejection and loneliness can grow bitterness and anger. The resentment and hate will destroy you more surely than your original trouble. Read Matthew 7:7-11. If you want release from these feelings, will God give it to you? What can you learn from the example of earthly fathers, that makes you sure God will answer you?

CHAPTER FIVE

Conquering Spirits and Superstitions

1. Horseback Ride Through a Graveyard

Key Verse - John 5:24

"For sure, I tell you, anyone who hears My Word and puts his trust in Him Who sent Me has life that lasts forever. He will not be guilty. He has already passed from death into life."

Some children are afraid of the dark. This Navajo boy had been taught to be afraid of the dead. Even as a man and later a Christian, the superstitions were still deeply planted in his mind. Then came a moment of crisis, and he had to choose between feelings and faith.

PATCHES OF CLOUDS hid the full moon, leaving deep shadows across the trail in front of me. It was not difficult to see, yet I had to be careful. To ride in the wrong places meant certain death. I knew, for it was the Navajo way. My parents had taught me well.

I was home from school for the Christmas break. My body had gotten soft while I was away. After a day of rounding up cattle, the insides of my legs were almost raw. It hurt so much, I had to ride sideways. Every step the horse took was painful. I thought I would never get home. Then suddenly, about a hundred yards in front of me, I saw something that made me catch my breath—the skeleton of a horse and, the remains of a saddle and some broken pottery. Beneath them, I knew, was the body of a Navajo. I was standing in the place of the dead.

Until this moment I had forgotten it was there. Years before, a terrible disease swept through the reservation killing many Navajos. The spot where they were buried was in front of me, blocking my trail. I felt myself grow cold and I started to shake. My heart was pounding. What was I going to do? It was too cold to stay where I was, and my legs were too sore to ride around the graves that seemed to stretch forever on both sides of me. My home was about a mile straight ahead, but the only way I could get there was to cross the place of the dead. I knew the moment I tried it, they would come out and grab me and I would be lost. I was in too much pain to fight back. Death was staring me in the face.

My family was deeply rooted in the Navajo ways. Since I was a child, I had been taught to worship the things around me—the trees, lightning, the moon and stars, and patches of sacred ground. We were told to be careful where we walked because, if we stepped on an unmarked grave, we could get sick or even die. Every year to protect us, my parents had a medicine man sing over us. It usually was an all-night event. And they would do this other times, too, like when we got sick or had the flu. As a Navajo boy, I respected my parents and my aunts and uncles. They were so much higher than I was. We children went along with whatever they said. I did not really have a religion of my own. I was just part of theirs.

One of the things that bothered me most as I was growing up was the fear of death and of those who were already dead. Our people believed the spirits of the dead could harm us in some way. Fears about this used to run in my mind. What if I accidently step on a grave and my parents can't find a medicine man to sing over me? Will I die before help arrives? This fear was always with me. Another fear that worried me was the future. No one seemed to know what happened to a person after he died. "Well, maybe they will live again, but nobody ever comes back to tell us," the old ones would say. But nobody really knew what it was like on the other side, and this really scared me.

When I was about twelve years old, one day I heard a Christian preacher on the radio. He said something that caught my ear. "For sure, I [Jesus] tell you, anyone who hears My Word and puts his trust in Him Who sent Me has life that lasts forever. He will not be guilty. He has already passed from death into life" (John 5:24). I thought about this for a long time. Then about two summers later, after I had gone away to school for the first time, the words of that radio preacher came back to me again. I was thinking about these words when someone invited me to attend a Christian camp meeting. I went to find out more and before I knew it, at the end of the meeting, I was walking toward the front and giving my life to Jesus.

I meant what I said, but because of my home situation I was never able to attend a church or read a Bible. It was about two years later when I ran into the graves and all my old fears came back to me. It seemed I had no choice but to ride straight ahead, so I did. As I inched my horse forward, I was shaking. I thought I was going to die at any moment. Then the Word of God came back to me. At the camp meeting I learned, "Whoever puts his trust in God's Son will not be lost but will have life that lasts forever" (John 3:16). That encouraged me and I began to pray, "Jesus, save me. I'm going to die tonight, but I want to be with You."

At that moment, when I whispered the name of Jesus, the fear that had almost been choking me left. It was gone! In its place came a peace that seemed to fill me. I could feel God's presence within my heart. It was like nothing I had ever experienced before. Just then the full moon broke through the clouds and it was almost as bright as day. I nudged my horse forward and walked right over the graves without the slightest fear. I knew the Almighty Creator God was with me and I was safe. After that night, I knew that I should live for Jesus. I began being hungry to know more of God's Word, to talk with Him in prayer, to be with His people at church.

One of the first things I did was tell my parents what Jesus had done for me. I also told my dad I could not give him any more money for the medicine man because now I was following the Christian way. He respected my wishes, though he himself still believed the old way. In the years that followed, I finished school and got married, was active in my native church, and went on to become a pastor myself. All this time I prayed for my parents to become Christians. Then one day my brother telephoned. When he started to talk, he broke down and cried, "Dad is really sick and he is going to die!"

Yet I praised the Lord, for somehow I knew He would bring good out of this terrible situation. It turned out dad had cancer. He tried every kind of help the Navajo religion offered. It cost him most of his sheep and cattle, but it did no good. Finally, when he was on his deathbed and weighed only 110 pounds, he called for the local pastor and asked for prayer. That day he decided to put his trust in the Lord Jesus. Dad was expected to die soon, but many people were praying for him and he recovered. That was more than twenty years ago and the cancer has never returned. Today my father is a very respected, very dignified elder. He is a strong Christian believer who is always ready to share how Jesus saved him. Because of him, most of his grandchildren have trusted Christ as their Savior.

My Heavenly Father has brought me a long way since that night when, as a frightened Navajo teenager, I cried out to Him among the graves. He has taken that burden of fear away from me and given me a deep peace within. What a comfort to know that, when the God of Creation is on my side, I can walk straight ahead through life without the slightest fear!

2. Searching Native Meets Great Spirit

Key Verse - Matthew 6:24

"No one can have two bosses. He will hate the one and love the other. Or he will listen to the one and work against the other. You cannot have both God and riches as your boss at the same time."

His family had moved far away and forgotten their Tarahumara Indian roots. He felt empty inside and tried to fill the void by reclaiming his native heritage and religion. But despite sweatlodges and sundances that were supposed to make him "pure and holy," he felt and acted anything but.

MEXICO CITY IS a cold, smoggy place in December. My wife and I, along with a handful of other native Americans, were here doing ceremonial dances and giving offerings beside the Pyramid of the Sun and Moon. The dancing has much to do with gaining power and pleasing the spirits, and I saw many people worshiping and offering prayers to the ancient gods. That's when I was really awakened to the spiritual, as well as cultural, realities of the Indian ways. This was not something I had grown up with—and at the time I had no idea what I was getting myself into.

I was born in a California town where I lived most of my life. Though my people come from the Tarahumara tribe of northern Mexico, we knew very little about our Indian traditions. Nothing was ever said to us as children about the old ways. I grew up thinking I was just a Mexican or Chicano. After high school graduation I became a musician. For the next fifteen years I played in bars and nightclubs. My life was empty and I sought fulfillment anyway I could get it—through money, alcohol and women.

To fill the void, my wife and I both wanted to "find our native roots." That's why we made the trip to Mexico City. Our tour host was an Aztec Indian, the lead dancer and spiritual leader of the native worshipers there. He began to teach us the ancient ways of the Aztecs. Our interest grew and during the following years we became more involved in Indian spirituality. Later we attended a college in California for American Indians and Chicanos. At this school we joined the American Indian Movement, a native political group that introduced us to sweatlodges, pipe cerermonies and the sundance.

I was pulled strongly in this direction because of my spiritual hunger. My training took me to South Dakota, where I was given my first pipe by a medicine man. I made a four-year vow for the sundance ceremony and began to learn the ways of the sweatlodge. All this time I was searching for a better way of life, hoping to find it through the traditions of the past. The native leaders taught me about healing, communicating with "spirit helpers," and the Vision Quest. We were even told that during the sundance, when men give pieces of their flesh as offerings to the spirits, it is similar to how Christ gave His life on the cross. When my body was pierced during the sundance, it would become "sacred and holy."

Much later I learned from the Bible that "Christ died once for all, for the forgiveness of sins." It is not necessary to repeat His death over and over, through ceremonies such as the sundance. But for now, though the medicine man told me I was holy and sacred, I sure didn't feel that way. My life was messed up and I was still searching. According to the Indian ways I was "purified," but that didn't stop me from going my own way and doing whatever I wanted to do.

About this same time my uncle got cancer and was dying. Yet God had a different plan—of which I was a part—and healed him. While I was still involved with spirit worship, my uncle would come over to talk with me and my family about Jesus. He would read the Bible to me in front of the sweatlodge. I hated it. Often I got angry and told my uncle to leave. But he never condemned me. Instead he just continued to share God's love, pray for me, and show by example how God works in a person's life.

During this whole time my marriage was on the rocks. My wife left me several times because I was not faithful to her. One of our separations was so stressful that I suffered a small stroke which left my face partially paralyzed. In those difficult days I had a Papago brother who was staying with me. Using the sweatlodge I had built in my backyard, we fired up the stones and held sweats regularly. I was proud of my place as a pipeholder, sundancer and lodge leader—yet I was miserable inside. These things had never brought any real Light into my life. Praying to "Mother Earth" or to any plant, animal or spirit only brought momentary satisfaction, not the longlasting peace and fulfillment I desired.

One day in the lodge, however, I got the biggest shock of my life. What happened was to change me forever. I had just closed the entrance flap, when I had the clear impression that Jesus was speaking to my heart: "I am Jesus, the Son of the Living God. Get out of this place! You have no business here! You don't need any spirit helpers. I want to give you My Holy Spirit. Leave this place now!" In a flash I climbed out, never to return. I poured out my heartaches to the Lord God and asked Him to forgive my sins and take control of my life. He listened and saved me, and soon afterward He saw fit to restore my health and my family to me.

I gave up the sweats and sundances, but letting go of my pipe and Indian medicine was harder. For awhile I tried to hold a pipe in one hand and the Bible in the other. But I read a verse of Scripture that showed I must make a choice: "No one can have two bosses. He will hate the one and love the other. Or he will listen to the one and work against the other. You cannot have both God and [things God hates] as your boss at the same time" (Matthew 6:24). After reading that verse I threw away the pipe and the medicine, and renounced everything that goes with it. I wanted to serve Jesus only. Neither my life nor my circumstances became instantly perfect, but I am free from fear!

My wife left me for good when she saw I had truly turned my life over to Jesus. As a single parent I am training my children to follow Christ, and together we are praying that one day my wife will come to the cross. Like my uncle, I don't condemn any of my Indian people in their search for identity and wholeness. I hurt for them because I know they will never find what they seek in the sweatlodges and spirits. You can never find the Light while worshiping anybody or anything else but Jesus.

Medicine Man Finds Cure for Sin

Key Verse - John 13:34-35

"I give you a new Law. You are to love each other. You must love each other as I have loved you. If you love each other, all men will know you are My followers."

When peyote led him to other drugs, he felt guilty. He prayed for peyote to give him power over weakness, then became a traveling medicine man. Yet his real motive was to make money and escape the world he hated. At last, even he admitted peyote gave no power over fighting and greed.

THE DOGS WERE running back and forth around the hogan. They were crying in their barking, as if talking to a ghost in the darkness. My grandmother was eating peyote and praying to her god, hoping this nightmare would come to an end. My mother was in labor, but did not know where she was or what she was doing. To help her, my father tied a rope around her waist. Then tossing the other end over a log on the ceiling, he pulled to keep her in an upright position. Finally it happened—I came into the world.

At the time I was born, peyote was strong among

my people. It was their religion, and it soon became mine. In school, at home, or as I herded the sheep, I learned that peyote had a great part in my life. We drank peyote juice each morning as we went to school. They told us it would make us learn better. Later, when I went to the city for three years, my boyhood involvement with peyote paved the way for drugs and alcohol.

Yet deep down I felt guilty. My lifestyle of parties and sex was wrong. Nobody had to tell me this, because in my heart I knew that I was a sinner. When I returned from the city to the reservation, I prayed for help at the peyote meetings our family held. I wanted to stop doing wrong and live a good life, and so I cried out, "They say peyote is powerful and almighty. Heal me now from my spiritual weaknesses!" But my attempts to change lasted only a little while.

At the same time I got involved with the American Indian Movement. First it seemed all right, but later I found myself disagreeing with some things that were happening in the group. Nevertheless, AIM made me hate the white man, especially the government. I didn't want to have any part in white society (except for its green money). To leave both the Indian movement and the white world behind, I decided to become a "road man" and peyote chief. "This way I can make a living and not really be part of the white world." I started going deeper into the doctrine of peyote, performing native religious meetings with my uncle. I felt that I had finally found myself as a true Indian.

At one of these meetings, something happened that

gave me a disturbing new idea about my Indian religion. My mother was accused of something she didn't do. She found no love, forgiveness or mercy in peyote; so she left the religion, and a year later she found Jesus. My mother would tell me about Christ, and this made me think about my life. At first I was angry at her ideas. I thought peyote was for Indians and the Bible was for white men.

Then I discovered the Bible was all over the world. There were not just white men, but all kinds of people who were following its ways. Even more, the Bible brought unity among these people, though they had never seen each other. They followed the command of Jesus, "You must love each other as I have loved you. If you love each other, all men will know you are My followers" (John 13:34-35). Peyote had never brought such unity and love among people.

I decided to become a Christian like my mother. And when I did, my whole life changed. Peyote had never given me the power to stop doing and thinking wrong things. Now Jesus gave me victory in my battle over sin. Before, I was confused by the hatred and strife that I saw in peyote and in the Indian movement. Yet with Christ, life made sense. Once I accepted Jesus as Savior, I was no longer a slave to the old religion and my old sinful ways. They had no more power over me and peyote became a thing of the past. Today I live a reborn life!

4. Trying to Walk Two Trails

Key Verse - Romans 12:1-2

"Christian brothers, I ask you from my heart to give your bodies to God because of His lovingkindness to us. Let your bodies be a living and holy gift to God. He is pleased with this kind of gift. This is the true worship that you should give Him. Do not act like the sinful people of the world. Let God change your life. First of all, let Him give you a new mind. Then you will know what God wants you to do. And the things you do will be good and pleasing and perfect."

He was brought up the traditional Navajo way, and she grew up the Christian way. When they got together, he could see the two ways were different. For years he went back and forth, sometimes to church and sometimes to the medicine man. It didn't work, and finally he had to choose one way or the other.

WHEN WE MET, I fell in love with her. When she got pregnant, we dropped out of high school and started living together. Right from the beginning we faced struggles over religion. She came from a Christian home, but my people followed traditional native ways. For me, having been brought up one way, it was hard to understand how others could believe differently.

We spent a lot of time living with relatives because I did not have a job and we had no home of our own. When we were with my wife's parents, I went along with them to church. This was a new experience for me and started me thinking. But with my own relatives, they told me to stay with our native religion. "Becoming a Christian is for the white man, not for us," they said. Yet there was something about the way my wife's people believed that seemed attractive to me.

As the months went by, I thought a lot about these two ways of believing. The Christian way was new, for I had grown up in a traditional Navajo family. It seemed there was always a lot of frustration and ill feelings in the old ways. Whenever we needed help, we had to pay money for the medicine man and the materials he used. This often created much financial difficulty for my parents.

In getting to know my wife's family, I could see the Christian way was different. My wife and her parents were very strong Christian believers. They talked to me a lot about it, and shared the Bible with me and sang hymns. Their lives were filled with joy. And it was all free! It didn't cost anything to have a Christian pray for you or help you with a problem.

About a year later, we all went to an evangelistic meeting at Navajo Mountain in northern Arizona. As I listened to the preaching and testimonies, I debated inside whether I should follow the Lord or stay with my traditional beliefs. One minute, something would overcome me and I felt that I should turn to the Lord. Then something else kept pulling me back, telling me to keep my old ways. In the end I listened to what God was saying and asked His Son Jesus to take control of my life. When I did, I was filled with joy.

Around this time our son was a year old, and my wife and I decided to get married. For the next eight years we followed the Lord off and on. Sometimes we would be in church. Other times we would go back to the old Navajo ways or to peyote. I knew what I should be doing but, because I had never really gotten serious about living for God, something was always drawing me away from Him.

For example, when we were married I was out of work. After living with various relatives, we ended up in Denver. It was here that we first noticed our son was having problems. Though he was already walking and talking, suddenly all he could do was crawl and he forgot how to speak. The doctors told us he had a hereditary disease that works on the nervous system. Slowly his body would stop working and he would die. For three years we watched our little boy grow weaker, and there was nothing anybody could do. My wife would stay up all night with him. She would cry and pray, but it seemed our prayers were not being answered.

Ever since my wife and I began a relationship, my own family was always trying to bring us back into the traditional ceremonies. Now that our boy was so sick, these pressures increased. We wanted our son to live and, when the Lord seemed to ignore our prayers, we finally turned to the Navajo religion for help. We went through a lot of Navajo religious ceremonies trying to find a cure for our son, and it cost money. Since I did not have a job, some of our relatives sold their jewelry to raise the funds. But even this did not help. When our son was five, he died.

From then on, we continued to play games with God. We were always going back and forth between the old ways and the Christian way. Finally one day I decided this had gone on long enough. I knew that I belonged to the Lord, that I was His child, and that He wanted me back. The way I lived was wrong and had to change.

My wife and I sat down and talked about what was causing problems in our Christian lives. We came up with three things: First, we would have to turn our backs on our traditional religion that denied Jesus Christ. Then I would have to give up the rock music and thirdly I would give up watching the dirty television movies that consumed my life. "Let your bodies be a living and holy gift given to God...[and] do not act like the sinful people of the world. Let God change your life. First of all, let Him give you a new mind. Then you will know what God wants you to do [to live for Him]. And the things you do will be good and pleasing and perfect" (Romans 12:1,2).

Since I first heard rock music, it had a hold on me. I listened to it almost every minute I was awake. When I should have been reading my Bible and praying, I was listening to rock music instead. I spent a lot of money, belonged to all the mail-order clubs, and every payday I would buy more tapes. The music and the words encouraged me to do sinful things and turned me away from God. The dirty movies on cable TV also had a hold on me, and I began to enjoy things that were displeasing to the Lord.

Once my wife and I admitted these things were causing us problems, we decided to get rid of them.

First we disconnected the movie channel from our television, and set limits on what we watched. Then we went through our home and gathered all our rock tapes and any possessions that had to do with traditional religion. With the help of our Navajo pastor we smashed each one and told the Lord we would have nothing to do with these things anymore.

This break with the old life was a tremendous, powerful experience. It has changed us, and things have been very different since then. For one thing, my wife and I are living a better and happier life. We are actively serving God in our local church and praying for His guidance as we consider going into full-time ministry. Wherever He wants to lead us, my wife and I will gladly follow.

5. Music Group Cleans Up Act

Key Verse - 1 Corinthians 8:11

"You may make the weak Christian fall into sin by what you have done. Remember, he is a Christian brother for whom Christ died."

They were nothing but pictures, religious symbols that were part of her native heritage. But when this Navajo woman began serving the Lord, she realized her home and even her clothing carried many native religious messages that made others wonder where she really stood.

I AM A NAVAJO, and my husband is a Chippewa. Together with our family we serve the Lord through music. We travel to native churches and communities across North America, sharing the message of salvation through good Christian Gospel music. As part of our program I would often wear outfits with Indian styling, or bring traditional crafts. After all, I wanted people to accept us as authentic native Americans so they would listen to our singing. But as much as I love my Indian heritage, God had to teach me that first I must be one of His people. And He used some hard lessons to get my attention!

One autumn, our singing tour for that season required a lot of driving. Our family seemed more accident prone than usual. It got so that my husband was getting uneasy about driving our bus. Then when we got home from one trip, we found our home had been robbed of several valuable articles. And soon I became ill as I had never been before.

Alone in the house that evening I went for my Bible, hoping to read something that would comfort me. I cried out to God, "Please speak to my hungry heart. You know how physically miserable I feel right now." Almost immediately I felt God was impressing a message upon my heart, "Have no other gods except Me" (Deuteronomy 5:7). What was that supposed to mean? I didn't have any other gods but Him. Yet I felt the Lord directing me to read Deuteronomy 4-12. Quickly I scrambled out of bed, grabbed my Bible and started reading.

It wasn't long before I noticed that in these Scriptures, God was telling His chosen people they must obey all He told them. He warned them not to intermarry with the ungodly nations around them and not to pick up any of their bad habits. If the people of Israel were not careful, they would soon be serving other gods. For their own protection, God told them to destroy all the ungodly things they had picked up and have nothing to do with those things ever again.

"Why was God so strict?" I wondered. Then I realized it was because the Israelites were a holy and chosen people unto God. They had a special duty to follow the Lord, because they were His representatives to the world. If they let sin rule their homes and lives, the other nations would mock God. So He would judge the Israelites to get their attention. Many would lose their health and become sickly. Their businesses would fall apart. Their prosperity would dwindle away into nothing, making life unbearable. Over and over again God warned them, "You must love the Lord your God with all your heart and with all your soul and with all your strength. Keep these words in your heart that I am telling you today. Do your best to teach them to your children" (Deuteronomy 6:5-7).

God's people had two choices. If they obeyed Him, they would prosper. If they allowed other gods to be in their homes, then they would be punished. As I considered these things, I really became convicted about several articles in our home and some practices in our singing performances.

The Lord brought to my mind an outfit I liked to wear when our family was singing. It had a border of *yeibicheis*, figures that are a powerful native religious symbol. "But that's okay," I tried to tell myself, "because they're just part of Indian culture and I certainly don't worship them." Yet God still pointed His finger: What would my audiences think, especially people involved in native religion for whom *yeibicheis* have great meaning? Would they be confused since I was supposed to be a representative of Jesus Christ, one of His chosen people?

Then I had a yarn "god's eye" picture of beautiful maidens dancing with feathers in their hands, according to Navajo religious ceremonies. Whenever our family went on tour in the bus, I took this beautiful native craft along because it matched the carpet. Among all the items in our home, why did I always choose to bring this with me. I had always thought it was harmless and a part of our culture, but now I understood the picture had great religious significance for many people who might see it in our bus. What would they think?

That night, the Word of God penetrated deep into my heart. I knew He was disciplining me as His child. "So know in your heart that the Lord your God was punishing you just as a man punishes his son" (Deuteronomy 8:5). I had some house-cleaning and some soul-cleaning to do! When my husband came home we both repented and renounced these things. God wanted our message as Christians to be clear and without any compromise, because He had chosen us to be His representatives to the world. So we burned these things that were in our home that did not please God. The next day my sickness broke and I vowed to share the lesson I had learned with other Christians.

A chapter of Scripture (1 Corinthians 8) explains it this way. Here we see a people who lived all their lives believing false gods. Their custom was to eat meat that was first given as an offering to idols. Then they became Christians, and eating that meat was horrible to them. Yet other believers said, "Those old gods are false, so the food is nothing but meat. Why not eat it?" The new Christians were confused, for they always associated the meat with idols. Shouldn't they have nothing to do with old ways, now that they followed Jesus? The Bible says the older believers should forget the meat, rather than weaken the faith of the newer Christians. In the same way, my husband and I don't want to cause confusion by using native religious symbols.

Some time after God taught us this lesson, we met a dear sister in Christ who was wearing a beautiful *yeibichei* ornament. When I told her about my experience, one lady standing nearby turned to me and said, "Don't tell me you're superstitious!" "No, I'm not superstitious," I replied, "but I believe the Word of God, and He has warned us about our making compromises for a reason." In the years since the Lord taught us this lesson, its impact has never been forgotten.

What about you? Are there things in your home that are not pleasing to God? If you are not sure, ask God to show you—as I did. We would not think of setting a big, fat idol in our living rooms. But many of us have gods of the old Indian religion hanging on our walls. And we have ungodly tapes and records and magazines. Why not replace them with Christian ones? The Bible says, "Let us put everything out of our lives that keeps us from doing what we should" (Hebrews 12:1). As Christians, we can continue to enjoy our beautiful Indian heritage. But anything contrary to God's Word should be put aside. Don't give Satan any ground in your home by clinging to things that displease the Lord and compromise your testimony as His child.

6. Boy's Heart Torn Apart
Key Verse - Matthew 10:34-39

"Do not think I came to bring peace upon the earth. I did not come to bring peace, but a sword. I came to turn a man against his father.I came to turn a daughter against her mother. I came to turn a daughter-in law against her mother-inlaw. A man will be hated by his own family. He who loves his father and mother more than Me is not good enough for Me. He who loves son or daughter more than Me is not good enough for Me. He who does not take his cross and follow Me is not good enough for Me. He who wants to keep his life will have it taken away from him. He who loses his life because of Me will have it given back to him."

His father said Jesus was for white people, not for Indians. "They have their beliefs and we have ours." But when this native boy heard for himself about Jesus, he believed. His father was the village medicine man and would not like it. Yet in his young heart he knew it was really true. What should he do now?

"DADDY, GUESS WHAT I did this afternoon," I called as I ran to my home. I was so excited my father answered back, "Caught a fish as big as a canoe?" I laughed. I liked my dad very much, and I respected him too. He was a tribal leader in our village. He took care of the people when they were sick or unhappy. He knew all the old tribal customs for healing.

"No, dad, I haven't been fishing. I've been listening to the visiting white man. I liked his stories about Jesus and, when he asked us to pray, I invited Jesus to come into my life." My dad was quiet for a little while. "Jesus is not for Indians," my father said. "He's only for white people." Then my father walked away.

I was very unhappy. I loved my father and I loved Jesus. What was I to do? I felt like a canoe that was being pulled apart by two strong men. Until that afternoon I had believed as my father. We knew white people worshiped Jesus and read His words in the Bible. But I never paid attention. White people had a right to their own gods, just as we had a right to ours. Now everything was changed!

Only that morning I had spotted the airplane, one that nobody recognized. I always loved to see airplanes ride down from the sky to land on the lakes in the far north woods. I would see them as specks in the blue sky, until all of a sudden they were closer and I could see their colorful markings. Everyone in our village noticed when an airplane came. Airplanes were important in northern Minnesota, for our small Indian village could only be reached by boat or airplane. Mail, visitors, newspapers—all kinds of important things came to us by airplane.

This day the airplane circled our village and landed on the lake. I ran down to see who was coming. A white man stepped out and talked to some of the grownups. I followed along. The village men did not seem very interested in the man. But they were polite to him, as they always were. One by one the grownups drifted away, until only we youngsters were left.

"Hi, there," said the smiling white man. "How are you today?" We all politely answered. The man introduced himself and told us, "I have come to talk to people about Jesus, God's Son." It was then I noticed the book the white man was carrying. I realized it was a Bible. No wonder the grownups were not interested! But the man continued, "I would like to tell you some stories later, after I talk to the grownups some more. I will teach you some songs, too." He had a happy face and seemed easy to like.

I got busy with my chores and almost forgot about the white man until later that day when I heard some singing. I joined the group of boys and girls, and listened to stories about Jesus. The white man stayed with us for several days and told us many more stories. At last I understood that Jesus was for Indians too, for He loved all people and died for them. That meant He died for my sins, and so I asked Jesus to come into my life and live with me. And that's when I went to tell my father.

Now inside me, my heart was breaking apart. It was a good thing the white man had taught me to pray. I prayed that God would show me a way to tell dad that Jesus is really for Indians. Over the years as I grew up, I prayed that prayer almost every day. The white man returned many times to help me and other young Christians in our village to study the Bible and become strong in our faith.

We learned Jesus expected each of us to "take up

their cross and follow Him," even when our families and friends were opposed to our faith (Matthew 10:34-38). The tribal leaders and many others in our village did not realize that Jesus died for Indians, too. Whenever the white man came they would say, "Why should we listen to a white man tell us about a white man's god?" But I knew Jesus loved Indians, because He lived in my life day by day. The greatest love I could show my dad was not to go back to his religion, but to keep speaking the truth of how Jesus could give him eternal life.

So I kept on praying for my father—and here is how Jesus has answered. One day I felt Jesus telling me that I should trust Him in every step of life. He reminded me that I can always ask Him for the things I need. And when I began to trust Him, Jesus gave me a desire to study and become a pastor. He has provided for all the needs of my family, for good food and warm clothing. Soon I will go back to my village. When I step off the plane I will say, "Before, a white man came to tell you about Jesus. You thought Jesus was a white man's god. Now I, an Indian, come to tell you that Jesus is God for all peoples."

I know they will listen as I tell how Jesus has proved Himself to me over and over again, how He has always helped me and loved me and guided my life. Ever since the day that strange airplane landed on our lake, I have known for sure that Jesus is for Indians.

7. Spirit Beings Battled for My Soul

Key Verse - 2 Corinthians 11:14-15

"It's no surprise! The devil makes himself look like an angel of light. And so it is no surprise if his servants also make themselves look like preachers of the Good News. They and their work will come to the same end."

His mind, reeling from peyote, was an open door. The spirits came, enticing him with secret knowledge and power to join them. And as this Havasupai man struggled to regain consciousness and life, they would not let him go! He saw the spirits for what they were. But was it too late to escape them?

I COULD FEEL THE peyote taking effect. I looked at my body and it was all red. Pretty soon I could hear voices singing old songs. They were coming through the sky toward me. As the spirit beings got closer I could see there were thousands of them. It took almost an hour for them all to arrive. Then I could see they were dressed in leather and bucksins. I tried to get up and run, but my legs were numb and I fell over. So I just lay there and waited.

The leader looked like my grandfather. He called out my name. "Come," he said. "We're going to show you what we do and what you need to know to be a spiritual leader for your people." Then the spirits came closer and said, "This is what we do. You should come and do it and we will teach you more." I looked and there was a big circle. All the spirit beings were singing, and inside the circle were people rolling around in the dirt. Their clothes were covered with dust and they poured it over their heads. They said I should do that, too, so I began rolling around and pouring dirt over my body.

That's what I was doing when my girlfriend found me. She tried to bring me back to the village. But I fought her and finally she just left me on the trail. I couldn't have followed her anyway because I had lost the use of my muscles. I had eaten too much of the plant. Soon the peyote began working again in my body. My grandfather told me it was time to go and I felt my soul leaving my body. It seemed I was walking effortlessly with the spirits of the sky. I was feeling good and enjoying myself as the spirits taught me songs I could take back to my people. Then suddenly the spirit guards came running. "Somebody is coming! Somebody is coming!" they said.

Around midnight a tourist, hiking to our village campground, found my body lying on the trail. He checked for my pulse and heartbeat. Then he ran to the clinic and told the doctor. Within minutes a four-wheeler came rushing down the trail toward my body. Right away, the crowd of spirit beings took off. I yelled after them, "Wait for me! I want to go with you!" My grandfather turned and said, "Come on, let's go!" I tried to follow but couldn't. Out of frustration I fell back on the ground.

As I rode in the trailer to the clinic, four spirit beings were beside me, including the one that looked like my grandfather. They said, "Jump! Jump! We're going to fall!" They all jumped out and I tried to follow, but I was strapped to a stretcher. All the way to the clinic the spirits tried to get my attention, but as I pointed they would duck behind the trees. When we got to the clinic, a spirit being stood right in front of me. "Come on, let's go. We still have a lot of things to show you and teach you." The doctor was trying to ask me some questions, but the spirit kept commanding me, "Say no! Don't tell him!" I couldn't speak but only lie there and shake my head.

For many hours the spirits kept bothering me. They pretended to want to help me, but never repeated anything so I could learn it. They just said it or sang it once. Then I began passing in and out of consciousness. Gradually I felt my struggles were going too long. That's when I knew the spirit beings had no intention of letting me go. They wanted to take me. It was scary! I was fighting to come back and they were fighting just as hard to take me away.

How had my life come to this? From the time I was a child on the Havasupai reservation, in Arizona beside the Grand Canyon, I wanted to help my people. When I was six or seven, I was sent away to a boarding school where I grew up. Even at a young age I knew there was a reason why I was put on the earth. But I didn't know what it was, and this bothered me. After graduating from a high school in California, I went home. But I had been away for so many years that I had trouble fitting in again.

In the back of my mind, I thought my family didn't like me and that was why they sent me away to school. This started me into drinking and drugs. The problems grew steadily worse. Soon I was drunk or high almost every day. At last my family stopped me and asked, "Why are you doing this? You're causing trouble for everyone." Then they explained why I was sent away. "We had no steady job. The only way we could be sure you were cared for was to send you away to school. We did it to help you."

This made me feel better. I started getting myself together, cut back on my drinking and worked a bit to help out the family. Yet there weren't enough jobs. I kept trying, but without much luck. Wanting to feel useful, I started thinking of becoming a spiritual leader for my tribe. I talked to different people about my desire, and someone told me to prepare by fasting and going to the sweatlodge. Then I was to eat a certain plant and wait. Deep inside I really wanted to get something positive out of this so I could help my people.

You've heard what happened that day I ate the plant. But my struggle wasn't over when the doctor brought me back to consciousness. He let me go home the next day, but the spirit beings still bothered me. For four days I would bump into barbed wire and get all cut up, or walk around and get lost in the cornfield. I didn't know where I was going. Eventually the spirit beings gave up trying to drag me away. But one of them, an evil spirit, stayed with me. Because of this I began doing bad things like stealing and causing fights. At last my wife left me and the government took our children to a foster home.

About this time my years of bad behavior caught up with me. I had been with a group of people and we were all breaking the law, but I got blamed for it and was put in jail. While I waited for my day in court, a local pastor heard of my case and came to visit. He listened and said, "That's a pretty big problem you're facing. But you've got a bigger problem and it's called `sin.' You need to accept Jesus Christ as your personal Savior. As for your problem with the law, I'm sure the Lord will see that the truth is brought out." We kept talking and I told him about my desire to be a spiritual leader and about the spirit beings who tried to take me away.

The pastor helped me understand from the Bible who all these spirit beings were. They were not my grandfather and other loved ones who had died, but evil spirits from Satan who made themselves look like my relatives. "The devil makes himself look like an angel of light...[and] his servants also make themselves look like preachers of the Good News" (2 Corinthians 11:14-15). They were very smart. Though they were evil, the spirits pretended to be nice and friendly. And once they had me, they weren't going to let me go.

The thought of it was like a crushing weight on my back. Five days later I was released from jail for a time and went to see the pastor. This time I invited Christ to come into my life and take control. I knew my real problem was now taken care of—and though it didn't happen right away, eventually my court problems were solved. A month later I located my wife and children in a shelter, and we all came home together. Back in the canyon, we started getting our marriage straightened out. My wife talked with my pastor friend and gave her life to Jesus, as I did. Later we dedicated our lives to serving Him, and in a year

I was asked to teach a Bible class for teenagers.

As I look back, I can remember how much I wanted to be a spiritual leader. I tried one way and it didn't work—in fact, it almost destroyed me! Then I tried God's way and my life began to turn around. He taught me patience. I learned that when you put Christ first, the Lord will take care of the rest. Now at last the Lord has given me a chance to help my people by working with the teenagers. I'm so glad! Following God hasn't been easy and there are still problems. But I don't ever want that old life back again. God's way is the only way for me.

THINGS TO THINK ABOUT

1. Horseback Ride Through a Graveyard

Perhaps you have "outgrown" old fears, or placed your trust in Jesus as Savior and Lord. You revere your native heritage, but the influence of the old cultural superstitions is still strong. Read John 5:24. Why can you know for sure that God has given you eternal life? How can that assurance help you live for Him today?

2. Searching Native Meets Great Spirit

Have you tried to have it both ways, to be a Christian but also go along with the old religion? Perhaps you are worried people will reject you if you don't? Read Matthew 6:24. Why is it impossible for you to go both ways? If you go along with the old religion, how will that affect your life as a Christian?

3. Medicine Man Finds Cure for Sin

Where the Spirit of God is present, it will produce love and unity. The man in this story saw no such love in his native religion, but found it among those who followed Christ. Read John 13:34-35. Why did the man decide that, since Christians loved each other, he could believe Jesus was truly God? Since he saw no such love among those who followed peyote, why did he decide God was not in that religion?

4. Trying to Walk Two Trails

Living as a Christian requires a commitment to put God first—even when people are pressuring you to return to the superstitious old ways, and when society is pressuring you to adopt its sinful new ways. Read Romans 12:1-2. God wants both your body and your mind. How can you do this? What kind of life will this obedience produce in you?

5. Music Group Cleans Up Its Act

Native religious items, symbols and ceremonies may only seem like art or culture to you. But they have great power over those who are drawn toward the old traditions. As a messenger of Jesus to your people, you cannot send mixed signals. Read 1 Corinthians 8:1-13 and Hebrews 12:1. When it comes to treating native religious items, how can your example affect others? What should you do with any items or practices that hinder your Christian testimony?

6. Boy's Heart Torn Apart

When you break from the old ways, it may divide you from your family and people. Read Matthew 10:34-39. Even if loved ones oppose your new faith, what does Jesus command you to do? What does He promise if you obey?

7. Spirit Beings Battled for My Soul

Native ceremonies such as peyote, sweatlodges and sundances, leave your mind open to attack by Satan and the spirit world. Read 2 Corinthians 11:13-15. Why does Satan try at first to appear as an angel of light? Why do his servants pose as preachers of good things?

CHAPTER SIX

Conquering Anger and Abuse

1. The Wedding that Changed My Life

Key Verse - 1 Peter 2:21-24

"These things are all a part of the Christian life to which you have been called. Christ suffered for us.This shows us we are to follow in His steps. He never sinned. No lie or bad talk ever came from His lips. When people spoke against Him, He never spoke back. When He suffered from what people did to Him, He did not try to pay them back. He left it in the hands of the One Who is always right in saying who is guilty. He carried our sins in His own body when He died on a cross. In doing this, we may be dead to sin and alive to all that is right and good. His wounds have healed you."

He dreamed about shooting and stabbing, and got pleasure from making people hurt. When they screamed for mercy, he got more angry. Nobody had ever given him a break! He dragged others down, and got straight people hooked on drugs, to make himself seem higher. Then he found out Jesus was no weakling either.

THERE WAS SOMETHING about the three of them that spelled trouble. I saw it the minute my girl and I walked into the bar. But they wanted to party, so I let them follow us home. We got a case of beer, opened all the bottles, turned up the rock music and got down to serious drinking. But I could tell our three visitors were planning something. Oh well, I had been a fighter all my life and they would get the worst of it if they tried anything.

When the first case of beer ran out, I wandered into the kitchen for some more. My girlfriend followed, took a bottle and walked back to the living room. As she walked out, one of our visitors slipped into the kitchen behind her. There was a loud bang and my girlfriend raced back to the kitchen to see what happened. When she opened the door, she was frightened half to death—and with good reason! There was blood all over, our visitor and I were fighting, and I had a knife in my hand.

I remember the blood and violence of that night, but everything else is hazy. An ambulance came, the cop cars arrived, and lights were flashing all over the place. I was handcuffed and shoved into the back of a police car. As we drove away, I saw the other guy on a stretcher but couldn't tell if his face was covered. It didn't bother me, except to know what charge I would be facing. After all, he started it.

Violence was not unusual for me. Even as a child there were just two main influences on my life— alcohol and hate. From the time I was five, I was always looking for money to go to the bootleggers. My dad left home when I was seven, and after that all the love went out of my life. To take its place I let hate build up inside. I spent my time dreaming of violence, stabbings and shootings. From the age of nine until I was twenty, I was always going in and out of court. Breaking and entering, car theft, assault and battery—all could be traced to the hate that raged inside me.

Rock music and drugs were a big part of my life. Then at age thirteen I got involved in satanism and calling up demons. I did this on purpose to make myself more violent. The more people I could drag down, the higher my position in hell would be. With that goal in mind I would hang around straight guys until I got them hooked on drugs. I got a lot of pleasure from beating and stomping on people. When guys begged me to stop, it just made me more angry. Why should I pity them? Nobody ever showed me any mercy! But my hate for Christians and Jesus was the worst. They were weaklings. Anybody who let Himself be nailed to a cross was a loser. Christians were just ripping people off to get their money.

By the time I was in my mid-teens, life had no meaning. I fully expected to be dead by my eighteenth birthday, and didn't care how many people I took with me. If I put somebody in the hospital, it did not matter. Violence was my way of life. Then my eighteenth birthday came and went, and still I was alive. Two years later I went to school for a few months in British Columbia, and it was here that those unwelcome visitors followed me home to my apartment.

A day or two after the fight, I was waiting in a jail cell to see a judge. An Indian guy came and offered to be my lawyer. After he advised me to speak only in court, he went away. Later I was charged for "wounding with intent to maim and disfigure a person" and bail was set at one thousand dollars. I did not have the money, so my lawyer telephoned my sister. She came down and signed over her pickup truck, and I was free to go home.

One evening as I awaited trial, my brother asked me to be the best man at his wedding. I did not know he was a Christian, or that the wedding would be a Christian ceremony, so I agreed. As it turned out, the day my brother was married was the turning point of my life. I was amazed at what I saw! People were getting up and telling what Jesus had done for them. They were quoting Bible verses and singing gospel songs. But most of all, I heard how Jesus stood by silently as He was whipped, spat upon, cursed, kicked and nailed to a cross.

"Christ suffered for us," the Bible (1 Peter 2:21-24) says, and "this shows we are to follow in His steps. He never sinned. No lie or bad talk ever came from His lips. When people spoke against Him, He never spoke back. When He suffered from what people did to Him, He did not try to pay them back. He left it in the hands of the One [Father] Who is always right in saying who is guilty. He [Jesus] carried our sins in His own body when He died on a cross. In doing this, we may be dead to sin and alive to all that is right and good. His wounds have healed you!"

This Jesus was no weakling, but a God of great power Who died for my sins. As I sat in that church, I felt His Holy Spirit impressing a message upon my heart: "Give your life to Jesus, or you will die the same way you have lived."

That night on the way home I prayed and asked Jesus to forgive my sins, set me free and take control of my heart and life. Right away I felt a total release, that my burden was lifted, and I knew God had answered my prayer. When we got home, I went to my room and gathered up all my ungodly posters, rock tapes, drug pipes and satanic books. Then I hauled them outside and burned them. That same night my girlfriend, who later became my wife, also prayed to receive Christ. Later we told her family and they all gave their hearts to Jesus that very same night!

My entire life had taken a new direction, but I still had my court hearing hanging over me. It didn't bother me anymore, though, since I was now free on the inside. Before my hearing a few months later, my Indian lawyer asked if anything had changed since the last time he saw me. I explained how I had become a Christian, and he just sat back in his chair and smiled. "I'm a Christian too," he said. "I used to be the town drunk, and then the Lord changed me. I went back to school and now I'm a lawyer."

We discussed my case and decided I should plead guilty to a lesser charge. At the hearing, a missionary from my area spoke on my behalf. Then my sister-in-law presented six letters from Christian friends who knew how much I had changed. The judge took the letters. "I need an hour to read these. Then I will pass sentence." When the judge returned he asked me to stand. "There appears to have been a change in your life," he said. "I hope you're not fooling anybody, because I'm giving you a one-year suspended sentence. That's one year without alcohol and drugs, and two years on probation." The Lord had set me free!

Today I am free from jail, and free from the prison of my own hate. For twenty years I had built that prison, until it very nearly killed me. Rock music and Hollywood movies make street life look fun, but they are wrong. It is no fun lying in the street bleeding, knowing you have to get up and keep fighting—or someone else will kill you. It is no fun sitting in jail again and again, thinking what a mess you have made. This was my life, nothing but a big circle of death, until I met Jesus Christ and found He alone had the power to free me. I am no longer looking for a chance to die or to hurt someone. Jesus has taken all that hate away, replaced it with His love, and given me a reason to live.

2. God's Spirit at Work Behind Bars
Key Verse - Romans 8:7-9

"The mind that thinks only of ways to please the sinful old self is fighting against God. It is not able to obey God's Laws. It never can. Those who do what their sinful old selves want to do cannot please God. But you are not doing what your sinful old selves want to do. You are doing what the Holy Spirit tells you to do, if you have God's spirit living in you. No one be-longs to Christ if he does not have Christ's spirit in him."

When it was over, he couldn't even remember the argument. But his brother was dead, and this Chippewa man had killed him. "It was the logical result of the way I was headed," he says, for a

man cannot escape the consequences of his behavior. He had to face God, and found something he never expected.

IT WAS NEW YEAR'S EVE. Everyone was celebrating. We each had a bottle and there were lots more in the case. Laughter filled the room. That much I remember, but exactly when the joking stopped and the argument began, I'm not sure. I only wish it hadn't happened, and so do a lot of other people, especially me. Because when it was all over, I had shot and killed my own brother.

Though I didn't know it then, the Bible has something to say to people like me: "You cannot fool God. A man will get back what he plants" (Galatians 6:7). That means the way you act will eventually catch up with you. I never thought it would happen to me, always to somebody else. But now I know the violence I did that night was the logical result of the way my life was headed.

I grew up in northern Minnesota among my Chippewa people. Like many of them, I figured Indian religion was for Indians, while Jesus was the white man's God and the Bible just another book of stories. Besides, Christianity seemed like an awful way to live, with all those commandments to keep and church rituals to follow. At that time I was an alcoholic, but I didn't need religion to quit. After a while I began to taper off and drank only three or four times a year. But each time I did, my temper would flare up real easy. Maybe that's because alcohol was supposed to drown my tensions and pressures, but still left me feeling empty inside like something was missing in my life.

On that fateful New Year's Eve the drinking, frustration, anger, bad temper and hatred for this kind of life all came to a head. What the argument was all about is really unimportant now. Perhaps I just didn't want to take another beating—not so much from my brother, but from life itself. In any case, that night in the first few hours of the new year, I shot and killed my brother. He was a good man and a believer in Jesus. We had a good relationship, shared a lot and always had time for each other. Now he was dead, for no good reason at all, and I was his murderer.

It is hard to describe my feelings as I sat in the county jail. Life seemed meaningless. "What hope is there? What's left after someone takes another man's life?" Questions like these were continually in my mind, but one kept coming back to me as I cried day after day: "What is God going to do to me now?" About two weeks later I was indicted for first degree murder. The public defender told me to forget about my wife and family. "You'll be locked up for a long time," he said. Not much of a future, but it was mine and there was nothing I could do about it. Suicide was out of the question, because I was a chicken at heart and too scared to take my own life.

To keep myself occupied in the county jail, I read a lot of books. One that I picked up was the story of man who was a prisoner and became a Christian. His main theme was that I should be thankful for anything, even prison, that would bring me to a knowledge and acceptance of Jesus Christ. That was a brand new thought to me, one that suggested a hope and a purpose for prison life, and so I kept reading. As I discovered that I could have a personal relationship with Jesus Himself, tears began to trickle down my cheeks. Jesus loved me, died for me, just the way I am. Though I was a murderer, He still wanted me as part of His family. Eternal life could be mine, said the author, because "if a man belongs to Christ, he is a new person. The old life is gone. New life has begun" (2 Corinthians 5:17).

That was enough for me. I got down on my knees, right there in the jail cell, and trusted Christ to be my Savior and to give me a new life. That night as I lay down to sleep, I felt the peace of God even behind bars. Christ at the cross had taken my punishment upon Himself, so "even though my sins are bright red, they will be as white as snow" (Isaiah 1:18). My testimony is not that I killed my brother, but that God has forgiven me for what I have done.

Looking back, I have often wondered what makes people do things like murder—or rape and robbery, dope and drink, pornography and perversion? It is because "the sinful old desires of the flesh...fight to get hold of your spirit" (1 Peter 2:11) as Satan tempts us to satisfy our cravings rather than think about God. That's why we always want something more or something better. The new car only looks new until we own it, then we see another one that looks nicer. The more money we make only leads us to believe there is more to be had. People became slaves, willing to kill and steal, do drugs or sex, just to satisfy their particular desires. Once I accepted Christ's new life, He gave me His Holy Spirit to help keep my desires under control. "We do not do what our sinful old selves tell us to do anymore. Now we do what the Holy Spirit wants us to do. Those who let their sinful old selves tell them what to do live under that power of their sinful old selves. But those who let the Holy Spirit tell them what to do are under His power. If your sinful old self is the boss over your mind, it leads to death. But if the Holy Spirit is boss over your mind, it leads to life and peace. The mind that only thinks of ways to please the sinful old self is fighting against God. Those who do what their sinful old selves want to do cannot please God. But you are not doing what your sinful old selves want you to do. You are doing what the Holy Spirit tells you to do, if you have God's Spirit living in you" (Romans 8:4-9).

Today I live in the state prison. Though God has freed me spiritually, man's law is still punishing me for what I did. Someday, when God is ready, He will deliver me from the bondage of this prison too. In the meantime, I am taking Bible correspondence courses to become a minister and more effectively share the Gospel of Christ with others. I have a long way to go, but I know someday I will make it. That's because of a promise from God that is very special to me as a prisoner: "I have given you an open door that no man can shut" (Revelation 3:8).

3. Anger Was My Addiction

Key Verse - James 1:19-21

"My Christian brothers, you know everyone should listen much and speak little. He should be slow to become angry. A man's anger does not allow him to be right with God. Put out of your life all that is unclean and wrong. Receive with a gentle spirit the Word that was taught. It has the power to save your souls from the punishment of sin."

Uncontrollable anger ruled his life, along with drugs and alcohol that made his temper worse. But it wasn't enough just to get rid of his anger, or to quit dope and drinking. He had to replace them, find something new and good that would take the place of his old thoughts and habits.

CRASH! I THREW another vase against the wall and it fell to the floor in pieces. I was yelling like a madman in a fit of rage. I was drunk and angry and I wanted everyone to know it...again. Just like my violent-tempered father before me, I was striking out at anything in my path. As a child I had vowed I would never be like my father. But now as a teenager I was following in his footsteps. All my money was used to buy alcohol and drugs, and I had been in trouble with the police several times already.

Then I met a girl whom I liked and respected very much. She was a sweet person and helped me stop taking drugs. Yet one night in a fit of anger I smacked her hard across the face. I drew back. What had I done? She left the house crying and I sat alone, feeling very small. Now I knew my anger was a real problem but I didn't know how to deal with it.

Perhaps the military would straighten me up, and so I joined the army reserves. But from there my life just went downhill. My drinking and anger went more out of control. Soon I found myself, once again, sitting in a jail cell. Yet that was a turning point for me. I was on the road to destruction, and I knew it. So I quit the army and joined Alcoholics Anonymous. After ten months they helped me quit drinking, for which I am thankful, but somehow that did not seem like enough. I was searching for more, something to replace my anger.

One evening at a friend's house I noticed a man who had been an alcoholic. He had such a peaceful look on his face that I decided to talk with him. The man shared his faith in Jesus Christ and how the Lord had changed his life. I was a bit frightened when he began reading Bible verses to me, yet I wanted the same peace that man had in his heart. From then on, the Lord brought more Christians into my life. Their peaceful spirits were attractive to me, for I wanted to find an escape from my anger. They invited me to a conference and, a month later, I too turned my life over to the Prince of Peace.

Since then Jesus Christ has helped me conquer my old angry, self-centered spirit. My greatest weapon against anger has been the Bible. "Your Word have I hid in my heart, that I may not sin against You" (Psalm 119:11). By memorizing the Word of God, and applying it to my life, I can have victory over my daily battle against anger. The favorite Bible verse I have memorized says, "Everyone should listen much and speak little. He should be slow to become angry. A man's anger does not allow him to be right with God. Put out of your life all that is unclean and wrong. Receive with a gentle spirit the Word that was taught" (James 1:19-21).

When this verse comes to mind, it helps me remember to think before I speak or react in anger. The last part of the verse also teaches an important Bible principle. It is not enough just to put away bad thoughts, and then replace them with nothing. I must put the anger out of my life, then replace it with the good things from God's Word. By memorizing Bible verses I am also following the example of Christ. When Satan tempted Jesus (Matthew 4:1-11) in the wilderness, He quoted Scriptures to put the devil on the run. I have found that overcoming anger is hardest when you are with the ones you love. There is no hiding from them! Sometimes if my old, angry spirit keeps fighting to get out, it helps me ease up if I whistle, hum or sing about the Lord's love. I know that I cannot be what I should on my own. Only through the Holy Spirit can I love as I should and have victory over anger. So when I am with my loved ones, I go to Jesus in prayer and ask His Spirit to stretch my tolerance level. He and I have come a long way together since I first asked Jesus to take control over my life. Yet every day that I live for Him, I find that I desire more and more to be the man God wants me to be.

4. A Truckload of Forgiveness

Key Verse - Philippians 3:8

*"Even more than that, I think of everything as
worth nothing. It is so much better to know Christ
Jesus my Lord. I have lost everything for Him. And
I think of these things as worth nothing so that
I can have Christ."*

He pretended to be a friend and asked to borrow a truck, with some money and clothes, to get a new job. But all the time it was a swindle. Yet the native man whose truck was stolen had a bigger problem. An angry spirit was stealing his joy and effectiveness as a Christian.

I COULDN'T BELIEVE IT when they told me. A man had just been checked into our hospital in Prince George, British Columbia. "He is very sick, paralyzed, can't talk and may not live much longer," they said, "and his name is the same as the guy who stole your truck." My first reaction was disbelief. "It couldn't be the same guy," I said to myself. "I must be dreaming. That guy isn't anywhere near here." But what if it was the same person? For months I had built up anger and resentment against this man who had betrayed my friendship and trust. Now he was going to die and I, as a Christian, might be the only one who could tell him the way of eternal life.

"Lord," I prayed, "what should I do?" My anger against this man was strong. I remembered when he first came to our town. He knew my nephew, called him "brother," and went with my nephew to our native church. The Indian believers made this white guy welcome, and he came back to the services and listened. I talked to him about the Lord and he seemed interested. Then one day he told me, "I have been promised a job on the Alaska Highway as a supervisor, but I have no way to get to the Yukon and no money. If I can go and take the job, I'll get your nephew a job there too."

My people are always ready to share with those who need help. We don't have much ourselves, but we understand about not having work. So our church got together and gave this white man some warm clothing, boots, a down jacket, and a $200 loan for travel money. I loaned him my 4x4 pickup truck along with extra tires, a chain saw and some of my nephew's tools. We all liked this man and were glad he had a job. The next Sunday we prayed with him, and he left on Monday morning with the promise that he would return my pickup the next weekend.

The weekend came, but neither our friend nor my pickup ever arrived. The second weekend passed and still nothing, not even a message. At church we began to fear he had some trouble on the road or perhaps an accident. We were all praying for his safety. At last we called the Yukon Highway Department. To our great surprise, they did not recognize the name of our friend and said nobody by that name had ever been promised a job.

Boy, was I ever angry! He had used me, ripped me off! In the old days, before I was a Christian, I would have wanted to take revenge and get even. Nevertheless, I was still furious. After waiting a few more days to be sure, I called the police and reported my truck was stolen. In time the authorities found the winch off my pickup—it had been sold to someone in the Yukon. Later they recovered the canopy, and some months later the truck itself was located. It had been driven 18,000 extra kilometers and was in pretty bad shape. So I made a cold bus trip up north to the Yukon in February to drive my pickup back home. Our "friend" was charged with the theft but didn't show up for the court case. I had not heard anything more about him until now, some months later, when he was in our local hospital—and given no more than 24 hours to live!

What this man had been through, I did not know. But during this time I had been through some struggles of my own. I knew a bitter heart could destroy my usefulness to God. It could take away my joy and testimony as a Christian. I did not want this to happen. So as I prayed for the man who stole my truck, I also prayed that God would help me deal with my anger. Then one day as I read my Bible, some verses got my attention: "I think of everything as worth nothing. It is so much better to know Christ Jesus my Lord. I have lost everything for Him. And I think of these things as worth nothing so that I can have Christ...[through Whom] I was made right with God by faith" (Philippians 3:8-9).

I began to understand that "things" such as my pickup truck were like "rubbish" compared to the eternal riches I had as a Christian. Yet God was not finished with His lesson. When I learned the man was in the hospital, my feelings were still confused and hurt. I sought out a mature Christian friend and together we prayed for the Lord to guide me. After talking about it, the two of us agreed to go see this man together.

The nurse explained the man had been arrested by the police, then transferred from the correctional center to the nearest hospital when his condition worsened. She said there was a limit on visitors and we couldn't stay long. The man was now on life-support, drifting in and out of consciousness, and not expected to live past tomorrow. When I put my head through the door of his room, it was indeed the man who had stolen my pickup. He looked like skin and bones, lost among a maze of tubes and bottles. From his expression I could see he knew me, and that he had not expected to ever see me again!

My Christian friend spoke first. "We love you and God loves you, and our native fellowship has been praying for you," he said. Then I knew the Lord wanted me to say something. "I forgive you for taking my truck. Because God forgave me, I forgive you and I'm not angry. I have been praying for you." Tears came to his eyes and, though he could not move or speak, I knew he understood. Then the nurse came to say our time was up.

We went back the next day and I brought my Bible and read to him. We told him again that God loved him and the native people were praying. I told him again that I forgave him. My wife had also come along and she couldn't believe that I was being so patient with the man who had hurt me so much. She saw the Lord had changed me!

Unexpectedly, the man's condition stabilized. He still couldn't talk and was often asleep or unconscious, but we kept visiting each day. I prayed that he would recover or that the Lord would give him enough time to understand His love and receive Jesus into his heart. Then one day the nurse told us his family back east had been notified and the doctor was going to remove the life-support system. It was just a matter of time.

That night all the Christians prayed again and the next day we went back to the hospital. All the tubes had been removed—but our friend didn't seem worse. The next day he seemed stronger, and each day afterward he improved. He began to recover his speech and slowly the feeling returned to his body. After five weeks he could talk well enough to tell us he wanted to receive Christ as his Savior! From then on he looked forward to us coming to the hospital to read the Bible to him. I could see that forgiveness has strong power.

One Sunday morning the native church was just beginning the service, when a taxi stopped in front of the building. The driver got out and assisted someone into a wheelchair. He was still very weak and pale. But he wheeled himself to the front of the church and with tears he said, "I'm sorry. Please forgive me." Then he publicly apologized to all the people he had hurt.

Later he went back east to his family and I received a letter from him at Christmas. He is still doing well. Today I am thankful he was part of an important lesson the Lord has taught me: "You must be kind to each other. Think of the other person. Forgive other people just as God forgave you because of Christ's death on the cross" (Ephesians 4:32).

5. Deep Hatred Masks Deep Hurt

Key Verse - Ezekiel 36:26-27

"I will give you a new heart and put a new spirit within you. I will take away your heart of stone and give you a heart of flesh. And I will put My Spirit within you and cause you to follow My Laws and be careful to do what I tell you."

The hate he learned as a child stayed with him as an adult. This Salish man hated everyone, even his wife and children for tying him down with responsibilities he resented. The downward cycle of anger, and then escape through alcohol and parties, continued until at last he hated himself most of all.

I LIVED TO please myself. Nothing else mattered, not even my family. When my children were born I soon learned they needed to be cared for, and I didn't want to be forced to do anything. Before long I resented them. Every dollar I had to spend on my wife and kids meant one less dollar to spend on alcohol and fun, and that made me mad. My wishes had to come first. Nobody else mattered.

Hate and hurt. That is what I remember about my youth. Much of it was spent in institutions—tuberculosis hospitals, boarding schools and prisons. Since I wasn't home much, things weren't too hot between my parents and me. I figured they ditched me in the boarding schools because they didn't love me. So I hated them from the bottom of my gut. And the hate I lived with in school stayed with me when I left. I hated people, people in general. I even hated my own people. Why was I born with brown skin? Why did I have to sit in school with white people? I always thought I was not prejudiced, but I sure was.

As a Salish Indian boy living in British Columbia, my dream was to do something big so people would look up to me. Out on the woodpile I could forget about my worries and just relax with my big schemes. Mom and dad were drinking a lot and our home was filled with turmoil. I wanted to get out of there, become rich and famous, and come back with a big car. But in real life I just quit school after tenth grade, and before long ended up in prison.

There I lived two different lives. In the day time I would be hard and solid like a rock, playing the tough guy. But at night I'd go back to my cell and cry, nursing my hatred and hurt and loneliness. After prison I wanted things to change, but they didn't. There was more drinking and fighting and wild parties—and more hate at the unfairness of everything.

I tried going to art school and did pretty good. But it wasn't enough just to learn how to make a living, when I hadn't yet learned how to live. After a while I was back on skid row. It was during this time that I got married, and those first eleven years were really shaky. I hated the way that a wife and children tied me down with so many responsibilities. I was always escaping through alcohol and parties, so that my wife never knew where I was. The cycle continued until I hated the only thing left—myself. I couldn't stand my life anymore and was even thinking of killing myself.

I wanted to pray to God but didn't know how. So I just talked. "God, I'm tired of living this way. I don't want to live like this anymore. I'm just so tired." No, I didn't become a Christian that day because I had never heard the Gospel. But from that moment the Holy Spirit began bringing me under conviction about my sin and hate. The next day I told my wife what had happened, but she didn't believe me. Just another one of those stories I had been feeding her all those years, she thought. "I've had enough, and I don't want to live with you anymore," she told me.

I kind of thought something like this might happen someday, so I wasn't really surprised. We talked for a while and I let her keep the house and the children, and promised to send support money. I moved out of the house and within a week we were legally separated. I could visit the children, but only if I was sober and called ahead. Now that I was alone, I saw how wrong it was to resent my family. Perhaps I had hated them for holding me back, the same way I hated my parents for holding me back as a child. Only when I lost them did I finally see my mistake.

For five weeks we were separated. My wife didn't expect anything about me to change. But the Lord was starting to get my attention. I sought treatment for my alcoholism and also started reading the Bible. I even took the Bible to bed with me. Then one day, during a visit, my wife wanted to talk. "I really believe you are serious this time about trying to change. You're not the same," she said. After a pause she added, "Is your rent paid up?" That got me excited. "Why, have you got a place for me to stay?" "Yes," she replied, "I'd like you back."

On our eleventh anniversary we were remarried and said our vows all over again. Our life together now took a turn for the better. But even with our family reunited, I found there was still a piece missing in my life. I wanted to know more about God, and saw that a Christian conference was coming to our city. For three days I listened to Bible teaching, and on the fourth night all the pieces fell into place. "Lord," I prayed that night, "come into my life and be my boss. This is what I need. I believe in You, and I believe in Jesus the Son who died on the cross to pay the penalty for my sins and was raised from the dead. I repent from all my old ways. Help me to be the man you want me to be."

After the prayer I felt like shouting to everybody, "Hey, I got Jesus in my life tonight! I'm a new person! I'm saved and I'm going to heaven!" At last I knew the missing piece in my life was filled. Jesus touched me with His love and took away all my old hate. The Lord had done as He promised, "I will give you a new heart and put a new spirit within you. I will take away your heart of stone and give you a heart of flesh. And I will put My Spirit within you and cause you to follow My laws and be careful to do what I tell you" (Ezekiel 36:26-27). The next morning I still felt like a new man. And my family knew what happened without me telling them. "We can see it just by looking at you," they said. "You are so different."

In the days following the conference, two Indian

missionaries began visiting with me. They came to my home every day, shared God's Word with me and answered my questions. Before long, other native people in my community asked Jesus into their lives and our little fellowship grew. We kept needing larger places to meet, until a native church was begun that today meets in Vancouver. As for me, I now work as a commercial artist and my greatest desire is for people to see Christ at work through my art and in my daily life. I want them to find the freedom I discovered when Jesus lifted me out of my prison of hate and gave me a new life.

6. Wife's Faith Breaks Vicious Circle
Key Verse - John 8:34-36

"Jesus answered them, 'For sure, I tell you, everyone who sins is the servant of sin because sin has a hold on him. And the servant does not belong in the house The son belongs in the house. So if the Son makes you free, you will be free for sure'."

From a life spent mostly in prison, this native man learned what makes people violent. It begins with anger and leads to hopelessness and despair, which only feeds the desire for violence. Marriages and families then break apart, deepening the cycle of anger and despair. From that prison there is only one escape.

I'VE SPENT MORE YEARS in prison than most people spend on their jobs. Leavenworth, Alcatraz, San Quentin—altogether I've done time at eight prisons in five states. Most of my adult life has been spent behind bars. And many of those years I was in isolation, for everything from knife-fights to prison riots. Twice I finished my time, and twice I came right back again for another crime. Prison did nothing to cure the anger and violence that ruled my life. Then the third time they let me go, I found out "if the Son makes you free, you shall be free indeed" (John 8:36).

My first brush with the law came at the age of thirteen. As a Cherokee boy from Oklahoma, I ran away with a carnival. The police got me a year later and sent me home. Before long, though, I was using dope and living on my own. Of course, my life did not fall apart right away. I even married a beautiful Christian woman and we had two little girls. But the violence and drugs eventually caught up with me, and I was sent to prison for the first time.

My first stop was Leavenworth, then Alcatraz, and from there to prisons in Georgia and Kentucky. Altogether my stretch lasted twenty years. At the last prison I got in trouble for a prison riot and spent the next five years in isolation. I seethed with angry and violent emotions over my treatment, and about the prison officials and guards who seemed to deny me any shred of dignity. Near the end of my time I was used for drug research. They gave me fifty grams of dope a day, then pronounced me an incurable drug addict. When they released me I proved them right, because I got right back on drugs going home.

Soon I was recaptured and given a long sentence at the state prison in Oklahoma. Most of the time I was in isolation again, over a knife-fight I had with another convict in the prison yard. Given my record of violence, they could not take the chance of letting me stay with the other inmates. Sure enough, they had me pegged right. When I was released and sent home, it was only a matter of weeks before I ended up in the slammer again. This time it landed me in San Quentin. It seemed I was a "lifer" in a prison of my own making, a prison of anger and violence, with no possibility of parole.

By now I had spent most of my adult life in prison. Hopelessness and despair were all around me. Some guys cracked up and got worse in prison than they ever were outside. Others got released and then a few weeks later I saw them back again. Nobody would hire them. If you admitted being an ex-con they chased you out, and if you lied they would find out soon and you'd be through. So what else was left but going back to crime?

I'm very sure I would have died in prison if it weren't for my Christian wife. She didn't enjoy the things I was doing, but because of her Christian faith she stuck with me. There was a lot of strain on our marriage, but she was consistent in her Christian living and that did a whole lot for me. An inmate just doesn't have much to live for if his family doesn't stick with him. I've seen guys crack up and commit suicide when their wives deserted them. They'd been in prison four or five years, and then the wife just gave up and quit—so they just committed suicide right then and there.

Eventually I was moved from San Quentin to Folsom Prison, and finished my sentence at the California Men's Colony. When they let me go, I had no reason to think my freedom would last very long. The old pattern of anger and violence still had a hold of my life. This time I wanted to break that vicious circle, but I didn't know how. I just lacked the power. On the bus ride home I was glad to be outside, but wondered how long it would last.

As the bus pulled up to the station, I was greeted by a sight that was more meaningful than anything else could have been to me. My whole family, wife and children, had come to meet me! The following Sunday they took me to church and insisted they had completely forgiven me. Even more, they said God would forgive me too. That meant so much to me! I got down on my knees and got right with the Lord. Today I can say that through the love of Jesus Christ my old hate and violence have been washed away and forgiven, and my death sentence has been commuted to eternal life with Him.

That was nearly twenty years ago. Since then God has given me a ministry with young people, and I have spoken to literally millions of teens across the country. I try to reach them before anger and violence, drugs and crime really mess up their lives. And to those who are in trouble now and want to go straight, here's what I found out the hard way: I never did myself or my family any good, as long as I stayed with the same old crowd. I needed to make a clean break from the people and things and attitudes that got me into prison. That break was only possible by a real, honest, sincere surrender to Christ. Whatever your prison, Jesus is the key that unlocks the door.

7. The Butterfly I Couldn't Catch

Key Verse - Jeremiah 17:9-10

"The heart is fooled more than anything else, and is very sinful. Who can know how bad it is? I the Lord look into the heart, and test the mind. I give to each man what he should have because of his ways and because of the fruit that comes from his works."

All the hate and bitterness in the heart of this Sioux man erupted, when he joined a native rights movement that turned from protests to violence. It was exhilarating at the time. But as he remembered all the damage and destruction, he knew such violence was no substitute for what he truly desired.

STANDING FOUR STORIES up on the roof, I looked down nervously as three hundred federal marshals arrived in full riot gear. We were told, " Vacate the building in one hour or be removed by force!" I was taking part in the American Indian Movement's "Trail of Broken Treaties," protesting the government's unjust dealings with native peoples. But when it was all over, it was I who had learned a lesson. Native rights are a just cause. Yet my actions that day were more about violence, and the need to vent the hate and rage I felt toward a world which had denied me a meaningful life.

Late on a November afternoon I joined with several hundred other native Americans in occupying the Bureau of Indian Affairs building in Washington, D.C. We forced everyone to leave, chained the doors and took over the building. As the war drums played and war songs were sung that night, a medicine man offered prayers and applied war paint to the men who were armed and ready for battle. We shouted the words of the great Sioux chief, Crazy Horse, "It's a good day to die."

When the federal marshals arrived, my heart was pounding with the thrill of the moment. We prepared ourselves for the charge of the marshals and their dogs, tear gas and guns, which could happen at any time. The threats to remove us by force only made us more angry and violent. We taped up windows and distributed water barrels with towels in anticipation of tear gas. We fashioned weapons of all kinds, spiked clubs, bows and arrows, deadly spears, gas bombs, a small arsenal of guns and other "articles of war."

It was a very scary, and yet very exhilarating, situation for a seventeen-year-old boy filled with hate and rage. Once I had to jump quickly out of the way to avoid a man swinging a pipe, and shattering every object he could. Another time I was given a dozen gas bombs and, along with several others, was instructed to start the Bureau building on fire if the federal marshals charged. In the end we ransacked the entire building, stripping it of any items of value. After eight tense days of threats, warnings and moments of mass confusion, the siege ended. The marshals never did storm the building. Even without them, we exploded with pent-up anger, bitterness and frustration. It all seemed like such a great thrill. I was sure we had made our point!

When I returned to my reservation in South Dakota, however, I had time to think. I had said a lot of righteous words about native rights. Yet the fact is that I helped cause more than $2 million worth of damage. Now that the thrill was over, I became disillusioned and disappointed. Is this what would give my life meaning? Being honest with myself, I had really acted like the fuse on a keg of dynamite— angry and frustrated and ready to justify whatever violence I thought was necessary.

Later I learned from the Bible why my violence, which at the time seemed so satisfying, at last left me feeling so empty. "The heart is fooled more than anything else, and is very sinful. Who can know how bad it is? I the Lord look into the heart and test the mind. I give to each man what he should have because of his ways and because of the fruit that comes from his works" (Jeremiah 17:9-10). Without God my heart had followed its wicked nature and been fooled. So the fruit my life produced was dry and unnourishing.

My search for meaning was like catching a butterfly. Every time I thought I had what I was looking for, it fluttered away. First I had tried to become a "real" native American. In the years ahead I became a counterculture hippie, and then a spiritual mystic. Any sense of a meaningful identity escaped me— and I raged at every minute of it!

My mom and dad divorced before I was born, so I never knew my father. When I was seven, my mother decided she didn't want us growing up on the Sioux reservation. So we left South Dakota and, after spending a year in Denver, moved to Oregon. During that time mom divorced again and raised our family alone. With all the pain and confusion of growing up in a troubled home, I looked for my identity elsewhere. In high school my life was wrapped up in sports—and in drugs and alcohol. My basketball career was cut short when an auto accident left my arm partially paralyzed. So by age seventeen I left home and traveled across the country, searching for some reality and meaning in life.

During those months I was drawn toward the American Indian Movement. Their powerful words about restoring native rights and culture gave me a sense of identity. When I was later disillusioned, I found myself drifting deeper into drugs and alcohol. I left the reservation and planted trees in Washington State for a while. After a brush with the law, I left with a friend for seven months to Maui, Hawaii. All the time I hated the world for denying the life I deserved.

Still searching, I was drawn into Eastern religions—Buddhism, Taoism, Hinduism and Yoga. I traveled the island and spent many nights praying to these gods under the stars. The combination of drugs and mysticism only led to more confusion. Even in the midst of parties with my friends, relationships with women, and all my pious mystical prayers, I felt empty inside.

While in Hawaii, I met some Christians who told me about God. I dismissed them as narrow-minded Jesus freaks and Bible thumpers. But one day, alone on a beach at Maui in the early morning hours, all my futility hit home. The things I had pursued—sports, drugs, native religion, Eastern mysticism—

had brought me to a dead end. I remembered what those Christians told me about Jesus and decided, right there on the beach, to give Him my life. Immediately the question of my identity faded away, for I knew that I was His child. My hate was gone because my answer was found.

After I came to know Jesus Christ, His Holy Spirit started working in my life, convicting me about my drugs and drinking. I did not have any Christian friends, so I went to visit a woman I knew in Alaska who had become a believer in Jesus. She got me involved in a Christian training center where I stayed for two years and dedicated my life completely to serving God. The center owned some businesses to help support the ministry, and I became manager of a bakery. When I met and married my wife there, we used that business experience to open a small vinyl and leather repair shop in Anchorage. Six years later, at the age of 27, I became a pastor in Washington State.

Since I truly surrendered my life to Christ, I have been at peace with myself and the world around me. I've learned my identity is not in what I do or accomplish, but in being a wholehearted follower of Jesus. Many Indians are filled with hate and rage at the way their lives have gone and how the world seems so unfair. I know, because I was one of them! But now I have learned that in Jesus Christ, native people can have a new life that replaces anger with divine love.

THINGS TO THINK ABOUT

1. The Wedding That Changed My Life

If you are angry at life, hurting other people can seem like a way to make yourself higher. However, that is not being tough but only trying to hide your weakness. Read 1 Peter 2:21-24. Because of Jesus' example, how should you handle hurtful or potentially violent situations? Do you have the right to "pay back" other people who have wronged you? Who does?

2. God's Spirit at Work Behind Bars

You have probably done some things in anger and were sorry later. Perhaps the argument was silly, or you don't even remember what it was about. But you had to live with it for a long time. Read Galatians 6:7-9 and Romans 8:4-9. When you do wrong, can you escape the consequences of your action? Why do people do wrong things? How can you have the discipline to do right things?

3. Anger Was My Addiction

It is not enough to simply "control" the anger in your heart. Instead you must replace it with something new and good. Read James 1:19-27 and Psalm 119:11. How does anger affect your relationship with God? What should you put into your heart to replace the anger? If you do this, how will it show in your behavior?

4. A Truckload of Forgiveness

Perhaps you have been wronged, like the man in this story whose truck was stolen by a swindler. Of course you're angry! That guy doesn't deserve to be forgiven! Read Philippians 3:7-11. What is more important than any wrong or loss you suffer? By giving it up, what do you gain?

5. Deep Hatred Masks Deep Hurt

Anger begins by hating people and circumstances, but ends by hating your own life—or at least by living a life you hate. Read Ezekiel 36:26-27. What is the root cause of your anger and hate? To remove and replace them, what two new things are needed? How can you get these two things, and where do they come from?

6. Wife's Faith Breaks Vicious Circle

The Bible says, "A man is tempted to do wrong when he lets himself be led by what his bad thoughts tell him to do. When he does what his bad thoughts tell him to do, he sins. When sin completes its work, it brings death" (James 1:14-15). As the man in this story discovered, sin begins with a thought that leads to action, and becomes a pattern that leads to destruction. Read John 8:34-36. When you sin, what is your relationship to that sin? What then becomes of your relationship to God? How can the situation be changed?

7. The Butterfly I Couldn't Catch

You may try to justify violence with words, especially when you join with other people. Yet when the thrill is over, what is left? Read Jeremiah 17:9-10, then go back and read verses 7-8. Why does a heart without God tend to do bad things? If you follow your own heart, why does that leave you empty? What makes your life fruitful instead?

CHAPTER SEVEN

Conquering Sickness and Handicaps

1. My Disability Became His Ability

Key Verse - Psalm 139

"O Lord you have looked through me and have known me.....You know all my paths very well..... All you know is too great for me....It is too much for me to understand.....Take me out of trouble and away from the many waters, from the power of those from other lands. .... I will sing a new song to you, O God.....
Happy are the people whose God is the Lord!"

Worse than the disability of cerebral palsy were the taunts of her classmates. Even after this Ojibwe woman became a Christian, the hurt and pain affected her attitudes toward others. Then she learned God does not make mistakes, and her identity is much more than just her physical body.

UNEVEN SURFACES like stairs and street curbs are hard on me. Often I trip and fall. Usually someone comes along and helps me up. When they ask if I'm all right, I just laugh and say, "It says in the Bible I can get on my knees and pray anytime. So I'm taking advantage of it!"

Having a sense of humor about my situation did not come naturally to me. You see, I have ceberal palsy. This disability causes lack of muscle control and affects limb movement, speech, hearing, vision and learning. When I started life, my cerebral palsy was severe and I barely made it. The doctor who delivered me told my birth mother that I would never walk.

At first my mother tried to take care of me. But babies like me don't come with special instructions. She couldn't handle it, and left me in the community hospital where I was born. I spent two years there and twice I nearly died of pneumonia. Yet God loved me and gave me foster parents who took me home with them. I spent a lot of time in hospitals after that, but it was never my "home" again.

I began physiotherapy and speech therapy when I was two years old—and continued until I was eighteen, along with visits to a lot of doctors, nurses, psychologists and social workers. When I started kindergarten at age four, my older brother had to carry me into the classroom. It was a regular school and I failed my first two years. Rather than repeat kindergarten a third time, I ended up in a special education class for slow learners. After that year, I entered regular classes again and never failed another grade. (I finished high school and have the diploma to prove it!)

At age five I started walking. Both my ankles had to be operated upon because I was born without a bone that supports them. Yet even when I didn't have to be carried to class anymore, my early school years were not easy. Whoever made up the verse, "Sticks and stones will break my bones but names will never hurt me," never had a physical handicap! For two terrible years I was called names and insults. For a laugh the kids would imitate the way I walked. Not knowing how to handle this, I tried to ignore my classmates and bury my feelings deep down inside.

The hurt that comes from name-calling cuts deep and can affect the rest of your life. But after those two years my family moved away to a different community. I was actually treated as a normal person most of the time. By this time I had five foster brothers and four sisters to keep me company, plus other foster children that came through our home. Early in my life I became aware that my foster parents were different from most other people. They prayed for me and with me, took me to church and encouraged me to memorize Bible verses.

When I was ten years old they brought me to an evangelistic crusade. I began to get interested when I saw a banner that proclaimed a Bible verse I had memorized, "I am the Way, the Truth and the Life" (John 14:6). That night the evangelist asked, "Where would you go if you died tonight? Heaven or hell? Are you ready? You can be!" He explained how I could accept Jesus Christ as my own personal Savior and Lord, and how I could have assurance from the Bible that I would go to heaven.

I wanted to go to heaven, and certainly not to hell.

So when the evangelist invited people to come down to the front and pray with him to trust Christ for eternal salvation from sin, I went forward. I'm not sure if I really understood what I was doing, but five years later I confirmed my decision during an invitation at a Christian concert. From then on I was hungry to learn more about the Bible and how I could live for Christ. My pastor and family helped me to grow as a Christian . Soon after, I followed the Lord in baptism and joined an active local church.

After high school graduation I enrolled in a native Bible school. When a counselor spoke to the first-year students, both as a class and individually, I told him about my past. The hurt and pain affected my attitudes toward myself and others, and yet I refused to ask anyone for help. "I know how you feel," the man said to me, but in my mind I thought to myself, "No, you don't, because you don't have a physical disability."

The counselor must have known what I was thinking. "My wife has a physical disability," he said, "so I'm very much aware of what you are going through." He explained that God made me the way He wanted, to glorify Himself through me. God didn't give me a raw deal, but knew what He was doing all along. "For You made the parts inside me, and You put me together inside my mother," he read from Psalm 139. "My bones were not hidden from You when I was made in secret and put together with care...(and) Your eyes saw me before I was put together. And all the days of my life were written in

Your book before any of them came to be."

Then the counselor challenged me, "Decide for yourself whether you want to accept that, or not accept it and continue to feel sorry for yourself." For two weeks I pondered those words, and I prayed and cried out to God. At last I realized God knew what He was doing, even though I didn't. He had given me an identity that had nothing to do with the limitations of my body.

Since that day I have been learning and growing. Some people don't feel comfortable to be with me, feel sorry for me, or are afraid to talk to me—and I am learning to be patient with them, especially when they fall short of my expectations. I am also learning to trust God with my circumstances, and not to compare myself with others who are more able-bodied. Today I also feel more freedom to laugh and share my feelings, rather than compensate for my disability by always being "strong" and never admitting any weakness.

Sure, I still have hurts sometimes. But even when the world doesn't understand me or my disability, God does. "He has chosen what the world calls foolish to shame the wise. He has chosen what the world calls weak to shame what is strong," for "in that way, no man can be proud as he stands before God." It was Christ Himself who "made us right with God and set us apart for God and made us holy," and so "if anyone is going to be proud of anything, he should be proud of the Lord" (1 Corinthians 1:26-31).

2. Bible Student Who Couldn't Read

Key Verse - Matthew 11:28

"Come unto Me, all you who work and have heavy loads, I will give you rest."

A childhood heart problem nearly claimed his life, then kept him from being like other boys. When this Navajo man got older, he decided to make up for lost time. But traveling became drifting, and he never could run away from his fear of death. His future was consumed by his past, until he learned to see life from God's point of view.

THE DOCTOR WAS talking to my mother as they stood beside my bed. She was upset and the doctor was trying to comfort her. "I'm sorry, ma'am, but we've done all we can for your son," he said. "He has a heart problem that we can't correct. I think you should take him home and let him rest. Make him as comfortable as you can so he can enjoy his last days with his family."

Although I was five years old at the time, I could not understand what they were saying. I only knew about this conversation because my family told me. Beyond that I have no memory whatsoever of those five years in the hospital—and of the several months that followed back home on the reservation.

My mother had a job where she could not look after me. So I went to live with my grandparents. Our home was in a Navajo village in the northeastern part of Arizona, and it was there I was supposed to spend my "last days." Each morning my grandmother took me outside and laid me on the sunny side of the hogan. As I rested day after day in the sun, breathing the fresh air, God slowly turned my life around.

By the age of seven I began to know what was happening around me. But though I was able to get up and eat, I could not do much else. As the months passed my strength and health increased, but even yet I can remember the frightening pounding and trembling in my heart. If I would do some work or run or get excited, it would beat wildly. The pounding was so bad that my brother could hear my heart thumping as we lay in bed at night. Yet I made it into the teenage years, and my health improved so much that I was able to do almost anything—riding and breaking horses, even wrestling cows. These things made my heart pound away, but since it didn't hurt me I just tried to ignore it.

Though my health worries seemed behind me, those years still left their mark. I'd always had to "take it easy" and stay away from the excitement and good times other boys enjoyed. So by the time I was fifteen, I was easily impressed when an older boy came to our trading post wearing brand new clothes and a real nice pair of boots. He'd earned the money working in the sugar beets, and was going back soon. "If you're interested in coming along," he said, "there will be a truck coming by here in a few days."

My buddies and I decided it was a good idea, and I got permission from my grandmother to go. That was the beginning of many years of drifting. That first time away from home I got lonesome and decided to run away with two friends. We hitched a ride to Phoenix where I saw a city for the first time. When our money ran out we got jobs on a vegetable farm where they taught us to understand English. One day in Phoenix I met a man who had been in the military. When he found out I knew nothing about the United States he opened up some maps, showed me how big the country was and told me what it was like. Right away I became curious. If our country was like that, I wanted to see it.

Remember, my sickness had held me back from exploring things that other young people could experience. So I decided it was my turn. First I went to California and then Oregon, Washington, Idaho, Nevada, Utah and Wyoming. Finally I found work on a farm in Montana—and after just a few hours I discovered this place was different. The farmer and his family were Christians. Right after breakfast on my first morning there, the farmer said, "Before we go to work, we usually have what we call devotions." Reaching over, he picked up a great big Bible and began to read. After he read for a while, he put the Bible away and told me, "We always pray together, too." The whole family knelt down right away and I felt foolish because I was still sitting. As quickly as I could, I knelt too and listened to everyone pray. Then we all went to work. That evening after supper, the farmer invited me into the living room and we had family devotions again.

Up to this time, my life was filled with problems. Because of my sickness I had never been to school, and so I couldn't read or write. And there were deeper problems. I had real battles with fear, everything from fear of thunder and lightning to fear that there was some evil inside of me. Those years I lived so close to death had left their emotional scars upon me. Though it seemed I had overcome my physical heart problem, I had yet to overcome my spiritual heart problem.

Over the next year, the farmer and his family often talked to me about the Lord and the importance of life. They took me with them to church on Sundays and, though I couldn't read, I understood English just as though I had been to high school. One day a missionary spoke at the church of how God had shown the great needs among the Indian people to hear the Gospel of Jesus Christ. I don't really remember much about the message. But when the missionary finished and then invited anyone to come down the aisle and talk about salvation, I slipped into the prayer room. It was there that I confessed my sins and asked Jesus to be my Savior and the Lord of my life.

You know, that night when I trusted my life to Christ, all my old fears vanished! Jesus said, "I give you My peace and leave it with you...(so) do not let your heart be troubled or afraid" (John 14:27). He invites anyone, "Come to Me, all of you who work and have heavy loads, and I will give you rest" (Matthew 11:28). These words are really true, because this is what happened to me. It was something very real in my heart.

That same night I met the principal of a native Bible school that was located in Minnesota. He said,

"I want you to come and learn about the Word of God." If the little I had heard from the Bible that evening was powerful enough to take away my old fears in one night, imagine how more of His Word could change my life! I didn't need anymore incentive than that. In a few weeks I was hitchhiking across North Dakota, all the way to Minnesota.

I was very nervous on my first day in Bible school. After all, if I told the truth about not being able to read or write, I figured they would kick me out. Sure enough, that first week all the students were given a test. While the others filled up their blank pages, I sat there drawing pictures. When the test was over I handed in my artwork. That afternoon I was called to the principal's office. I knew what was coming. "Look," I admitted, "I've never been to school in my life. I can't even read or write. But I really want to study the Bible. That's why I came all the way over here." There was silence for a while, then the principal spoke. "If you want to study the Bible," he said, "you must be able to read and write. We will help you all we can. But it will be slow, hard work."

They were right. The school had a three-year course, but I flunked all three years and had to take three more. Finally I got my diploma and was asked to be the pastor of a native church in South Dakota. Later I even became principal of my old Bible school! As I look back over the years, I am glad for all God has done. I could have gone through life trying to make up for my sick childhood. Instead I now see life not on my terms but on God's terms. It is God who gives me life, so my life belongs to Him to use as He pleases. And the Lord has been good. He has given me a wife and four children, and led me back to minister among my own Navajo people, helping to build strong native churches to reach more Indians with the Gospel.

And my heart? God took care of that. Years later, when the doctors who wanted to operate checked me over, they found I did not have a problem anymore. Only God could do that! He has given me not only a healthy body but also a new spiritual life. If it wasn't for God, I could never have proved the doctors wrong.

3. Loss of Limbs a Stepping Stone
Key Verse - Hebrews 13:5

"Keep your lives free from the love of money. Be happy with what you have. God has said, 'I will never leave you or let you be alone'."

When she survived an airplane accident, this Cree woman was sure God would make everything turn out all right. But when doctors had to remove her right eye and both legs, her career dreams were shattered. It all seemed so unfair, until the hardships made her Christian faith come alive in a way it never had before.

THE ONLY WAY to reach the village where I was born is by airplane. For native people like me who have grown up in northern Manitoba, bush planes are a fact of life. You just take them for granted. Whether in winter or summer, my people think nothing about visiting family and friends by airplane. So the idea of any danger never occurred to me.

When my plane went down during a winter flight, a friend who was flying with me was instantly killed. Somehow I survived the impact, but the possibility of rescue seemed remote. With my legs broken it was too painful to move or find shelter from the terrible cold and snow. Even when I was rescued and rushed to the hospital, the doctors feared I might not live. But I was convinced God had spared my life for a reason. Though there would be many obstacles to overcome in getting my life back together, I was determined not to give up.

The initial crisis passed and the doctors told me I would live. That good news, however, was soon followed by a series of personal losses—the first being my right eye. When the plane hit the ice, a piece of plexiglass injured my eye beyond repair. The doctors said I must have it removed to prevent infections that could lead to total blindness. When I realized how bad it was, I gave them permission to operate. Then the doctors informed me I had suffered severe frostbite and must have some toes removed. Upon hearing this I broke into tears for the first time since the accident. With so many people praying for me I was certain God would make my body all better. Now I knew things would be different. The Lord had other plans for me, and I was scared. A few days later I got more bad news. The poison going through my system from the injured toes was so bad, the doctors would have to amputate higher up. There was no choice. It was either lose both my legs below the knees, or lose my life.

Six weeks after the accident I was moved from the hospital in Winnipeg to another hospital in the small northern Manitoba town where my parents lived. Before the accident I was training to be a nurse, and now that I could get around in a wheelchair I wanted to resume my studies. But because I missed the scheduled day for the exams, I was not allowed to enroll. This was perhaps the hardest blow of all to take! All my life I had wanted to be a nurse, and now I couldn't. It seemed so unfair. After all, it was my eye and my legs that had been injured, not my brain. I was still a full person with hopes and dreams for my future.

Three months later, once my legs had a chance to heal, I returned to Winnipeg to learn how to walk again. Within two months I was able to walk easily and with good balance. Since then I've learned to drive a car, go ice skating and mountain climbing, and even bought a horse I love to ride. With the door to nursing closed, my education took a new direction. First I went back to Bible college and got a diploma, because I needed a solid foundation in God's Word to pursue whatever plans He had for my new life. Then I enrolled at the university where I am now pursuing a bachelors degree. At the same time I volunteered at a Christian ministry that reaches out to native peoples, and ultimately God led me to join the staff full time. Today I just keep busy doing the work of ministering to my own people, and leave it up to God to meet my needs.

After all, God met all my needs when things seemed darkest. He fully prepared me for even my worst losses. Just before the accident I was at a Christian youth conference where I met a soldier who had lost his legs in combat. He was the guest speaker and really impressed me with his commitment to the Lord. Six weeks later I wrote him a letter saying, "Guess what happened to me?" His attitude about his loss was a great help. Another time I was in the hospital, feeling especially low about losing my legs, when a stranger suddenly walked into my room. The man took off his artificial leg and handed it to me. "This is what your legs will look like, when you get them," he said. It shocked me but it boosted my spirits too, and I thanked God for sending him.

I love living, but the greatest gift God has given me is life in Jesus. Before my accident I was a born-again Christian, but it took the crash to make my faith come alive. What was a tragedy has become a blessing, because I have experienced God's love for me in ways that would not have otherwise happened. Though I'm sad about the loss of my friend in the crash, because he was a model follower of Christ, I will never regret the accident—and I know my friend would not. Without the accident I would not know God as I know Him today. And perhaps other native people I have touched with the Gospel would not know Christ today, either.

Humanly speaking, I've had some major losses. But spiritually I have had some major gains. Jesus Christ promises, "I will never leave you or let you be alone" (Hebrews 13:5). That assurance is a real comfort and the reason I have been able to keep going. Not with my own strength, but through His strength I will carry on.

4. In a Hospital Bed for a Reason

Key Verse - Romans 8:28

"We know that God makes all things work together for the good of those who love Him and are chosen to be a part of His plan."

When a pinched nerve landed this busy Ojibwe pastor in a hospital bed, he blamed God for "wasting my time and His." There was so much work to do, and this delay was so unexpected and inconvenient. Then he discovered the Lord's work doesn't go by a schedule, but according to His own plans.

"WHY, LORD?" I questioned. I was lying flat on my back in a hospital bed, my legs in traction. "You know I've got a lot of work to do. I'm a busy pastor with letters to answer, cassettes to duplicate, next week's sermon and radio message to write, and a lot of people to visit. I hope You know what You're doing, Lord, because I sure don't."

As I lay there, I thought about Romans 8:28 a number of times that day. "We know that God makes all things work together for the good of those who love Him and are chosen to be part a of His plan." In fact, I had even preached on that verse a good many times. But that was small comfort as I lay there fighting the pain and fretting about all the work that was falling farther behind on each day.

As the hours passed, my thoughts went back to the many ways God had blessed me. During my early teens I had developed a severe case of tuberculosis. The doctors had not expected me to live. But God by His grace had brought me through it. Later while serving in the armed forces, I got an overdose of chlorine gas. I was discharged from the service and again the doctors were doubtful if I would recover. But once more God brought me back to health. I was not a Christian at the time and did not see those recoveries as God's hand upon my life. But later I came to see how God, in His mercy, had spared me from an eternity in hell without Christ.

Some years later I trusted Jesus Christ as my Savior at an evangelistic crusade in Toronto. Within six years the Lord led me, with my family, to undertake mission work among my own Ojibwe people. Besides pastoring a small congregation, I became involved in a radio and counseling ministry carried on several stations across northern Ontario.

It seemed God had given me a steady green light through sixteen years of ministry, until this latest accident had put me in the hospital. It was winter and I had been tobogganing with the children, when I took quite a tumble that severely wrenched my back and made my left leg almost useless. I hobbled around using a cane for a few days until I finally gave in and went to a doctor. He discovered I had a pinched nerve in my back and put me in the hospital right away. For treatment I was tied down to a bed with my legs up in the air. There was to be no activity until the pressure on the damaged nerve was relieved and healing had begun.

All day Friday I fretted and stewed about the situation. On Saturday I was still complaining and blaming God for wasting my time and His. After all, I had commitments to His work that needed to be kept. By Sunday my resistance came to an end. I told God, maybe not too cheerfully but at least willingly, that I was satisfied to stay in this situation as long as He wanted me here. At that moment, peace filled my heart and I was able to get the rest I needed for the healing in my body to begin.

Early Monday morning the hospital staff brought a man into the empty bed next to mine. It seemed as if all the gloom in the world had settled upon him. His depression was so deep I could feel it as soon as he entered the room. He sobbed and cried all that day and most of the night. I tried to talk to him, but he would not respond to anything I said. This went on through most of Tuesday, until in the evening he finally began to open up. He had been having severe family problems and become so depressed that he had decided to take his life. There seemed nothing to live for, so he had gone outside with a gun to end it all. A neighbor saw the man and talked him out of it, then called the police who brought the man to the hospital.

I began to talk to this man about God's concern for him and of his own spiritual needs. He was quite bitter toward God. "If there really is a God who is personally interested in me," he declared, "then God has sure given me a dirty deal." We argued this back and forth until the early hours of the morning. I was exhausted and didn't seem to be getting anywhere with this man. As simply and forthrightly as I could, I explained God's plan of salvation. Then as I went to sleep, I silently released him to God's wonderful mercy and to the working of the Holy Spirit.

I awoke early the next morning. There my roommate sat on the edge of his bed, with a smile on his face as bright as the morning sun. Immediately I knew what had happened. "You don't have to tell me," I said, "because I know." "Yes," he replied, "I've accepted the Savior, Jesus Christ, to be the God and King of my life. I just feel as if all my burdens have been lifted." In the following hours before his release we rejoiced together in his newfound freedom.

I stayed in the hospital a few more days before I was well enough to go home. However, I was content and continually thanking the Lord that He controlled my life. He knew best where I could most profitably serve Him each hour of the day. I found out later that the doctor who had admitted the desperate man had requested he be placed in my room. The doctor quickly recognized the man's real problem was spiritual, and that as a Christian pastor I might offer the needed help. I still marvel at God's grace and perfect timing. My own ministry has become better since I learned that lesson about waiting on the Lord. And if the whole situation had occurred any differently , who knows what might have happened to that man?

5. Pain Was My Teacher
Key Verse - Luke 18:7-8

"Will not God make the things that are right come to His chosen people who cry day and night to Him? Will He wait a long time to help them? I tell you He will be quick to help them."

God controls the nations, but it took a ruptured appendix to show this Sioux man that God cared about him personally—and that when Christians pray for another believer who is in need, those prayers do make a real difference.

PAIN. TERRIBLE PAIN. Not even the needles helped. And to make matters worse, the doctors could not decide what was wrong. "Oh, God," I screamed in my mind, "why are You doing this to me?" It was not until many days later that I found the answer.

The day before had been busy. Besides having company, I had just been working in the field in our farm in South Dakota. By the time we had supper and said goodbye to our guest, I was ready for bed. Almost as soon as my head hit the pillow, I fell asleep. But several hours later I was awakened with sharp pains in my stomach. For a while I tossed around trying to go back to sleep. It was hopeless. Finally I sat up and looked at the clock. It was three in the morning.

"Now that I'm awake," I thought, "I might as well go downstairs and get some medicine." Slowly I swung my feet to the floor and made my way to the kitchen and then to the couch. But time only made the pain worse. By seven o'clock it was so intense that I realized this must be something more than a stomach ache. Unable to bear the pain any longer, I walked down the hill to my neighbor and asked him to take me to the doctor. When we arrived at the hospital, the doctor came out to examine me. "I think it's just a case of intestinal flu," he said, "but to be sure, we'll keep you in bed until we complete some other tests." Before he left, the doctor gave me a needle to relax my stomach muscles and ease the pain.

A short while later, another doctor came on duty. By then I was in so much pain that I was in no mood for humor. But I could not help smiling at the doctor's first question. Thinking perhaps I had been on a long binge, he asked, "How long have you been drinking." To that I replied, "Thank God, I haven't been drinking for eight years. When He delivered me from drinking, He also set me free from the things that tempted me to drink." The doctor didn't answer but continued to examine me. Sensing I had something more than intestinal flu, he decided to send me to a specialist. "I think it's appendicitis," he said, "but I want to be sure."

By this time, the pain was so bad it seemed to cover my whole body. Though they gave me painkillers, the medicine wasn't doing much good. Out of my agony I remember crying out to God with a mixture of praise and complaint. Then suddenly, though I realized my condition was worsening, my resentment toward God stopped and I began to praise Him without hesitation. In the midst of all the pain, the Lord gave me the assurance that He was in control.

Because I was a veteran, they took me 120 miles away by ambulance to the veteran's hospital in Fargo, North Dakota. When I arrived the doctors reexamined me and ran some more tests. The doctor in charge agreed it was appendicitis and gave orders to prepare me for surgery. They had just moved me to the waiting area when my wife came in. She had driven behind the ambulance all the way from South Dakota. "I've called a bunch of friends," she said, "and they are all praying for you." I knew one of those friends was my mother-in-law, a dear woman who was always a faithful prayer warrior on my behalf and like a "spiritual parent" to me. As my wife and I talked, I felt a peace come over me and the pain began to subside.

The operation went ahead and was successful. Afterwards I learned my appendix had started to seep. If the doctors had waited any longer it would have been a tragedy. As I recovered in the days that followed, I had a lot of time to think. During those quiet moments God showed me that He had allowed that terrible pain to teach me two valuable lessons. The first one is that He is concerned about our every need. Sure, He cares about countries and nations and world affairs, but He is also concerned with our individual hurts and smallest needs.

The other lesson I learned is that intercessory prayer is a command of God, an order every Christian should obey. God promises to help believers "who cry day and night to Him," but challenges us with the question, "When [Jesus returns], will He find faith on the earth?" All over the world there are Christian brothers and sisters who need the uplift of our prayers. There come times in every Christian's life when he is down or beaten. It doesn't matter whether the problem is physical, mental, emotional or spiritual. The fact remains that he needs help. This is where our prayers come in. Our duty before God is to pray for this brother until he can get on his feet again.

Though I would not want to have that pain again, I am glad God sent it my way. Through it, He has taught me to be more mindful of people around me and their needs. Being thankful for those who shared with me in my need, I want to give to others as I received.

6. God Waited For Twenty-Five Years

Key Verse - Psalm 38:21,22

"O Lord do not forsake me; be not far from me, O my God. Come quickly to help me, O Lord my Savior."

For more than thirty years this Pima woman had drifted away from the Lord. She had been a Christian believer since childhood, but married in rebellion and went her own way. Now her children were grown and, after losing her leg to diabetes, she thought her life would never count for God.

IT WAS NOT EASY to go home. With my right leg amputated, I was helpless. Even to eat or use the bathroom, I had to wait for someone to carry me or push my wheelchair. I couldn't get to church. I wanted so much for someone to talk and pray with me. I asked God, "Why did You spare my life?"

All my life I had lived on the Pima reservation in Arizona. My parents brought me up in a Christian home, but I wandered far from the things they taught me, and I was an old woman before God used sickness to finally get my attention and bring me back to where I belonged.

I was born the oldest of ten children in a Pima Indian family. Father had a small farm on which we raised vegetables and a few animals, and he made extra money by selling firewood. We had very few possessions, but we were happy because my parents knew Jesus as their Lord. Every morning before breakfast we prayed as a family. After my father left to chop firewood, mother would stay at the table a while longer and sing Christian songs with us. I learned God loved us so much that He sent Jesus, His only Son, so that "whoever puts his trust in God's Son will not be lost but will have life that lasts forever" (John 3:16).

Because we were poor, I quit school after eighth grade to get a job and help make ends meet. When I was 15, I met a young man who was also from the Pima tribe. He treated me well and I liked him. Though my parents didn't approve—because he was not living for Jesus—I decided that I could choose my own man. We were married when I was 18.

Everything seemed fine, and within a year my husband began attending church and appeared to accept my beliefs. He even became a deacon. But then he was drafted by the army and served in combat for four years.

After my husband came home his life was changed. He was bitter and angry and quit going to church.

He asked me to stop as well and, because I didn't want to displease him, I obeyed. In the next 25 years I went to church only three times, once after each of my three children were born. Instead we struggled along on our own, forgetting about God as our family grew up.

Along the way I suffered a great deal with diabetes, until at last my right leg was lifeless. By the time I was 52, with my children all grown, I went to the hospital to have it amputated. After the operation I lay in my hospital bed in pain, feeling very alone, drifting in and out of consciousness. Yet the God that I had cast aside was still with me in my time of pain. I began to feel His presence, and somehow got the impression that I should read Psalm 38. Later when I awoke again, I reached for the Bible on the bedstand and opened it.

The passage certainly described my situation: "I have sorrow all day long for my body is filled with burning pain. There is no strength in my body. I am weak and broken" (Psalm 38:6-8). But it wasn't the amputation that caused me to feel defeated. Something more was making me unhappy with my life. The psalm explained that if "I cannot stand straight," the reason was not a missing leg. "My sins are gone over my head. Like a heavy load, they weigh too much for me. I cry because of the pain in my heart" (38:4,8).

Yet as I read further, I could see that "all my desire is before You, and my breathing deep within is not hidden from You" (38:9). Then I felt joy because God knew and cared for me and heard all my cries and groaning. But I also felt sorrow because I had failed

Him. He had to wait 25 years for me to come back to Him. He had given me a long life and fine children, but I had been blind to His goodness.

I read on and found that if I would confess and repent of my wrong attitudes toward God, then I could come to Him and ask, "Do not leave me alone, O Lord! O my God, do not be far from me! Hurry to help me, O Lord who saves me!" (38:18,22). I remembered what I had learned as a child. Jesus was waiting with open arms ready to put them around me. I asked Him to forgive me and cleanse me—and He did!

7. Trials of Life Become Tools

Key Verse - Matthew 6:34

"Do not worry about tomorrow. Tomorrow will have it's own worries. The troubles we have in a day are enough for one day."

Tuberculosis and meningitis had broken up his family, left him paralyzed, and took him from one institution to another. The nurses could only prop him up beside the window to stare outside all day. Then Christ came along and taught him that the secret to a meaningful life is putting God and others first.

"WORRIES ABOUT tomorrow's hardships are only in your imagination. Walk with Christ today." These are the closing words of a meditation I recently composed. Each week the pastor reads one of my devotionals from the pulpit of our native church in Saskatchewan. People seem to appreciate them—perhaps because I write from a life of experiences that few natives would wish to share! Though confined to a wheelchair, I have learned the keeping power of a personal faith in Jesus Christ.

I was born in northern Saskatchewan. Our whole family lived in a caboose while my father worked in a sawmill. When he was killed and mother remarried, there were thirteen of us. But we weren't together for very long. My stepfather often beat my mother, yet that wasn't the reason for our break-up. Tuberculosis was discovered in all the family, except for one sister. One by one, the provincial Department of Health and Welfare removed us. Finally they took three children on the same day and sent them all by barge to the sanitorium in The Pas, a city in northern Manitoba. By then the family was down to three.

When it was my turn to go, I had many unanswered questions. All I knew for sure were two things—that I was sick and away from home. I had difficulty swallowing and I often staggered. In those days people with tuberculosis were also considered mentally retarded, and that's how the sanitorium treated me. After a few days the doctors discovered I had cerebrospinal meningitis and sent me to another institution. One night I fell down there, and the next morning I awoke almost totally paralyzed. I could only mumble and had just limited use of one arm and a hand. From then on, my world became like a strange dream.

Over the next three years I was shuffled from sanitorium to hospital to training school. I lived in four different cities and lost track of my family and my native heritage. I was alone. Eventually my life became a dull routine. The nurses would prop my paralyzed body in front of a window every morning, and for several months I did nothing but gaze outside for endless hours.

I found myself in front of that window one Christmas Eve night, watching the falling snow. In the distance I could hear the carolling of children. I wanted to see more, to enjoy the blessings of the season. I wanted so much to move. At that moment, I saw the window sill glide away. Then I was shouting, "I'm sitting up! I'm sitting up!" What a Christmas present!

Later I recovered enough to take a trip home. My mother was unprepared and I spent an entire year living in her attic. Yet my body continued to regain some strength, enough to begin a series of operations to correct the deformities brought on by tuberculosis. First the surgeons worked on my club feet and mangled knees, and then my hip. The last operation, and the most difficult and painful, was to correct my badly hunched posture.

By age 22, I was at last able to live on my own. It was spooky, but once I got used to things I was determined never to allow my life to be ruled by institutions again. For awhile I lived pretty high, off the money that had accumulated over the years from the Compensation Board, in the city of Regina. When the money ran out I ended up in Saskatoon, moving from place to place, living off welfare. As the novelty of my freedom began to wear off, I began for the first time to think about life. Where was it all headed? Why was I here?

After two years of drifting, I moved in with a Christian family. In the three years I lived with them—the longest I had ever stayed anywhere—they gradually helped me understand the Gospel of Christ. Later, when a lady explained the way of salvation more directly to me, I was ready to listen. Gently and simply, I prayed a prayer of confession and repentance, and trusted Christ as my Savior.

Though I was a "new man" in Christ, my life was still a roller coaster for the next few years. My faith began to grow as I joined my host family at occasional church meetings. But other times I lapsed into my old habits. I needed to "get stabilized" as a Christian. Two years after leaving my host family, the Lord led me to a Christian group home for the handicapped, and there I learned humility, obedience and, most of all, responsibility. My pride and selfishness were broken. And as I began to put God and other people first, I felt more purpose in my own life.

By now I had a growing desire to serve the Lord among my own people. I heard of a native church in Saskatoon and found there a "family" where I could share my feelings honestly—and have a ministry through the writing of weekly devotional meditations. The trials of my life are now the tools of this ministry. Through my writing, Indian people are taught the truths of Christ's abiding faithfulness.

One of my favorite meditations says it this way: "Are you afraid—afraid of what tomorrow may bring? Jesus is asking you to trust Him by refusing to be afraid. `So don't be anxious about tomorrow. God will take care of your tomorrow, too' (Matthew 6:34, TLB). Worries about tomorrow's hardships are only in your imagination. You don't know if you'll live another day. Trust—respond by an act of your will—in Jesus, and fear nothing.

"Satan can put wrong thoughts in your mind if you live by feelings. He can make your wrong desires attractive, and so impair your judgment. He slowly leads you as he pleases. You will walk blindly on the road to hell through your false feelings and imaginations. But you will never make this mistake if you trust in your Savior. Listen to His words and follow His guidance by daily meditating on Holy Scripture. Why worry about tomorrow when you can walk with Christ today?"

THINGS TO THINK ABOUT

1. My Disability Became His Ability

When you experience rejection because of a handicap, you may start to question your own worth and identity as a person. Read Psalm 139:13-16 and 1 Corinthians 1:26-31. Can you be sure God knew what He was doing when He created you? Why should you accept that?

2. Bible Student Who Can't Read

Even when you recover, a serious illness can leave you afraid of dying and restless to make up for lost time. Read John 14, especially verses 1-4 and 26-29, and Matthew 11:27-30. Why should death and danger no longer be fearful? How can Jesus replace your restless feelings with peace?

3. Loss of Limbs a Stepping Stone

When sickness or injury strikes, perhaps you expect God to make everything normal again. But if you lose the old things that were once important to you, God can show you how to live by the things that are important to Him. Read Hebrews 13:1-10. What should be your priorities? How does God promise to help you live thay way?

4. In a Hospital Bed for a Reason

Sometimes a sickness or injury seems to happen for no reason, except to be annoying and inconvenient. Perhaps you know the familiar Bible verse, Romans 8:28, that says, "God makes all things work together for the good of those who love Him and are chosen to be a part of His plan." Now read Romans 8:31-39. According to these verses, how can you be certain God will bring good from what seems a bad situation?

5. Pain Was My Teacher

Though your need is great, the opportunity to see God at work is also great. And He allows other Christians to have a part in that work by praying for you. Read Luke 18:1-8. What does this parable tell you about the effectiveness of prayer? What promise does God make?

6. God Waited for Twenty-Five Years

When you disobey God, He has many ways to get your attention. Sometimes He allows physical suffering for that reason. This is not for punishment, but because He loves you and wants to bring you back to Himself. Read Psalm 138. If you feel defeated, is sickness or sin the real reason? How do you know God still cares and will forgive?

7. Trials of Life Become Tools

It is easy to focus on yourself, when a sickness or handicap causes your body to have so many needs. However, the key to your well-being is putting God and other people first. Read Matthew 6:31-34. Why is focusing on your own physical needs a wrong attitude? How does the right focus help you to stop worrying?

CHAPTER EIGHT

Conquering Tragedy and Fear

1. I was Blind But Now I Can See

Key Verse - Acts 4:12

"There is no way to be saved from the punishment of sin through anyone else. For there is no other name under heaven given to men by which we can be saved."

A brush with death made this Cree man see his need for Christ who then helped him clean up his life. Shortly after, God became less important as his old problems faded. If he acted like a good person, was church really necessary? It took another tragic accident and the loss of his sight to make him see the truth.

IT BEGAN AS a normal day. I was working the night shift and it was now five in the morning. My job was driving an 85-ton, truck-type loader. It was not all that difficult, but at this hour it was about all I could do to stay awake. What happened next I will never forget! And as I look back, I realize it fits in with the kind of life I was living. Though I was a Christian, I was asleep at the wheel and headed for trouble.

When I least expected it, the heavy loader I was driving slipped and turned over. As it hit the ground, the batteries came flying out of the side, splashing acid all around. One of the batteries knocked me on the head, soaking my face. Soon everything went black. I could not see. The fiery battery acid had made me blind. I was frightened and in pain. But then God stepped in and did something that helped penetrate my spiritual blindness. At that crisis moment He flooded me with a peace like I had never known before. I really sensed that God was with me and I was grateful to be alive. And I saw He was intimately involved in my life, and not just in the background where I had been trying to put Him.

I grew up in northern Alberta in a mixed community not far from a Cree reservation. My parents professed to be religious but did not practice it. There were always a lot of parties. I learned to drink from the time I was eight and with each passing year the habit grew stronger. By my late teens, alcohol wasn't enough and I started doing drugs. Keeping a job became a problem, so I moved to Edmonton hoping things would get better. They didn't, and two years later I moved back north to another new town. Soon I found a job and felt more at home in the north. But even though I held that job for six years, I was still unhappy. Thoughts of my past, and of two children I had fathered and abandoned, got me very depressed.

I had a girlfriend, and one day her sister took me

to a church volleyball game. The truth is I only hung around that night for the food. But the pastor must have thought I was interested about God. So I saw him quite often in the weeks that followed. He would drop by my house and, though I was not much interested, he showed love and concern and was patient. Sometimes the pastor arrived when my girlfriend and I were drinking or arguing. Yet I could not turn him away. I would make some coffee and we would talk. We often talked about hunting, a favorite topic of mine, and then he would change the subject and share some Bible verses. I did not mind, but did not care much either.

My life went on as usual—which means it continued to get worse. I was missing a lot of work and asked my supervisor for help. He suggested Alcoholics Anonymous and gave me time off to attend meetings. The program sobered me up for a while, but did not remove my desire to drink. After a really bad argument with my girlfriend, I picked up a few cases of beer and headed off with two friends on a motorcycle. The next thing I remember is waking up in jail and being told I had been in a motorcycle accident. I could have killed myself and my friends! Ashamed, it was as if God let me see how horrible I was. Then one of the pastor's Bible verses came to my mind. "There is no way to be saved from the punishment of sin through anyone else [except Jesus]. For there is no other name under heaven given to men by which we can be saved" (Acts 4:12).

A day or so after I got home from jail, the pastor came over. I had a lot of questions. He shared with me from the Bible how I could know Jesus in a personal way, and how He could change my life. I admitted the longest I had ever been sober was the last four months, and now it had ended with me making a fool of myself. I really was helpless. When the pastor asked if I wanted to trust Jesus to save me, I said yes—and right away! We got on our knees and prayed together. I received Christ and also asked Him to take away my desire for alcohol and drugs. He did that, and since that day He has filled my needs in those areas.

However, the time after I became a Christian was difficult in another way. My girlfriend and I were living together without being married, and I knew that was wrong. Yet I was scared to lose this girl. I loved her very much. After about a year, my prayers were answered when she came to know Jesus. A few months later we were married, and God has blessed our commitment and given us three beautiful daughters. Things were starting to go well, and so I began thinking I did not need to spend time with other Christians anymore. I figured it was all right if I just read the Bible by myself. I had no interest in church or in sharing the Gospel with others.

And that's when my accident with the 85-ton loader happened. After the rescue squad loaded me into the ambulance, a real race began! Somehow the ambulance caught fire and, only seconds after I was removed, it exploded and eventually burned to the ground. I was put in a second ambulance and rushed the rest of the way to the hospital. At last the doctor told me I had a broken rib and a punctured lung. For three days I was in the hospital and remained totally blind. But that did not really seem to matter, since God was removing my spiritual blindness. My second day in the hospital was even my birthday, and that was a very humbling lesson. Then on the third day God restored my physical sight.

After being released, I lost my job since the accident was my fault. But I did not really care. Now that God had opened my eyes, literally and spiritually, I had a strong desire to serve Him. For that I needed training. So my wife and I applied and were accepted for Bible school. During our first Christmas break I will never forget how I preached only my second sermon in our pastor's church, and had the joy of seeing my grandmother come forward to trust Christ! Since Bible school my wife and I have gone to serve God among the native people of southern British Columbia. None of this seemed possible when I was lying beneath that 85-ton loader, wondering if I would ever see again. But except for that, I might still be blind.

2. I Forsook the Traditions of My Forefathers
Key Verse - Ephesians 6:12-13

"Our fight is not with people. It is against the leaders and the powers and the spirits of darkness in this world. It is against the demon world that works in the heavens. Because of this, put on all the things God gives you to fight with. Then you will be able to stand in that sinful day. When it is all over, you will still be standing."

Once she enrolled in Bible school, this Chipewyan woman thought her life as a Christian was on track. It was, and that's why Satan

was working overtime to defeat her. That same
year she suffered two terrible auto accidents, but
God gave her the victory.

THE DOCTOR SAID I should have been thrown
from the car and instantly killed. My head hit the
windshield and shattered the glass. The engine was
torn right out of the car. He just shook his head: "I
don't understand how you survived." But I know it
was God who let me live—and I know why the accident happened. In fact, it was my second car accident that year. You see, all my life Satan had worked
hard to keep me from Jesus. Now that I had become
a Christian and wanted to tell others, the fighting
had really started!

My struggle with Satan began, in a sense, even
before I was born. I am a Chipewyan from the Northwest Territories, and our society is very family ori-
ented. For generations my family had been the medicine people in our village. Now I was the child they
expected to carry on the tradition of our forefathers.
As a little girl I used to wander in the bush for hours,
speaking to the gods of the earth and enjoying the
peace of the land.

But if our village was surrounded by such peace,
why did people fight and get drunk and break down
doors to get high on glue and paint? One day when
I was five years old, a terrible fight occurred in our
home. I hid under the bed and for the first time
prayed to God with as much understanding as I had.
"If I grow up, God, my life won't be like this." I
didn't become a Christian that day because I had
never heard the Gospel of Jesus. Yet God was already

calling me and leading me to Him.

Soon after that day I was taken from my home to attend an Indian residential school. There I had a dream one night about three eagles that flew over my teepee and disappeared. Somehow I couldn't get that dream out of my mind. "What does it mean?" I kept asking myself. At first I thought the dream was telling me to become a medicine person like my father. Yet I wasn't sure. So again with my best understanding, I asked God to show me the right way.

As I grew up, the desire to help my people remained strong and I enrolled in college to obtain a teaching certificate. However, at the time I was also abusing alcohol. But God was watching out for me, because He gave me a Christian roommate. She was very friendly—but I wouldn't even say hello. Yet she prayed faithfully for me. Four months later a native evangelist was coming to her church for some meetings and she asked me to hear him. "Well, just the first night," I thought. Besides, my roommate had always been so nice, and it would be a favor to her.

So I went, and though nothing happened it made me think about my life. The meeting wasn't too bad, so I agreed to go the next night. That evening, the evangelist clearly explained the Gospel of Christ. He said that Jesus freely offers eternal life to all who admit their sinfulness and trust Christ to save them from hell. When he said, "Is there anyone who wants to give his life to the Lord Jesus Christ?", I felt God directing me to walk down the church aisle and pray with the pastor. I didn't know anything about the Bible or how to pray. The pastor even had to give me the words as we prayed together. Yet I truly meant those words in my heart as I offered them to God.

For the first year I struggled with my old life. How could I break the traditions of my family, who had been the medicine people of our village for generations? Now, please don't think I always go by dreams. Yet God is in control, and we never have a dream He doesn't know about. As I wrestled with my old life, one night I dreamed of an eagle that flew into the sky, leaving a feather behind. When I touched the feather, which is a powerful native religious symbol, the eagle was struck by lightning. The dream was so vivid it made me start to think. "Who made the eagle? God did," I said to myself. Then I prayed and felt God was impressing something on my heart. "If I made the eagle," He seemed to say, "why do people worship the things I created instead of the Creator?"

It was clear to me that the sweatlodge religion of the medicine man was not the way. Neither was any church, for my family had attended Catholic mass when I was growing up, and I knew rituals did not bring true peace. Only Jesus Christ is the Way, as we have a personal relationship with Him. Breaking from the old ways was very difficult, for I dearly love my family and my people. Yet to be the person God wanted, I had to put Him first. I felt God leading me to Bible school for more training—and Satan went into overtime trying to defeat me, for that's the year I had my two car accidents. But the more I live for Jesus, the more peace and strength He gives me.

"Our fight is not with people," the Bible says, but "against the leaders and the powers and the spirits of darkness in this world. It is against the demon world that works in the heavens. Because of this, put on all the things God gives you to fight with. Then you will be able to stand in that sinful day. When it is all over, you will still be standing. So stand up and do not be moved. Stand against the devil and he will run away from you. Stand against him and be strong in your faith" (Ephesians 6:12-14, James 4:7, 1 Peter 5:9). Satan is playing for keeps, as I learned through two terrible accidents. But the God Who lives in me is stronger than my enemy who lives in the world (1 John 4:4).

3. Praise God For My Paralysis
Key Verse - James 1:13

"When you are tempted to do wrong, do not say, 'God is tempting me.' God cannot be tempted. He will never tempt anyone."

Paraylzed by a stroke, his left hand and leg useless, his career as a musician was gone. This Cherokee man refused any help or friendship. Then God impressed a question on his heart. Would he rather have gone to hell as a whole person, or lose his limbs yet find the way to heaven?

MY WHOLE LEFT SIDE was useless. They called it a paralytic stroke. But I wasn't worried. Being a confirmed alcoholic, I thought this condition was only temporary, the result of drinking too much. I thought it would go away in a little while, like a hangover. Then the doctor came and explained the seriousness of my condition. A stroke such as mine, which occurred while I was asleep, resulted from a burst blood vessel in my brain.

"Your condition could very well be permanent," he said. And that was when the real shock came, followed by despair and depression. I imagined myself, a proud Oklahoma Cherokee, confined to a wheelchair or bed-ridden for the rest of my life. Over the years I had faced some pretty tough situations and always managed to handle then. But paralysis! That was different. The words "possibly permanent" took all my hope away and left me feeling helpless. My future looked cloudy and bleak. By profession I was a western guitar player and bookkeeper, both of which required the use of my left hand. After having led such an active life, being paralyzed was a crushing experience.

I withdrew into a shell of self-pity, became completely unreasonable and refused to communicate. I hated myself as well as the world and people around me. I would not speak unless spoken to, nor would I cooperate with people who tried to help me. Music became unbearable because it reminded me of my lost career. Anytime I saw someone walking or using both hands, I boiled with hatred inside. At the same time I was searching deep within myself, searching for some reason for my suffering. The thought came that maybe this was punishment for going against God—though I could not figure out why.

"God, what have I done to deserve this? I know I haven't lived according to your will. But there are many others who have committed much worse deeds than I have, and they are still well and healthy." Then I remembered something I once heard from a radio preacher, how God is the source not of misfortune but of love. He was explaining a Bible verse that says, "When you are tempted to do wrong, do not say, `God is tempting me.' God cannot be tempted. He will never tempt anyone. A man is tempted to do wrong when he lets himself be led by what his bad thoughts tell him to do. Whatever is good and perfect comes to us from God" (James 1:13-14,17).

As the weeks passed with no apparent improvement, I was transferred to a veterans hospital. Here I could think and concentrate. And as I was thinking one day, it suddenly seemed strange to me how people so often forget God until some terrible event makes them desperate. I was not a born-again Christian, but I believed in God as much as the next guy. Could the Bible have something to say about my suffering? With plenty of time to think, I was ready to consider any explanation. So I began reading the Scriptures, searching for passages that would provide some answers for my condition.

Then I found a verse that greatly impressed me. "If your hand or your foot is the reason you sin, cut it off and throw it away. It is better for you to go into life without a hand or a foot, than to have two hands or two feet and to be thrown into the fire of hell" (Matthew 18:8). After meditating on that verse, I knew it was better to lose something if that brings you to God, than to keep those things and go to hell. Before my stroke I never gave any thought to

God. Though I was a whole person physically, I was on my way to hell. In His love, God allowed my stroke to happen, taking me aside where I could hear Him calling.

I answered that call by putting my trust in Christ. And my life began to change. There was a complete reversal of my attitudes. Hope and faith took the place of frustration and depression. I began to see the people around me as the caring and concerned individuals they really were. Before I had treated them badly, but now I treated them as friends. Until this time I had never fully cooperated with any aid that was offered. I had not tried to do anything, not even walk. Now I said, "Lord, with your help, I am going to walk." It was not easy. I was very clumsy and off-balance to start with, but I kept trying and believing. I thought often of the apostle Peter, when he walked on the water. As soon as he took his eyes off Jesus, he began to sink (Matthew 14:22-33).

Strength slowly returned to my body, and I can walk fairly well now with a cane. Though I am not completely healed, I have much to be thankful for. After all, God spared my life, for that stroke could have been fatal. He left me the use of my right hand and allowed me to write this story and many other articles that have been published. I have not touched alcohol for several years now. But most of all God has healed me spiritually, forgiven my sins, and made me His child. The life I was leading would have definitely ended in death by this time. It took a stroke to bring me to my senses. Today I look at my paralyzed left side and praise God for it!

4. My Accident was No Accident

Key Verse - Hebrews 2:18

"Because Jesus was tempted as we are and suffered as we do, He understands us and is able to help us when we are tempted."

A crippling childhood disease, a stray bullet in the eye, a tragic accident to his infant son, and now a car accident that crushed his upper body. This Lumbee Indian had a few months to think it over in the hospital. Was he being punished for sin, or should he trust that God loved him and had a plan?

RETURNING HOME LATE one night, a big Cadillac crashed into the back of my Toyota, totalling the car and almost killing me. My collarbone and shoulder blade were broken. Both arms were fractured in two places. My lungs were crushed. Six ribs were broken in the front and five in the back. One broken rib had struck my heart, stopping a portion of it from functioning. I should have been dead. When my mind cleared after the accident, the doctor came in to explain my condition. "They tell me you're a minister. Well, you'll never be able to preach again. You might as well forget it and concentrate on trying to live. That's about all you'll be able to do."

The doctor said I would need about two or three months in the hospital. That gave me a lot of time to think. I knew that sometimes God allows His children to suffer. Some people always say it's because of sin. But I didn't see where Jesus did anything wrong, and yet He suffered more than I ever would. The only answer that could explain my accident was that sometimes God just lets things happen—and I had to trust He would show me why in His own time.

The Lord doesn't delight when we suffer. "You are not a God Who is pleased with what is bad" (Psalm 5:4). Instead He sympathizes with us. "Because Jesus was tempted as we are and suffered as we do, He understands us and He is able to help us when we are tempted...[so] let us go [in prayer] with complete trust to the very place of God's loving-favor. We will receive His loving-kindness and have His loving-favor to help us whenever we need it" (Hebrews 2:18, 4:16).

Later, God did show me why my accident happened. But as I lay then in the hospital, I remembered many other times when the Lord used seeming tragedies to do a work in my life. When I was one year old, I had a disease that caused me to swell so large my parents had to cut my clothes off. Then I was sickly most of my childhood, until I got another disease that affected my muscles and made my body jerk around. I could be walking along or even just sitting in a chair, when I would fall down and not be able to get up again. But I was healed in such a way that I knew God was involved. After that I became a born-again Christian and promised to live for the Lord.

As the years passed, however, God became less important. I dropped out of school, got married and started a family. Though I felt God calling me to preach, I told Him I didn't have enough education. When the church asked me once to teach Sunday School, I made excuses until they got somebody else. The next day I couldn't shake the feeling that I had failed God. I was sitting on my front porch, thinking. Across the street some men were doing target practice in a neighbor's yard. Suddenly a stray bullet hit the edge of my eye and lodged in the tissue of my brain.

I was rushed to the University of North Carolina hospital, not far from where I lived among my Lumbee Indian people. Some of the best surgeons in the world worked on me. After careful examination, they decided it was too dangerous to remove the bullet. It is still there today, but gives me no pain and has done no damage. God helped me recover so completely that I later was cleared for service in the United States Army. This brush with death should have got me thinking, but I still resisted God's call to give my life to His service. Even when, several years later, my toddler son survived a serious accidental head injury, I kept on resisting the Lord. I should have known God meant business but, instead of coming closer to Him, I began to drift further away.

To make big money, I opened a beer joint and sold illegal whiskey. My wife and children begged me to come to church, but I wouldn't listen. Though I still drove the family to Sunday School, I made them come out right after class because I didn't want to hear about what the pastor was preaching. Then a year after my son's accident, he said something that finally got my attention. "Daddy, what do you want me to be when I become a man?" I paused a moment and answered, "Whatever you want to be, that's all right with me." Then he looked at me and said, "Dad, if you're going to sell beer and whiskey, then I want to sell beer and whiskey too. But if you were a preacher, then I would want to be a preacher."

Those words burnt me like fire! The very next Sunday morning I ran down the aisle of our church, got on my knees and prayed, "Lord, I'm ready now to surrender my life to You. Please take me back, and give me back your joy. Whatever you want me to do, Lord, I'm willing!" From that time, God began opening doors for me. He led me to become pastor of a small Indian church, and two years later I was ordained as a minister in my denomination.

Then came my car accident. I had been serving in my church for about six years and the Lord had given us a fruitful ministry. Why was He setting me aside now, at least for a time? What purpose did He wish to accomplish through this tragedy? After I was released from the hospital, I sat at home pondering that question for nearly four months. Day and night, I sat in a chair unable to go anywhere. Over the next two years I saw my doctor week after week. Then on one visit, though the waiting room was full, the doctor called me right in.

"Preacher," he said, "I want to tell you something." He had been on vacation. During his flight, the engine malfunctioned and forced the plane to make an emergency landing. "As we were coming down," he said, "all I could think of was that smile you always wear. After every operation I performed on you,

you would come out of the anesthesia smiling and praising the Lord that you were still alive. Well, Preacher, something happened to me on that plane. I accepted Christ and the Lord has saved me. I'm not the same man anymore."

That doctor was precious enough for Jesus to die for. So if He saw fit to use two years of my life in bringing that man to Christ, that was proof to me that God never makes mistakes. Today with the Lord's help, I am back to preaching full-time. Both my arms are now healed, though one is a bit disfigured and the other has a steel plate that pains me a little. A portion of my heart still does not function, but I feel fine and my lungs are 100 percent. All told, I really am blessed to be alive!

5. Surgery Reveals Surprise Answer to Prayer

Key Verse - 1 Corinthians 10:31

"So if you eat or drink or what ever you do, do everything to honor God."

This Chippewa woman heard the words a mother most fears, that her daughter might die. But she did not need psychologists. Instead she read a Bible verse and simply decided to do what it said. Whether or not her daughter was spared, the Word of God promised they could both triumph.

"I BELIEVE WE are dealing with cancer in the brain," the doctor told me in a kindly, quiet voice. "I recommend that your daughter have immediate surgery." I felt sick with weakness as strength drained from my body. I covered my face with trembling hands and wept. "What will I tell Esther? She's only eleven years old." The doctor offered to tell my daughter the news, but I shook my head. My emotional reserves were nearly spent, yet I felt Esther should hear the news from her mother. "I'll think about it and then tell her myself."

I went to the restroom to gather my strength and control my emotions. Then I walked into Esther's room. She was lying in a big white bed and her brown eyes watched me closely. How attuned children are to their parents' emotional signals! I could not hide my fears from her. I sat down next to Esther and she reached up to embrace me. For several minutes we sat holding each other. Then I told her the doctor's instruments had allowed him to see something growing in her head. "You will need an operation very soon," I told her.

Next I explained the things Esther needed to know about the surgery. Her head would be shaved. She would have things attached to her body that would help the doctor in his work. I talked to her about everything, but did not confess the possibility of cancer. The doctor was not certain, and I thought the word "cancer" might scare my daughter and shake her faith.

My sister meanwhile called our church friends and many people began praying for Esther. Then as I was packing our things for the hospital, I decided to call one of the elders in our church who had been a special friend to us. But as I got to the phone, it rang and our friend was on the line. He invited us to his home that night to read from the Bible and pray together.

He shared some Scriptures that were a great comfort to me in the ordeal that lay ahead. "Is anyone among you suffering? He should pray. Is anyone happy? He should sing songs of thanks to God. Is anyone among you sick? He should send for the church leaders and they should pray for him. They should pour oil on him in the name of the Lord. The prayer given in faith will heal the sick man, and the Lord will raise him up. If he has sinned, he will be forgiven. Tell your sins to each other. And pray for each other so you may be healed. The prayer from the heart of a man right with God has much power" (James 5:13-16).

Now, I do not believe pouring oil on someone's head will cure them. In Bible times, oil was used to soothe sick people and make them more comfortable. When we give comfort, then, the Word of God tells us to do so "in the name of the Lord." Also, I do not think these Scriptures say if we pray for the sick, then God must heal them. That is like saying we can command God to do what we tell Him. God has the authority to do as He wishes. But these verses are a great comfort in letting us know we CAN pray, and if we keep our eyes on the Lord then He will hear and answer. The answer may not always be what we want, but God loves us and His answers are always what is best.

At last it was time to leave our Chippewa reservation in northern Minnesota, and drive to the hospital in Fargo, North Dakota. The night before the surgery, Esther and I did as those Bible verses said. We had a private song service and prayer session in her room. Our voices blended in the darkening room as we sang words of praise to the Lord. They were only simple songs like "Our God Reigns," "Come Bless The Lord" and "Hosanna, Hosanna." But my daughter's childish voice sounded so sweet that I knew God was pleased.

Then Esther asked me to lay down with her while we prayed. I got in bed with her and laid my arm over her. We prayed for our friends and family, and for the hungry and oppressed. We thanked God for His faithfulness and for all those people who were praying for us. Then we prayed that God would give Esther a successful surgery and recovery. After she went to sleep, I made a bed in the recliner chair so I could be close to her. Then I myself began to pray, "Lord, I know something is wrong in Esther's head and she needs surgery. But when the doctors find the problem, I pray it turns out not to be cancer after all." In a few minutes, I went peacefully to sleep.

I was awakened early in the morning when a nurse came to record Esther's condition. Before my daughter was taken into surgery, she looked up at me and said, "Mom, I don't think this surgery is going to be such a big deal." That made me feel I was right not to tell Esther about the possibility of cancer. And as the orderlies rolled my daughter down the hall, a young nurse approached me and said softly, "We met in prayer for her this morning." Once more my spirit was lifted up and I thanked God for blessing us with so many caring friends.

After surgery, the doctor took me to the hospital chapel. In that quiet room, with the sunlight spilling on the carpet between us, he told me how the surgery had gone. "Everything looks good," he said. "We removed a large blood clot. There is no cancer." Later when I returned to Esther's room to see her, my heart was full of rejoicing. Little did I know that my daughter was going to teach me a lesson about real faith.

A short while after I entered, a young girl with kidney problems was brought to share Esther's room. We got to know this girl and, on the day of her surgery, Esther and I were very concerned for her. Then my daughter quietly confided to me her own morning prayers. "Mom, this girl is only nine years old and she's more scared than I am. So this morning I spent my time praying for her."

I had worried so much about my daughter's faith, whether it could withstand the thought of cancer. Now she had taught me a lesson. Esther had discovered that faith isn't just something you exercise to get things for yourself. She had complete faith God would not only take care of her, but He was big enough to take care of anyone and anything. I am still gleaning lessons from this experience. Life is full of trouble, yet God is faithful and does not allow us to suffer more than we can endure. (1 Corinthians 10:31). He loves us and is concerned about our needs, great and small.

6. Injured Woman Prays For Help

Key Verse - Matthew 21:22

"All things you ask for in prayer, you will receive if you have faith."

The telephone was dead. Her only neighbor was too far away to hear her cries for help. She lived on a dead-end road where nobody ever came. The pain of stumbling and cracking her ribs seemed more than this elderly Sioux woman could bear. There was nothing else to do but pray and leave the rest to God.

I DON'T KNOW which I felt first—the pain, the cold, or Rusty's tongue licking my face. I seemed to be drifting back into nothingness and fighting to stay awake, both at the same time. Then I remembered what had happened. I was moving my things from the tiny old house where I had been living, into a new trailer home. My arms were full of looms and beads, and I must have stumbled on one of the frozen ruts in the driveway. I must have fallen face down because the pain in my chest was really awful. Bones break easily when a person is past seventy and, like it or not, I must have cracked some ribs. My arm and hip both hurt too, though not as badly. It was only a few steps to the door of the trailer. If only I could get up and take them! But every movement drove new jabs of pain deep into my chest. So I looked around at the snowy hills. There were few neighbors and our road was a dead end. Only one house was in "yelling" distance, and it was getting dark.

How long had I been lying on the ground? An hour? Or more? The sinking sun did not tell me exactly. But it warned me that I could not stay outside much longer without freezing. Again I struggled to move. The rocky driveway dug into my bruises. What was I going to do now? I cried out to my neighbor on the slim chance she would hear me. But I couldn't keep it up long. Every breath seemed to stab me, and yelling out made it worse.

With a desperate effort I reached for Rusty's wagging tail. It seemed a little crude, but I needed help getting up, something to hang onto. At least I did not weigh much. My friends said I was hardly more than a toothpick, that I could hide in a mousehole. When I grabbed Rusty's tail, he did not yelp much. He seemed to know I needed help, and let me use his big back to brace myself. Slowly I got to my feet. But it wouldn't do to leave my looms and fresh beads on the ground. I stooped to pick them up, though it hurt terribly.

Then carefully and painfully, I edged toward the trailer. Shuffling and resting, shuffling and resting, I finally reached the steps. How would I ever get to the top? Slowly I hoisted myself up the first step. Then the second. Only two more to go! Then one. Now I had to find a way of opening the door. Shifting the looms and beads to my left hand, I reached for the latch and pulled.

Painfully I moved inside. But what would I do now? The trailer was new and had no telephone. I had no car, and did not know how to drive one anyway. What I needed was a doctor and something to kill the pain! My neighbor was not likely to visit on a cold night like this. She might not come tomorrow— or the next day. People did not think of me as a little old lady who needed help. I had always been independent and looked young for my age. Even now my dark black hair was only lightly threaded with gray.

I had noticed my neighbor's clothes still flapping on the line. Maybe she would take them inside before dark. Then she might be close enough to hear me call for help. Slowly I inched my way into a chair by the window facing my neighbor's house. The clock ticked on and on. Had my neighbor forgotten her clothes? No! At last her door was opening. With new hope I climbed to my feet and moved as quickly to the door as my pain allowed. Then I shouted with all my might. But the wind was in the wrong direction. Again and again I cried for help. My neighbor was enjoying the brisk air as she casually unsnapped her clothes from the line. Finished, she ambled back into the house and never heard me.

Now I was close to despair. If only I had some aspirin to help me through the long night! But that was back at my old house, and there was none in the trailer. Then I thought of something. A voice inside me was saying, "Pray and ask the Lord to send help." God was always ready to listen, even though I did not always pray as much as I should. Shifting my weight to one foot, and using the couch to steady myself, I knelt slowly and closed my eyes. I could have prayed without kneeling, of course, but somehow kneeling just seemed appropriate.

"Lord, I'm all alone and need help. Would You send me someone?" Then I glanced out the window, not knowing what to expect. Again and again I looked. When I had lost count, I glanced again and this time a car was coming. I could see the headlight beams in the distance. Not many cars came over our hill since the road was a dead end. There was not much to see. Just snow and hills and more snow and hills.

Then I thought, "The car will probably stop at the big house down the hill. The people there have a car." But, no, it was coming up our hill. It did not stop at my neighbor's house either. Would the car come up to the dead end and turn by my trailer? Yes, it would—and it did! The car stopped in front. The dome light came on as the driver opened the door, and the man looked like my pastor from the Sioux Indian church. It was him! Nobody else was so tall and thin.

Maybe he heard I was moving today. But whatever was the reason he came, I knew my pastor believed in prayer. Whether he knew it or not, he had been brought here by the Lord. Our pastor often told us a verse from the Bible, "All things you ask for in prayer, you will receive [an answer] if you have faith" (Matthew 21:22). Well, my answer to prayer was knocking on my door that very moment!

7. The Fear That Haunted My Life

Key Verse - Revelation 20:15

"If anyone's name was not written in the book of life, he was thrown into the lake of fire."

An accident left her with a fear of death. Then the priest at the village church said the world was coming to an end. Her fear became even greater and for years she had terrible nightmares. But a voice on the radio explained how death and the world's end need not be feared.

IT WAS THE FIRST time I had ever called out to God. My life was in danger and there was no one else to hear me. I was four years old, almost five, and my parents had taken me to the trapline in northern Quebec. We were camped at the mouth of a river leading into a lake. It was winter with lots of snow. Two older children and I decided to go set some rabbit snares. We started into the woods, but the bush was so thick I could not keep up. They sent me home and I turned to go along the river bank. It was covered with snow and very smooth and steep. About fifty feet below me was the water. Suddenly I slipped and began sliding down the bank on my tummy.

My snowshoes were still on so I tried to stop myself, but the bank was too steep. Then I managed to grab a willow sticking out of the snow and held on for my life. I looked at the black water below. If I fell then I would drown, because I could not swim. I knew the little willow would not hold me forever. And that's when I first called on God. Then slowly, I kept reaching for more willow branches until at last I was at the top of the bank. But though God helped me that day, I did not really know Him. Nobody had ever told me that He loved me.

After that incident, I became afraid of dying. The next year it got worse when I heard my mother and aunt talking. The priest had told them the world was going to end. I could not stop wondering about this. It really frightened me because we would die if that happened. When I asked my mother about it, she did not know any more than I did. My parents belonged to the priest's church and went there every Sunday if we were in the village. But there was never any Bible teaching in our home.

Then I started having bad dreams about the end of the world. It would get all dark and I would think, "The end has come!" A man in a white robe said I could not go with him, and showed me a dark black hole where I would have to stay forever. I was very frightened and kept wondering about these dreams. They haunted me for years, even as I grew older and went to school in the city. I was there four years, and then spent two years in the hospital. A nurse used to have Sunday School for us, but I could not understand how the Bible stories could fit into my life. God was only needed for real trouble.

Yet I knew something was missing in my life. At nineteen I got married, but still I searched for something more that would bring me happiness—and release me from my fear of death. One day I was lying down on my bed, reading my Bible, when I came to the last part of the Book of Revelation. Awful things would happen at the end of the world, and these things were for me! I was crying when I read, "If anyone's name was not written in [Jesus'] book of life, he was thrown into the lake of fire" (Revelation 20:15). I knew in my heart that I would be one of those, if I did not find help. I was crying so hard I had to leave the house before my mother saw me.

For the next four years I kept worrying. Then one autumn I went out to the trapline, only three weeks after my fifth baby was born. One Sunday I was alone in the tent, listening to the radio, when a preacher started talking about the end of the world. "For the Lord [Jesus] Himself will come down from heaven with a loud call," he said, reading from the Bible, "and the head angel will speak with a loud voice. God's horn will give its sounds. First, those who belong to Christ will come out of their graves to meet the Lord. Then, those of us [believers] who are still living on earth will be gathered together with them in the clouds. We will meet the Lord in the sky and be with Him forever" (1 Thessalonians 4:16-17).

Then the preacher explained how, when Jesus returns, He will leave behind those who do not belong to Him. He also said that mothers will be holding little babies in their arms, and the babies will be taken and the mothers—those who had not believed in Christ—left behind. At that time I was holding my baby in my arms, so the words of the preacher really spoke to me. As he talked, I heard for the first time that I had to be sorry for my sins and turn away from them. He also said I needed to ask Jesus to be my Savior. Then I would belong to His family.

I wondered about this all day. It would not leave my mind, this true message of salvation. Would this be the "something missing" in my life? Would this release me from the fears of death that had always haunted me? It was the first time I understood that Jesus died for me on the cross. I found it so wonderful that He loved me that much. I could not sleep after I went to bed, for I had a heavy burden on my heart. I had to ask Jesus to be my Savior! So I got up in the dark and knelt down beside my bed. I asked the Lord to forgive me, a sinner, and to save me from my sin. And I asked Jesus to take control of my life and be part of me. After I prayed, my great burden of sin and fear was taken off me and forever gone!

The Bible says, "Have loving-kindness for those who doubt. Save some by pulling them out of the fire" (Jude 22-23). I was saved not only by seeing the love of God, but also by seeing the everlasting fire that awaits those who reject His Son. Now, no matter what happens, I am no longer afraid. I have peace in my heart, even when I go through the trials of life. Many years ago I lost a baby. Yet I am happy to know I will see that baby again some day in heaven. And it may be soon because the Bible says nobody knows the hour when Jesus will appear. Once I dreaded that day, but now I look forward to it. For I belong to Jesus, and at last I will see Him face to face!

THINGS TO THINK ABOUT

1. I Was Blind But Now I Can See

Not until tragedy or danger strikes do people call upon God. And when the trouble is passed, then they forget about God again. Read Acts 4:5-12. Why is God the only One Who can bring real help? Why do you think the people in this Bible passage wanted to deny Jesus?

2. I Forsook the Traditions of My Forefathers

As a Christian, you are in a spiritual war with Satan and sometimes casualties do occur. But though Satan may bring tragedy or danger to defeat you, the Bible promises you will have the victory by resisting him. Read Ephesians 6:10-13, James 4:7, 1 Peter 5:8-11. Where does your real danger come from? How can you resist? What will result if you do? How can you overcome fear?

3. Praise God For My Paralysis

When tragedies happen, you may ask, "Why me, God?" You may blame Him. Probably you are afraid of losing something you want and think that's unfair. Read James 1:13-17 and Matthew 18:8. Does God deliberately cause hurt? What things do come from God? If a tragedy occurs, what is more important to gain than anything you have lost?

4. My Accident Was No Accident

Perhaps you have an idea that God enjoys watching you squirm. That if you step over the line, nothing will please Him more than to "zap" you. Read Hebrews 2:18 and 4:15-16. Why does the Lord understand your suffering and trials? Because of His sympathy, how will He respond if you come to Him?

5. Surgery Reveals Surprise Answer to Prayer

Perhaps you think a tragedy or danger is more than you can bear. Your faith in God does not seem enough, and you want to give up in defeat. Read 1 Corinthians 10:13 and James 5:13-16. What promise does God make about troubles in 1 Corinthians? What helps does God describe in James for dealing with troubles?

6. Injured Woman Prays for Help

The woman in this story was in trouble. She did not have a neighbor to help, nor did she have a telephone or even any medicine. But she did have prayer. Read Matthew 21:21-22. Does Jesus really mean you can move a mountain? Will He give you "all" things? If you live in Christian faith, for what kinds of things will you ask and pray?

7. The Fear That Haunted My Life

Danger and tragedy make you pause and think about death and what comes afterward. Perhaps that is why He sometimes allows these events to occur. Read Revelation 20:15 and 1 Thessalonians 4:16-18. Is hell a real place? What hope do you have beyond the grave? Do you know where you personally will go after death?

CHAPTER NINE

Conquering Pride and Self

1. Grand Chief Brings Ego to Altar

Key Verse - Mark 8:36

"For what does a man have if he gets all the world and loses his own soul?"

He was Grand Chief of the Cree Nation, the top native representative to the federal government, a man whose every word and deed made headlines. But he pursued power for a selfish reason, to escape his humble village and family. With enough power he could live as he pleased and nobody else could stop him.

I WAS BIG NEWS. Wherever I went, television crews followed me. Reporters were constantly shoving microphones in my face. All the talk shows wanted me. I was traveling across Canada, giving speeches in as many as three cities a day, pressing and pushing for native rights. As Grand Chief for one of the largest tribes, I was made the top negotiator for all First Nations in seeking constitutional reforms from the federal government. Yet what I enjoyed most was the fame and fortune that came with my power.

Not bad for someone who came from a Cree village in Quebec with 100 percent alcoholism, 100 percent unemployment and 100 percent welfare. My people lived in tarpaper shacks with plywood siding, and five-gallon drums for heat. Eight or ten people often lived all year in spaces of 14 by 16 feet. We drank from Wednesday night to Friday morning, then bought raisins and sugar from the trading post to make home brew for the following week. We had nothing but tea and bannock for breakfast, lunch and supper. Shamanism ruled the village and filled us with fear and superstition.

But I made it to the university, then came back and was elected band chief at 21 years of age. I had big plans to show what I could do, and use my office as a stepping stone to bigger and better things. Though I was elected to serve my people, my real goal was to get out of that village and seek my fortune elsewhere. That's why I was pretty upset when an Indian preacher came to our village and began intruding on all my big plans. He wanted to use the bingo and dance hall for church services and asked me for permission. Though I had no reason to refuse, I thought he was crazy. Besides, I was going to take my people in a different direction that had nothing to do with "white" religion.

The preacher began to minister, and one by one the people went to the services. The first person who became a Christian at those meetings was a great uncle of mine who was considered a very powerful shaman. Word spread like wildfire and more people began going to the church. The band council and I made plans to run the preacher out of town. But the more persecution the church had, the more meetings they had. The more welfare we took away from the Christians, the happier they seemed to get. As a young chief, this preacher really bothered my ego!

Later, a big hydroelectric project was being built on the James Bay near our village. I was trying to unite our people behind my leadership, as I negotiated with the government over terms and conditions respecting our land. So I announced a meeting of every adult in the village, more than 600 people. But when I called the meeting to order, the preacher stood up and said, "Before we do anything, we should put this matter to God in prayer." Silence fell over the hall. I conferred with the council to see if the preacher was a registered band member and had the right to speak. When I found he was not on the list, I turned to the councillor who represented the area where the preacher lived. "Tell him to sit down," I said. But the councillor replied, "Last night I gave my heart to the Lord, and I'm not telling him to sit down."

By then I realized most of the band council had become Christians. I had to be a smart politician if I wanted to stay in office. So I called the meeting back to order and told the preacher, "Why that's a great idea. Why don't you go ahead and pray!" From then on, God was mentioned in prayer at all our council meetings. One by one, all the other councillors became Christians. "But I want fame and fortune," I told myself. "I'm not interested in their religion. Why should I take the white man's God? If I throw away my Indian heritage, my political career will be over." I continued on with my life, working on land claims, making agreements and establishing a business.

Pretty soon alcohol, tobacco and pills had control of my body. My marriage fell apart and my children became distant. By now I was Grand Chief of all the Cree. When I was called to the constitutional negotiations, I was glad to leave my village behind for the world of national politics and power. Yet God was at work in my village, where my wife became a Christian. And He was at work in my life, though I did not know it then. All I could think about was politics, and how a successful negotiation would be my stepping stone to more fame and fortune. Then I could cut off my ties to the village for good, including all the relationships I had there.

While I traveled across the country trying to help all native people, I had no such thoughts for my own people. "God can have the village for all I care, if that's the way they want it! If they want to throw away their culture, let them go ahead and do it!" While I was seeking fame and fortune, I found nothing but bitterness and loneliness. Tremendous hatred swelled up in my heart. Alcohol was in control of my life. Finally, when the constitutional negotiations were over, I went home figuring this was the end. I'd go home and make a clean break, cutting the ties.

When I walked into my house, my wife took my hand. She said, "I know you've come to say good-bye and that our family life is over. Before you do that, just sit with me for a minute on the couch." She said a short prayer, then continued speaking. "I love you very much. But there is Someone who has a greater love for you than I have. His name is Jesus Christ, and I know He is dealing with you right now." I sat there trembling and my wife prayed again, this time asking the Lord to send someone who would talk to me.

Five minutes later a Christian man, who sometimes went hunting and fishing with me, walked into the house. Right away he sensed why I had come home, perhaps because the village church was praying for me. "You're not running away from your family," he said, "but away from God. It's time to make a decision, heaven or hell. Are you going to serve the devil or the Lord?" I was still trembling, but with anger as I thought, "How dare he come into my home? How dare all the preachers and evangelists come into my village and take over my people? We were doing okay before without them."

Yet, were we doing okay? I remembered the 100 percent alcoholism, unemployment and welfare—and how that began to change when the Gospel came to our village. Yes, we were poor, but we had also tied chains upon ourselves. I had always vowed to never been seen in church, yet now I was curious. So after lunch the following day I told my wife, "I think I'll go to church with you." At the next meeting I took a seat near the back, just in case things got too hot. As soon as I sat down, I began to get the shakes. Throughout the service (and today I can't even remember what the preacher talked about) I couldn't shake the feeling that Someone was speaking to my heart. I had a clear impression that God was choosing me, that today was my day, and now the decision was up to me.

Native people are proud, and I thought crying was for weaklings and wimps. Chiefs like me just didn't do that. But I was wrong. Chiefs need to get right with God just like everyone else. To people who seek fame and power, the Bible says, "What does a man have if he gets all the world but loses his own soul?" (Mark 8:36). With tears flowing down my cheeks, I made my way to the altar. There I met Jesus Christ and surrendered my life to Him. I needed forgiveness for all my sins against God, and the way I persecuted His people, and He gave it to me. I was washed clean by the blood of Jesus Christ. And though I went into that church a drunk, I came out sober.

When a Grand Chief gets saved, people notice! A mighty revival broke out in our village, and today 75 percent of the people are born-again Christians. The 100 percent alcoholism, unemployment and welfare has been cleaned up. For myself, I am no longer driven by a lust for fame and power. Instead I am using my skills in a business venture owned by the Quebec Cree that is truly helping our people. If God can turn around a defeated village like ours, and redeem a wicked man like me, than He can do it for every native person and community anywhere.

2. A Rodeo Cowboy's Greatest Thrill
Key Verse - Psalm 1:1,2

"Happy is the man who does not walk in the way sinful men tell him to, or stand in the path of sinners, or sit with those who laugh at the truth. But he finds joy in the law of the Lord and thinks about His law day and night..."

Everything came so easy, the awards and the acclaim of rodeo fans across North America. First he wanted to join the "cool" crowd, but that was empty and he came to Christ. Then in the excitement of winning, this Blackfoot-Cherokee man got caught up in acting like a celebrity and not like Jesus.

WHEN SOMEBODY RIDES a bull, he's got to be half crazy. Riding a horse or roping a steer seems natural, but climbing on the back of a powerful 2,000-pound bull isn't something normal people do. Yet there is nothing that compares with the thrill! That's why rodeo fans love to watch, and why the guys who ride are so admired. With success comes fame and money. When I started bull riding as a professional, it all came so easy—rookie of the year, four national finals, then world champion. I was having the time of my life. Sometimes I'd hop on a plane, or drive eight hours in a car, and ride two rodeos in a day. Competition was the love of my life and what I lived for.

As a Blackfoot-Cherokee growing up in California,

rodeo had always been my dream. My parents encouraged me from the beginning, and even bought me a horse for my fifth birthday. They took me to riding events and rodeos all the time I was growing up, and played a major part in my eventual success. Mom and dad were both spectacular, and provided all the love any child could hope for. But when I grew up and had a life of my own, something was missing that my rodeo fame and money did not satisfy.

After rodeo competitions I would go out partying with my friends and fellow cowboys. It's not that I enjoyed it so much, but it seemed like the thing to do. Besides, life on the road was lonely and empty, and I was searching for fulfillment. Sometimes I would remember an old friend I had growing up, who was like a mentor to me. We used to sit around and talk. He knew a lot about the Bible and told me a lot about God. Though I never went to church, somehow I never doubted that God existed. I just wasn't aware, or didn't care, that I could know Him in a personal way.

The year I turned professional, at first it seemed my dreams had come true. I was named rookie of the year and a great career was ahead of me. But something was still missing. The Lord stepped in, however, and shortly after I won the rookie award I got to know some Christian rodeo cowboys. They belonged to a Christian athletes' group that ministered to sports people who lived on the road and had no church of their own. I began attending the chapel services they held at rodeos and soon met a missionary who acted as their pastor. He told me it wasn't enough to believe in my head that there is a God. In my heart I needed to know Him personally.

Late one night, after a rodeo performance, the missionary invited me to his trailer. We talked together about my search for real fulfillment, and at last I made a decision that changed my life. I admitted to Jesus that I was a sinner, that I had pursued money and fame rather than Him. Then I asked Christ to be my personal Savior and come take charge of my life. The thrill of becoming a new man in Christ was more than I'd ever gotten from riding a bull!

After my rookie season I kept working hard. Bull riding requires mental toughness, because of what you put your body through. You must block out the rest of the world every time you get on a bull. And if you're ever injured, which happens at some time to most professionals, it becomes even harder to concentrate. Over the next four years I continued to have success, made the national finals, and at last won the world bull riding championship. For that I was given the gold championship belt buckle that's the goal of every rodeo cowboy. But in all the tough training and the excitement of winning, I started to drift away from my commitment to living for Jesus.

Only a year after being the best, I hit bottom and experienced the worst. That season I was stomped on by a bull, breaking two ribs and puncturing one of my lungs. Today I'm glad God used that injury to get my attention, because Satan had been using my previous success to deceive me. I got caught up in acting the part rodeo fans expected, rather than being like Jesus. In that way, Satan made me an ineffective Christian. However, God stepped in again by bringing another special believer into my life. This time it was a girl I had known most of my life, yet now we saw that God was putting us together so we might serve Him with all our hearts. As that desire grew within me, I turned my life back to the Lord for good.

After my injuries healed, I faced the challenge of getting back on a bull. When you've been hurt, it's hard to have that same fearlessness you had before. In bull riding even a momentary hesitation can be the difference between winning and losing, or between living and dying. Having surrendered my life to Jesus, I decided to keep my mind on positive things like Bible verses I had memorized. One of my favorite verses is, "I can do all things because Christ gives me the strength" (Philippians 4:13).

By reading and studying the Word of God, He has given me peace and shown me how to be one cowboy who lives for Him. A man who trusts in God "is like a tree planted by rivers of water, which gives its fruit at the right time and its leaf never dries up. Whatever he does will work out for him" (Psalm 1:3). Yes, I still love the competition and enjoy being in front of the fans. But when they ask me what it takes to become a world champion, I tell them my life was a loser until Jesus gave me the "inside" edge—and He can do the same for anyone who trusts Him.

3. College Eroded My Faith

Key Verse - Colossians 2:8

"Be careful that no one changes your mind and faith by much learning and big sounding ideas."

As a scholarship athlete, his education and status as a college star was assured. He was so proud that, despite what his mother taught him, this Seminole man would rather listen to the big professors who said Jesus was a myth. So he rejected discipline and authority, and as a result lost everything.

DURING MY HIGH SCHOOL years I made decent grades and was active in all sports. Soon I had offers of scholarships to play baseball and football at many colleges and universities. That meant they would pay for my whole education! I chose to play baseball at the state university near my Seminole reservation in Florida, and became a regular player my very first year. Any Indian would be glad for the things I had—a baseball scholarship and a university education all paid for.

But off the baseball field, the university was not always such a good place for me. Most of my professors hated God, and ridiculed what my mother had taught me as a child about Jesus. They made us students read books that said Jesus did not die and rise again. Some of the material they gave us made fun of Gospel preachers and evangelists. One professor told me there was no such things as God. All this was during a troubled time in the United States, when drugs were everywhere and young people were rebelling against society.

The Bible warns, "Be careful that no one changes your mind and faith by much learning and big-sounding ideas. Those things are what men dream up. They are always trying to make new religions [that]... leave out Christ" (Colossians 2:8). That is the trap I fell into at school. The professors began to change my way of thinking. But during my first year at the university, I kept one good habit I learned from my mother. I went to church every Sunday.

I spent most of my childhood on the Seminole reservation, living in low-rent houses with a lot of dogs and cats and chickens. My mother was a Christian who loved the Lord. Although my father was an alcoholic, she tried to bring me up as a Christian. Because of her I made a profession of faith at an early age. However, I did not really understand what I was saying. It was something my mother said I should do, and all my friends in church were doing it. I was afraid of death, so I just went along hoping God would be pleased. But none of this really changed my heart.

After one year at the university, I changed to another school where I could play more sports. That's all I cared about, just making it big and having a good time. The new school brought more new ideas, and I felt that I no longer needed to attend church on Sunday. I only went when I felt like getting up. Like the other students, I began to search for what I thought would be the truth. And as I tried different schools and the sports they offered, I found that I was always looking for something more.

Two years and three schools later, I ended up at an Indian college. Here I saw the terrible problems of native peoples. By the time I graduated with a degree, a year and a half later, I was convinced that Christianity was a white man's religion. To my way of thinking, Indian Christians were people who sold out, and the church was for old folks and sissies. I disliked the whites and their society. Yet the answer to my own search still escaped me. Not knowing what else to do, I soon was in school again playing football and baseball while I worked on another college degree.

My search eventually brought drugs and alcohol into my life. I began to hate anything to do with discipline and authority. Before long I quit school and wandered around the midwestern states, working when I could. Many times during these years, as I got into dangerous situations, God laid His hand upon me and spared me from hell. But the real test was yet to come. After quitting school I got married. Soon a child was born and my life became more complicated. I resented all the responsibility and my morals began to hit bottom. As a husband I was a flop, and as a father I showed no respect. I began to take trips out of state, just to have a reason to escape my family.

On one of these trips, God started to speak to my heart and convict me of my wrongs. The "new" ideas and habits I had picked up as a college sports star had only torn my life apart. Despite my success as an athlete and my college degree, I knew that I was a sinner. All my search for "truth" could not deny that fact. I began to realize there was only one thing left to do. I had to get right with God. I didn't want to do it, but my soul was wrestling with the Lord and He won.

I came home to Florida and met a missionary who lived on our reservation. We read the Bible together, and I found his own struggles had been much like mine. At last I told God that I could not take it anymore and that I could not make it without Him. I knew that I was a sinner in need of repentance, and asked Jesus Christ to be my Savior and come into my life that very night. And praise God, He did! Today I love my wife and sons, and I am thankful for my home. But even more, I am thankful God took away my confusion, forgave my sins and removed my guilt. And He has promised me a place in heaven. What more could any person want?

4. Former Chef Now Feeds Souls

Key Verse - Luke 5:11

"When they came to land with their boats, they left everything and followed Jesus."

After years of training and sacrifice, he reached the top of his profession. But despite success, the problems in his life and marriage continued. Trusting Christ made him a new man, but also brought another problem. God was calling him, and that meant giving up the job he had worked so hard to gain.

THE HALLWAY AT Ottawa's Chateau Laurier Hotel seemed long, and I had an uneasy feeling in the pit of my stomach. I tried to think of something I had done wrong, but nothing came to mind. Still I knew there must be some reason why an apprentice cook was being called to the head chef's office. He did not let me wonder long.

"You've got a great future in the food business," he said. "How would you like to take your training in France? You'll have a chance to study under some of the world's greatest chefs." He did not have to ask twice! It was a great honor and I accepted at once—little knowing that I would soon see things much differently.

When I was very young, I began drinking and smoking. I was never an alcoholic, but I was headed in that direction. To me, weekends at my home in northern Ontario were made for drinking. I especially liked Christmas and New Year because everybody was in the mood for parties and opened their homes to give you a drink. Then I met the woman who is now my wife. That was the greatest thing that could have happened to me. She did not want to date me if I was drinking, so I quit when I was seeing her. My friends kidded me a lot, but I figured she was better than a drink any day. To this day I am amazed how I quit, and the only thing I can say is that love is very strong.

A year after we were married, we decided to go to Ottawa where I could upgrade my education and learn a trade. Ottawa is a good city and we enjoyed being there. By studying hard I managed to do well in school. Then came time to choose a trade and I decided to be a chef. After six months of classes I was hired at the Chateau Laurier Hotel, the most famous hotel in Canada's capital city where many visiting dignitaries stay. There I began two-and-a-half years of on-the-job training. I worked hard and won the approval of my supervisors, which led to my chance to take advanced training in Europe.

But as the months went by, the pressures of training and shift work began to build up. As a cook, I had to prepare food when people wanted to eat. And in Ottawa, like in most big cities, a lot of people want to eat at night. I was assigned to the night shift. For days on end I had to work from three until midnight. And the longer I worked, the more depressed I became. It seemed life was passing me by while I was sweating it out in the kitchen.

One day, with only six months of training left, things finally reached the breaking point. After working my courage up with a few drinks, I walked into the head chef's office and declared, "I've had it with nights. I'm quitting." He looked at me for a moment, then let me have it. I could tell he was very angry. "You quit now," he said, "and you can forget about Europe! And I'll see to it you never get your chef's papers!" I knew he could do it, because at the time he was president of the chef's union for all of Canada. But I didn't care. I just turned and walked out.

As I was leaving his office, one of my fellow workers told me the National Arts Centre was looking for a cook. It was just across the street, so I walked over and applied. They hired me, which made me feel better about going home to tell my wife the news. Even though some pressure was applied by my old boss to make me lose my job, my new boss told me not to worry. A year later I finished my apprenticeship, wrote my exam and got my chef's papers.

While I was working at the National Arts Centre, the Lord began to draw me to Himself. First, my whole family became Christians. Then my older brother and his wife came to visit us. They wanted to go to church, so we found a good Gospel-preaching place and went along with them. I found that I enjoyed the service very much and could not forget it. That fall, when my two younger brothers came to live with us for a while, I discovered they had become Christians over the summer. Somehow I knew Christians should go to church. And even though they did not ask us to, we took them each Sunday to the same church we visited with my older brother.

Over the years of our marriage, drinking had gradually worked its way back into my life. One evening at church I was nursing such a bad hangover, I felt that I was going to die. As I sat in the pew, I began wondering where I would go if I did. About that time the pastor invited anyone, who wanted to accept Jesus Christ as his Savior, to come to the front of the church. I leaned over to my wife and said, "Let's go." She told me later she was ready to go without me, but God allowed us to give our lives to Him together.

After receiving my chef's papers, I cooked at a hospital in Quebec for a few months. While there, I had the feeling God was calling me to preach and sent an application to a well-known Bible Institute in Saskatchewan. Weeks went by without hearing anything, so we made other plans. Returning to Ottawa, I got a job as cook in the Royal Parliamentary Restaurant in the House of Commons. It was an ideal position with lots of security and the thrill of cooking for all the members of Parliament. But God had other plans. A week after being made a permanent employee, I received a call from the Bible school telling me I was accepted as a student. While they waited on the phone, I had to decide. Would I quit my wonderful job, travel far from anywhere I had ever been, and go to Bible school that fall? Then I remembered the story of Peter and how Jesus called him to be His disciple (Luke 5:1-11). Peter was doing honest work and busy with his trade, like I was. But he had heard Jesus teach, had seen how Jesus worked in his life. So when the Savior called, he "left everything and followed Jesus." I could do no less!

Four years later my wife and I both graduated and began our ministry of sharing the Gospel with native peoples. Though God enabled me to train both as a chef and as a pastor, He has chosen to use me in feeding the spiritual needs of my people rather than their physical hungers. To me, both jobs are worthwhile. But the one I have now is the most satisfying, because it is the job God has chosen for me.

5. Rock Star Disillusioned with Lifestyle

Key Verse - 1 Corinthians 10:4

"They all drank the same holy drink. They drank from a holy Rock that went along with them. That holy Rock was Christ."

Finally the gigs started coming. His rock group was a success, and he was making good money and playing in the best clubs. The beat, the applause and the fans all made him feel great! Then the fights began—about money, about who in the band should be in control, and who should be the biggest star.

ROCK MUSIC WAS in my blood. I loved the heavy beat, the wild emotion-filled vocals, the turned-up amplifiers. And the attention of the crowd, that was great too. But as much as anything, I liked the money I was making. I figured if I had a lot of money, I would be happy. But soon I found that the more our rock group made, the more problems we had with each other. Still searching, I tried other things but none gave me the peace of mind I wanted.

Things had not always been like this. As a child on my small home reservation in northern Manitoba, my dad tried to start me off right. He always took time to read the Bible to us kids in the morning, and at night as we went to bed. He taught me how to live a right life. But as I got older, I began to lose interest in what I was taught. My own ideas seemed better. I could hardly wait until I was old enough to run my life the way I pleased. As this desire grew, I soon found rebellion and hatred building up inside me. I started to hang around with other boys and stay out late looking for trouble. To make myself part of the gang, I began smoking, drinking, stealing and sniffing gasoline and glue.

Then it was time for high school. It brought a real change to my life. Because high school was not offered on our reservation, I had to leave home. This was a new experience. I had never been away from my parents before and I wasn't used to white people. Although I had a lot of friends, I felt pretty lonely at times. For the first year or so I did okay, but in the third year my grades went way down. Finally I decided to quit.

After I dropped out of school, I joined a rock group. We played in bars and in the surrounding areas. For the first time I was making money and things were looking up. But I soon found that along with the money came problems. When we were a struggling band trying to make it, all of us were united and working together. Now with success, we were arguing most of the time as each group member wanted to "do his own thing" musically. Yet in spite of the problems, we stayed together five or six years before breaking up.

The year before our rock group ended, I got married. I figured that as a married man, things would be better. Nobody would be telling me what to do. But a year later I was still searching for peace and happiness. As the days went by, our marriage kept getting worse. We tried moving to southern Manitoba for a year. While there, my wife and I took a life-skills course with a psychologist, but it did not help. Life kept getting more miserable, so bad that my wife at times would threaten to leave. Yet even this did not bother me. Money and applause had proved empty, and marriage did not make me a happy person. What was the use? So I just stopped caring and stopped loving.

Then one weekend an old friend came by to visit. I knew him well because we used to hang around a lot together. To me he was just a drunk and a thief. But as I watched him, I could tell he was changed. He had a peaceful look on his face. Later he told us what happened, and in so doing he shared the story of Jesus who took our punishment that we might have eternal life. "For God so loved the world that He gave His only Son. Whoever puts his trust in God's Son will not be lost, but will have life that lasts forever" (John 3:16).

My friend explained how each person needs to admit he is a sinner, then ask Jesus Christ to forgive him, save him and change his life. I thought about what he said, knowing someday I would have to face God. It was a struggle, but at last I did what my friend suggested and gave my heart to Jesus. In that moment I found all the joy and peace I had been looking for but could never find.

Jesus brought unity to my marriage, and now my wife and I love and understand each other. It gives me great joy when we hold hands together and pray. Over the years I have learned God works from the inside out. Once I allowed Him to take care of my inner spiritual needs, my other problems began to take of themselves. Today, instead of singing songs I don't understand, I am singing for Jesus Christ and His glory. I have found that Jesus the Holy Rock (1 Corinthians 10:4) offers things that all the rock music and money and applause in the world cannot give.

6. Businessman Forms Partnership With Christ

Key Verse - Proverbs 23:4-5

"Do not work hard to be rich. Stop trying to get things for yourself. When you set your eyes upon it, it is gone. For sure, riches make themselves wings like an eagle that flies toward the heavens."

When he left his Cree village for a successful career, he also left God behind. He had it made and didn't need religion. And since he was in control, drinking was no problem either! This native man at last learned the truth, but had to lose his position and career before the lesson hit home.

TO LOOK AT ME, anybody would think I had it made. Three years with the Hudson's Bay Company in Manitoba, and manager of my hometown store by the age of 22. Then an accounting certificate, and six years in Ontario as assistant district accountant in the Department of Lands and Forests. At last I came back home to Manitoba for a high accounting position in the provincial government. But on the inside my life was crumbling and my career was soon to follow.

When I was nineteen, I made my first trip to the

city. To get my job with the Hudson's Bay Company, I had to leave my small Ojibway village in northern Manitoba and travel three hundred miles to Winnipeg for an interview. Once the airplane landed, I saw a car for the first time. The ride into town was frightening, because all the cars on the highway seemed to be coming at us. Yet I was glad for the opportunity to improve my life. Back home there were no roads and all travel was by foot or dogsled. We had no running water and had to fetch what we needed from the lake. For heat we had to cut wood from the bush all around us.

Things got even harder when I was six. That year my father died, leaving mother to take care of us three children. She used a net to catch fish every day, and sometimes managed to get vegetables and make bannock bread. We never went hungry, but now I realize how hard it was for mother to raise us alone for six years until she remarried. Even then life was not easy. My mother and stepfather lost three children to tuberculosis, and I myself spent 18 months in the hospital with the disease. So my job with the Hudson's Bay Company was a ticket to a better life. They placed me in my home area and eventually I became manager of my hometown store.

About that time I became interested in accounting and bookkeeping. I quit my job and moved to Winnipeg to attend accounting school. Accounting was enjoyable for me. It meant order and there was a science to it, a sense of perfection. When an accounting solution worked, I knew that I had done the right thing and the problem was solved. Yet my new life in the city was not so tidy. The city was a strange setting to me and I could not seem to fit in anywhere. The only place I was comfortable was in the bars, where I could feel equal with the people sitting there. Before long I had a serious drinking problem.

In my desire to begin a new life, I also left my religion back at home. As a child I had a deep respect for God. But I was also very afraid of Him and glad to leave God behind when I left home. As the years went by, it seemed I had made a good choice to go my own way. I kept advancing in my profession, got married, started a family, had a nice home. My drinking was nothing to worry about, because I had everything under control.

But finally the inevitable happened. I became living proof of the warning, "Do not work hard [wear yourself out] to be rich. Stop trying to get things for yourself. For sure, riches make themselves wings like an eagle that flies toward the heavens" (Proverbs 23:4-5). At last, alcohol took away my big government job. Eventually my drinking was so bad that I could not work at all and had to go on welfare. Later, even the welfare office would not give me money, but only grocery vouchers that could not be spent on alcohol.

When that happened, I finally came to my senses. I put myself in a drying-out center, then started going to Alcoholics Anonymous. In time I went back to work, stayed sober and started a new native business of my own. Yet even though I stopped drinking, my basic problem—wanting to go my own way without God—was not solved. I knew that I was not living the kind of life I should.

Then my wife became a Christian. Whatever I did, she prayed for me and remained peaceful. That's the kind of peace I wanted! I would drop her off at church and then drive around town. But that burned up a lot of gas, so I started to sit and wait in the church parking lot. Before long I got curious and would sneak inside and listen from the back. As I listened to the messages, I learned that I could have a personal relationship with Jesus Christ. This is what I was looking for! I had always wondered why, if I had stopped my drinking, that I still had problems. Now I knew the answer—I didn't have Christ.

I went to the pastor and told him I wanted to become a Christian and give up my business. That way I could start all over. But the pastor said, "The Lord set you up in a business for a reason. Now you need to find out what He wants. But you can't do that until you accept Jesus as your Savior. First you've got to do business with Him." That night in the quiet of my basement, I turned everything over to God—and when I make a commitment, it's all or nothing! Though it's taken me time to grow up as a Christian, I decided that I better not wait until I was perfect to serve Him. The very next day I told someone else about Jesus, and since then my business has given me many chances to share my faith with native people all over Canada.

Today I know my life must first show I serve God and have trust in the Lord Jesus Christ. Business, married life, church and my relationships with other people all stem from that. "A godly life gives us much when we are happy for what we have. We came into this world with nothing, we will take nothing with us. If we have food and clothing, let us be happy" (1 Timothy 6:6-8). Once I was committed only to what I could gain for myself, and ended up losing everything I had worked for. Then by faith I committed my life to Jesus. Since I made that decision, there is no way I would ever go back to my old life. When I made up my mind it was all or nothing, and that's the way it's going to stay!

7. Hockey and Rodeo Were Empty Gods
Key Verse - Luke 15:11-32

"...Father I have sinned against heaven and against you. I am not good enough to be called your son. But may I be as one of the workmen you pay to work...But the father said...let us eat and be glad. For my son was dead and now he is alive again. He was lost and now he is found."

This native man lost a career in hockey and nearly lost another in rodeo. And it all happened for the same reason. For a while his victories came first and celebrations after. But then the lifestyle became more important and sports was only an excuse to live it up.

IN ELEVEN YEARS, I made the Indian National Rodeo Finals five times. It's not easy to do, and making it that many times is an honor. What strikes me most is the difference between my first appearance and the last. Both times I competed in the calf roping event. But the last time I went, my two daughters and my son came with me. The girls were in the barrel racing event, and my son competed in team roping. It was a great time together, and as a family we all praised God for blessing us so wonderfully.

However, my first rodeo final eleven years earlier was very different. It was exciting, of course, and I finished second in calf roping. Back then, however, I celebrated my trophies not by praising the Lord but by drinking with my cowboy buddies. In those days, rodeo was just an excuse to party afterward. Because of alcohol I already had lost a promising opportunity to play professional hockey. Now the same thing was happening with my rodeo career. Soon after those finals my life was out of control, my marriage was going down the drain, and my own children didn't even know me. From being within reach of the top in two professional sports, I had hit bottom. I didn't return to the rodeo finals until six years later, when Jesus had made me a new person and brought my family back together.

Growing up on a reservation near Calgary, Alberta, sports was everything to me—especially hockey. In the long winter months there wasn't much for boys to do except play on the ice. Over the years I rose through the ranks of league competition. During my teen years I played in the local Junior B Hockey League. In those days few natives made it that far, so I seemed only a short step away from the national level. Hockey was my life, and I dreamed of playing professionally. Those dreams were dashed, however, by an innocent ritual that ended up dominating my life.

Once a player reaches the level I had achieved, hockey takes a lot of time and the other players became your main friends. It became a tradition on our teams to end each game with a celebration. My buddies and I usually went "out on the town" partying and drinking. It became such a ritual that whether we won or lost, I would be drinking with my buddies. Before I knew it, I no longer played hockey to win. I was just playing to drink and be part of the "cool" crowd. Hockey was just my excuse.

Without thinking of the responsibilities, I got married and had four children. But I still carried on my carefree lifestyle. Sure, I worked at a store and drove a schoolbus, and looked after my family quite well. Yet I never had any time for them. My evenings were spent practicing hockey, and on the weekends I was off to games or tournaments. I brought home plenty of trophies, but missed out on those precious early years of my children's lives. To make matters worse, I talked myself into believing I was really a good father. Wasn't I providing for them? I was good at sports, never committed a serious crime, and only drank a little to have a good time. Surely that was good enough, and better than most native fathers I knew.

Yet deep down I must have known there was more to life than I was experiencing. Though I was playing hockey and part of the cool crowd, I was not happy. My relationship with my family was strained. Finally one night, after a big victory celebration, I stood up in a drunken stupor and looked around. Here we were, the champs, lying sprawled out across the floor. We looked and acted more like losers trying to forget an anguishing defeat! "This is not for me," I said. "Hockey or no hockey, I don't want any more of this." I stumbled to the door and walked out into the night, never to play hockey again.

Soon, I was into rodeo full-time. My father was a small rancher on our reservation. I had grown up as a cowhand and learned all the tricks in riding and roping. Now I joined the local cowboys' association and traveled throughout central Alberta to compete in rodeo events. I rode bulls for a few years, and placed high in the competitions. But what I really wanted was a championship. So I switched to calf roping and soon became the proud owner of numerous trophies and trophy buckles.

Even though I was busy and doing well in my rodeo career, there was always an empty feeling. In my search to fill that void, I tried Indian religion but still found no peace. Then one night, I saw Jesus in a dream. I was very happy and tried to tell others I saw Him, but they didn't believe me. I'm not claiming this was a vision. But have you ever had a really vivid dream? One that just stays with you? My dream was like that. When I woke up the next morning, I couldn't get the dream out of my mind. That same day I went to Calgary and bought a Bible. Once in a while I would try to read it, and for a few years I stopped drinking as much and concentrated on my rodeoing.

I didn't yet know Jesus Christ as my personal Savior

then, and before long I was back to my old habits. Yet, during those days I made the National Indian Rodeo Finals for the first time. But three years later, after our fifth child was born, everything began to fall apart. At home the children would want my attention, but they could have been a thousand miles away. I would be thinking of my personal glory, my rodeo competitions, my drinking—and my adultery. At that point it looked like my wife and I were heading our separate ways, and our family just couldn't live together anymore.

The pain dragged on for another year. I was still as determined as ever to be a champion, and had made it to the regional finals that would decide who qualified for the national event. During the competition I noticed a poster inviting people to attend a breakfast service sponsored by a Christian cowboy fellowship. The next morning my wife and I decided to attend. Since I was a rodeo celebrity, they asked me to say a few words. What came out of my mouth surprised even me: "In the western world there are athletic heroes. Some of these are Christian athletes. When people get into the wrong crowd and they fly too high, God will clip their wings and they will not fall too hard." Of course, I was really talking about myself!

I don't remember much about the rest of the meeting. But it spoke to me in a powerful way. The way I was going, I would lose my rodeo career and my family the same way I lost hockey years ago. I was like the Prodigal Son in the Bible (Luke 15:11-32) who went away for pleasure and fame, and lost all his inheritance. Like him, I needed to get right with God and get back on the right trail. When the invitation to accept Christ as Savior was given, I went to the front and committed my life to Jesus. I knew my sins were forgiven as His Spirit filled me with peace and contentment.

Because I used to think happiness came from my own efforts, there is a Bible verse that is very special to me. "For by His loving-favor you have been saved from the punishment of sin through faith. It is not by anything you have done. It is a gift of God. It is not given to you because you worked for it. If you could work for it, you would be proud. We are His work. He has made us to belong to Christ Jesus so we can work for Him" (Ephesians 2:8-10).

I returned to the Indian National Rodeo Finals four more times, including the last time with my whole family. Today I still rodeo on weekends, though on Sundays I'm usually at church worshiping the Lord. Rodeo is no longer my God and my competing is not for personal glory. I enjoy it, but my relationship with Jesus comes first and my family second. I do not say that sports and winning will destroy a person. But I know how Satan can control and destroy a person's God-given talent, until that talent is surrendered completely to Christ. With Him, I'm always a winner!

THINGS TO THINK ABOUT
1. Grand Chief Brings Ego to Altar

As for fame and power, the native man in this story had it all. Yet without the Lord he really had nothing. Read Mark 8:34-38. What must you do to follow Jesus? If you cling to your own way, what will be the result?

2. A Rodeo Cowboy's Greatest Thrill

In the excitement of success, it is easy to think God is not important. Even if you are a Christian, prosperity can be the time you become lazy and start drifting away from the Lord. Read Psalm 1:1-6. How does a godly man live, and what are his results? How is a sinful man different?

3. College Eroded My Faith

The "experts" sound so reasonable when they dismiss the claims of Christ. If you want to join the "educated" crowd, prepare to leave your faith at the door. Read Colossians 2:8, then go back and read verses 6-7. What tactics do the "experts" use to plant doubts in your mind about your faith? How can you guard against them?

4. Former Chef Now Feeds Souls

Perhaps you have worked hard and are doing an honest trade. God can certainly use you there. But when His plans are different than yours, which way would you go? Read Luke 5:1-11. What convinced Simon Peter, along with James and John, to follow Jesus? What thought did they give to the careers and families they left behind?

5. Rock Star Disillusioned With Lifestyle

Because the man in this story was once deceived by rock music, he was moved by the Bible verse that calls Jesus the "Holy Rock." That verse comes from an interesting Scripture story. Read 1 Corinthians 10:1-6, then go back and read 9:24-27. According to the passage in chapter 10, why did the people of God go wrong? How should you live instead, when you practice the verses in chapter 9?

6. Businessman Forms Partnership With Christ

Because native people often come from deprived backgrounds, the desire to escape poverty and achieve riches can be very strong. Read Proverbs 23:4-5 and 1 Timothy 6:6-10. What errors can you fall into by making riches your biggest goal? When you do that, why is it really pointless?

7. Hockey and Rodeo Were Empty Gods

Being successful can make you feel like you don't need anybody else. You begin believing you can do anything, even winning God's favor, by your own efforts. Read Luke 15:11-32 and Ephesians 2:8-10. What are the main points of the story of the Prodigal Son in Luke 15? According to Ephesians 2:8-10, what should—and should not—be the purpose of your efforts?

CHAPTER TEN

Conquering Apathy and Indifference

1. A Comfortable Life But No Joy

Key Verse - James 2:14

"My Christian brothers, what good does it do if you say you have faith but do not do things that prove you have faith? Can that kind of faith save you from the punishment of sin?"

This Navajo woman trusted Christ as a child. But her college professors said different people meet their needs in different religions. How could she claim that only her way was right? And when she got a husband, a wonderful child and a good professional job, things were going pretty well without God anyway.

THE WAY THINGS were going, it looked like our marriage would end up on the rocks. And yet when I looked at my life, there was not any one thing that was wrong. I had my education, a good teaching job and a good salary. My husband and I had a good family, a nice home and everything to go with it.

But something was not right. I asked myself, "You have all this. Why aren't you happy?" I had all the right things, but somehow there was something missing.

I was born and raised in Arizona. My parents are from the Navajo reservation, but brought me up in the city. I learned about my culture from the many visits to my grandmother, where I helped with the sheep and other chores. When I was about ten, I attended a Christian summer camp for Indian kids and asked Jesus to be my Savior. I was young but understood the Gospel and made a definite decision to become a Christian. The camp was run by missionaries in our city, and over the next few years they helped me study the Bible and learn to live for Jesus.

But things changed when I got to college. I began having doubts about my faith. All students were required to take a course about world religions and it really shook me up. It seemed there were many educated people who had chosen not to believe in Christ. I decided maybe they were right—every religion met somebody's need, so maybe every religion was okay. Who had the right to say there was only one true religion? That's when I decided that I did not need church or even God anymore.

Of course, I would call myself a Christian if anyone asked. In the back of my mind, I knew the decision I made as a girl was still true. On that day God promised me eternal life, a promise based upon His Word that never changes—no matter how much I might. But now that I had a husband, a delightful baby boy and a good teaching job, things were going pretty well without God. Yet deep down I felt empty. The joy I had years ago, when I was growing in the Lord and having fellowship with His people, was missing from my life.

My husband was also struggling. He was not a Christian, but the things he saw in the world did not satisfy him. He is a Chippewa from Minnesota, but grew up in the Southwest. His father was a teacher and school administrator for the Bureau of Indian Affairs, who eventually settled among the Navajo. When I met my husband he was working rodeos. After we got married and moved to the city, he decided to get a job helping native people. For five years he worked at alcoholism clinics but was discouraged by the lack of results. "There is nothing concrete you can tell a person," he would say, "no straight answers for a guy's problems. In the end, we basically tell people they have to solve it themselves." Finally he got tired of it and quit. He decided next to train horses for the rodeo, but could never find enough work to succeed.

That's where we were, when God brought a special friend into my life. She was also a teacher at my school and a very strong Christian. One day as we drove together to school, she said to me, "How would you like to go look for a church with me? I think you are a Christian. Am I right?" I just kind of looked at her and said yes, but I was groaning inside. Wanting to be friendly, I went with her. The Lord led us to a small independent mission church. The people opened their arms and, after a few Sundays, I knew something had happened. I had found, or rather rediscovered, what was missing in my life. That summer I publicly rededicated my life to the Lord.

I knew God was working on my heart, but I didn't know He was also working on my husband. Business was slow and he spent most days alone in our barn. To pass the time, he turned up his radio and some Christian programs caught his attention. My husband had never heard anything like this, and the messages began to touch his heart. Yet he was afraid people would find out and think he was a religious fanatic. Being "one of the guys" was important to him. His buddies liked to sit around the campgrounds, drink beer and shoot the breeze, and he did not want to lose these friendships.

But still he listened to the radio. God seemed to be asking him, "Is the Bible just a story or is it really My Word?" My husband could not reject the Bible, since it has too many undeniable facts. Once he admitted the Bible is God's Word, he had to deal with Jesus—for the whole Bible is built around Him. One day my husband simply trusted Christ as his Savior. Slowly his faith grew, though he never told me about it! He just kept listening to the radio and reading his Bible.

Then one evening he shared his story with me. I was so excited, it was all I could do to keep from jumping up and down! But my husband doesn't like being fussed over, so I looked calm on the outside and praised God on the inside. He had a real hunger to learn more from the Bible and told me, "I don't think I'll go to church, but I think I'll go to a Bible study." We went to a Bible conference that came to our area, and the people there accepted my husband

and acted like he belonged. He was so pleased with that.

That conference was a turning point for us. For one thing, we saw the need to obey the Lord and be baptized. And for another, my husband learned how the Bible says a man should work and support his family. Right away he started looking and got a good job with a drug treatment center. The program had a spiritual emphasis but was not specifically Christian. So after a year he resigned and, because his mother was sick, we moved to her town to look after her. The very first week a lady invited us to church. We met a man who had a ranch where retarded people can live in a Christian setting. He offered my husband a part-time job, then made him ranch director when the position opened up six weeks later. Today we are still there serving the Lord.

One thing my husband learned is not to be afraid of standing up for Christ. He had worried about losing his friends by seeming "too" religious, but he still has many of those friends and they still visit. One friend was curious about our faith, to see if it would last, and now he and his family have all become Christians too.

I have learned, "What good does it do if you say you have faith but do not do things that prove you have faith? Can that kind of faith save you from the punishment of sin? A faith that does not do things is a dead faith" (James 2:14,17). The faith I put in Jesus as a girl was enough to give me eternal life, for when I made that decision God gave me His promise (Romans 10:9-10). But when I drifted away from God and stopped living for Him, I had to live with the results of my disobedience—an empty life and marriage, despite all the nice things I had. And I became dead, as far as doing anything for God. Only when I turned my life back to the Lord could He use me and bless me. And that blessing has been so very great. God has given me a Christian husband and now we serve Him together. I'm so glad that I came back to God!

2. My Sister's Prayers Changed Me

Key Verse - 2 Corinthians 6:14

"Do not be joined together with those who do not belong to Christ. How can that which is good get along with that which is bad? How can light be in the same place as darkness?"

It began when she was a teenager, drifting away from the Lord and into drinking and parties. She married in haste, not seeking God's direction, and now this native woman had only a broken relationship and a broken life. But when her own way came to an end, that was really the beginning.

VISITING MY SISTER was like touching an electric fence. It did not take much to send a little shock through your system. Everything was "praise the Lord" for this and "praise the Lord" for that! Two years earlier, after drifting away from God, my sister had recommitted her life to Jesus. The change in her life was great. I had never seen her happier.

I longed for that same happiness and peace. Oh

yes, I had heard of Jesus. As a matter of fact, at age twelve I trusted Christ as my Savior and was baptized. I'll never forget how clean I felt that day, knowing my sins were forgiven and I had been born again. Then like my sister, as a teenager I started drifting away from God.

I continued going to Sunday School until the age of fifteen, but I was only there in body. My mind drifted to other places. Slowly I lost interest in the whole thing. Christianity was professed but not really practiced in our home, so it was easy to take the wrong path. Soon it was drinking, smoking and partying almost every weekend.

Life held pretty much the same pattern for the next eighteen years. I grew into a woman, lived on my own, and stayed as far away as ever from the Lord. In my relationships I only wanted to please myself and have a good time. The thought of marrying a Christian man, so that we could serve God together, never entered my head. I never read the Bible so I didn't know the warning, "Do not be joined together with those who do not belong to Christ" (2 Corinthians 6:14). Instead I just married for "love" and didn't care whether my husband was a Christian or not.

Now I was 33, sitting in my sister's home and crying over the mess my life was in. I ran to her because alcohol was causing such misery in my home that I couldn't stay there any longer. My husband continued to drink more than ever. Through these times it seemed that alcohol—the very thing that had led me away from the Lord—was now being used by God to get my attention. Each day was worse than the day before. I was at the point where I never wanted to see, smell or drink alcohol again. Since I didn't know where else to turn, I was ready to turn back to God.

During those days my sister and I prayed together. She would pray for me and pray for my husband, that God would give us both the help we needed. After talking with the Lord in prayer, my burdens always seemed lighter and an inner calmness settled over me. Because of my sister, I was encouraged to attend the native church that was holding services in her home. It was there that I recommitted myself to living completely for Christ. In the months and years that followed, Jesus became my closest Friend, always listening and guiding. And by joining with other Christians who "help each other in troubles and problems" (Galatians 6:2), my brothers and sisters in our native fellowship were a great help with their prayers and concerns in my times of need.

Today I no longer throw up my hands in despair, but start each day with a little prayer that goes like this, "Lord, help me remember that nothing is going to happen today that you and I together can't handle." This prayer makes each day a little easier when anxiety and worry begin to creep in. I rest in the fact that God is in control of everything in my life and "makes all things work together for the good of those who love Him" (Romans 8:28). Like the apostles in the Bible, I want to say, "I have learned to be happy with whatever I have" (Philippians 4:11) and to "be happy when you have all kinds of tests...[because] these build your faith" (James 1:2,3).

The best news is that my husband now sometimes attends our native fellowship meetings. I believe that even if you marry outside of God's will, once you're married it is God's will for you to stay married (1 Corinthians 7:13). My husband has been willing to attend church because I learned to accept him as he is, just as Christ accepted me. I had to discover that I couldn't change him myself. Instead I have turned him over to the Lord daily, and trusted God would make whatever changes are necessary.

As I've realized this, two Bible verses have become very special to me. One verse says, "Wives, obey your own husbands. Some of your husbands may not obey the Word of God. By obeying your husbands, they may become Christians by the life you live without you saying anything. They will see how you love God and how your lives are pure" (1 Peter 3:1-2). The other verse promises the Holy Spirit will do a special work to show my husband his sin, because "the husband who is not a Christian is set apart from the sin of the world because of his Christian wife" (1 Corinthians 7:14).

Today my friends say visiting with me is like visiting with my sister. The tremendous change in my life and attitude sends a thrill rippling through them. I thank Jesus for that change in my life and pray I can continue to be an example to my husband and others.

3. Christmas Was Almost a Disaster

Key Verse - 1 Timothy 6:10

"The love of money is the beginning of all kinds of sin. Some people have turned from the faith because of their love for money. They have made much pain for themselves because of this."

When this native man and his wife accepted Christ, it was the best day of their lives! But things got going "too good" and, over the next two years, God became less important. Money was the answer, even if that meant smuggling bootleg liquor. He struck it rich, but not the way he expected.

IT WAS ONE WEEK before Christmas. As I stepped into the small plane at the edge of our northern Ontario reservation, I could feel my heart beat faster. Everyone was excited about flying out to shop for presents, but my excitement was even greater. In a few hours my friend and I would put our plan into action. If all went well, we would be back in a few days with enough illegal bootleg alcohol to wet the whole village.

I was raised in a Christian home. My parents taught me to go to Sunday School and church, and to love the Lord. But even though I did all these things as a boy, they did not make me a Christian. I had to make my own confession of sin and my own decision to trust Christ as Savior. This did not happen until I was an adult and had been married for a year. One day I woke up around 3:00 a.m. with my heart pounding. I don't know if I was dreaming or not, but I had an overwhelming feeling of being lost, of living in darkness and being condemned to die. I was more frightened than I had ever been in my life! I could not get rid of this feeling, so I went next door to my dad for help. Right there my wife and I accepted Christ.

It was wonderful! Our lives were really changed and, for the next two years, we were very happy. Then my wife and I began drifting away from the Lord. This is called "backsliding," and it was our own choice. Soon we began to have a lot of trouble, until there was only misery in living. During those years I sometimes thought about going back to God, but never did. Though I had eternal life in heaven, Satan was determined that on earth I wouldn't be any good as a Christian.

Then came that fateful Christmas and my plan to smuggle illegal liquor into our village. The plane would take us to Sioux Lookout where my wife would stay, then my friend and I would continue by train to Winnipeg. I had several hundred dollars in my pocket and was supposed to shop in the big city stores for Christmas presents and other things my wife and children needed. Instead my friend and I would use a lot of our money to stock up on liquor. But none of that turned out the way I planned.

While my friend and I waited for the train, we had a couple of beers. Those few beers turned out to be the beginning of several days of solid drinking. The only time I didn't drink was when I was sleeping. Then in the morning I would start all over again. I thought that I was really having fun. Almost all the money I had was spent on drinking. When I finally got back to Sioux Lookout, I was in terrible condition. Somehow I had managed to save some liquor for smuggling back home. But my wife was afraid I would get in trouble and, while I slept in a drunken stupor, she poured all my alcohol down the motel sink. And with it went my plans to smuggle booze.

Two days before Christmas, our plane landed back at the village. I was pretty drunk. Later that night I got very sick. I realized the way I was living was worth nothing. The devil made it look good, but that was just lies. I had come to the end of my own way and was ready to try God's way again. "Some people have turned away from the faith because of their love for money. They have made much pain for themselves because of this" (1 Timothy 6:10). That sure was me!

That night I invited our pastor to come over, and right then I turned my life back to the Lord. My wife and I held hands as we asked forgiveness from God and from each other. Then we prayed together and rededicated ourselves to living for Christ. I'm so glad I meant business with God that night! He took me back, despite everything I had done. I knew right then I was free. Even though I was still sick the rest of the night and throughout the next day, I still had this true happiness inside. I thanked God for changing my plans, for who knows where smuggling might have led me? But because of God, we celebrated Christmas His way instead of mine. And it was the best Christmas we ever had.

4. I Put My Dream On Hold

Key Verse - Jeremiah 29:11

"For I know the plans I have for you, says the Lord, plans for well being and not for trouble, to give you a future and a hope."

Does a person have to give up his friends and his career to live as a Christian? This native teenager didn't know the answer, and just went on as before. When he got that dream job after graduation, his future seemed assured. Then he ran into a friend who had a knack for asking awkward questions.

ON THE DAY I became a Christian, I knew Jesus wanted me to trust Him as my Savior. But as a young person who had not experienced very much, it was hard to understand how I should turn everything over to the Lord. Was I supposed to give up all my friends since they were not Christians like me? So for a year after I received Christ, I continued to party with my friends. After high school I applied and was accepted to the Royal Canadian Mounted Police. That had been my lifelong dream! My training would begin in the fall, and it seemed my life was mapped out with God somewhere in the background.

As long as I can remember, I had wanted to be an RCMP officer. As a small boy I dreamed a lot about being one of these men. I could picture myself in those sharp uniforms and broad-brimmed Stetson hats. What a thrill it would be to join this noble force! Growing up in northern Saskatchewan, the

RCMP officers were very often our contact with those living in the south.

Life in the north was difficult. I was one of ten children, five boys and five girls. Though my father was a tourist guide during the summer, and hunted and trapped during the winter, sometimes there was no food in the morning. When I went to school, many times I had no food to take there either. As we got older, we were able to work and make some money to help our parents. Yet growing up in a large family could also be fun, for we did a lot of things together.

When I was about seven, our family was asked to leave the reservation. My parents had both Indian and European ancestry, so the chief told us we could no longer live on land reserved by treaty only for Indians. We moved into town, and as a teenager I was sent about 450 miles south to attend tenth grade in Prince Albert. To get into the RCMP, I was required to complete this grade. After I did, however, my friends convinced me to stay another two years and finish high school.

During those years I played a lot of sports—football, hockey and track. I also got involved with the wrong crowd. I wasn't a rough guy and never did drugs or got into trouble with the law. But I liked to have a good time! My buddies and I would drink on special occasions. Our sports teams were good and we traveled on the weekends to tournaments around the province. We won a lot of games and afterward we'd always go and have a drinking party.

One of my friends was going out with a Christian girl, and one day she introduced me to a girlfriend of hers who was also a Christian. This other girl asked what school activities I did and so I told her about all my sports. Then she asked me something I did not expect. "How would you like to come to our Bible study?" At first I was not sure about getting together with others to study the Bible. "I mean, what dude spends his time studying the Bible?" I told myself. But wanting to be friendly, I said that I would go.

After I had gone to the Bible study for about four weeks, this girl asked me another surprising question. She invited me to a teen retreat weekend being held at a native Bible school. Since the Bible studies weren't so bad, I agreed to come. At the conference I heard how Jesus loved me, how He gave His life so I could receive forgiveness of sins and eternal life. All my life I had never heard such news. The Lord began working in my heart, showing me how my pride and my lifestyle were wrong.

Just before we left the conference, the girl who invited me asked still another surprising question. Would I give my life to Jesus and then come attend the Bible school? At that point I didn't know what God might have ahead. After all, I wasn't even a believer yet! So I told her, "Bible school? Naw, I'll never go to Bible school. I'm going to join the RCMP." Yet back in Prince Albert, I kept going to the weekly Bible studies and my friend kept talking to me about Jesus. Before long I realized that I really did need Christ, and at last I trusted Him to be my Savior.

That was the greatest day of my life! But though I understood God wanted me to live for Him, I wasn't sure how. It was hard to give Him complete control, when I was full of youthful pride and confidence in my own future. So for another year, despite good intentions, there wasn't much change in my lifestyle. During the summer after my graduation from high school, however, the Lord began to show me I was living a two-faced life. Little did I know that it would come down, literally, to making a choice.

Once again my friend asked if I was thinking about going to the native Bible school. I had already been accepted by the RCMP, but told her I would pray about the matter. The rest of the summer I prayed, and it seemed two voices were trying to get my attention. Once voice said, "If you go into the RCMP then you'll have all the money you need and a vehicle besides." But God's voice told me, "For I know the plans I have for you, plans for well-being and not for trouble, to give you a future and a hope" (Jeremiah 29:11).

The last week of August, I finally said yes to the Lord. I sent in my application to the Bible school, and also wrote the RCMP to tell them what I was doing. I was afraid when they got my letter, the RCMP officials would simply trash my file. But they wrote back and said, "Whenever you're ready to join, we'll be glad to have you." Shortly afterward I found out the Bible school had accepted me as a student. I knew this was the right decision, because God was putting a tremendous excitement in my heart about going to learn more of the Bible.

I arrived at Bible school not knowing how to pay for my courses. I had only $40 in my pocket. The first thing I did was go to my dorm, put down my stuff, then kneel beside my bed and pray. "Lord, if this is where you want me, then I'm not going to worry about anything. I'm not going to worry about the money to pay for my schooling. I know you can do it." And God did. People sent in money for me, and by the end of my first year I even had $500 toward tuition for the next year! What's ahead? After Bible school I plan to enlist in the RCMP. I do not think it is wrong to make plans because God wants Christians to be wise. But the difference today is that my plans are in His hands. I live for Christ today and let Him take care of tomorrow.

5. A Boring Roller-Coaster Ride
Key Verse - John 10:10

"The robber comes only to steal and to kill and to destroy. I came so they might have life, a great full life."

Church became a routine, and Christian fellowship boring. Since she was going to heaven anyway, why not have some fun? Besides, this Navajo woman wasn't going to marry some nerdy Christian man, or serve God in some foreign country. But boarding school could be lonely, and she needed Someone to lean upon.

I AM A NAVAJO, born among the Chippewa of Minnesota, who grew up among the Sioux of South Dakota. You see, my dad was a native pastor who worked among various Indian tribes ever since I was born. Wherever the Lord called him to pastor a church, the family would follow. I was very close to my parents, but many things about our reservation bothered me. I was especially frightened of the night, when I would hear drums beating and voices singing in the dark. I sensed evil forces and would run to my parents' bedroom, where we prayed together for the Lord's protection upon me.

It seemed like people were passing away so often. When I was five, I went to a little girl's wake. Night after night, her loved ones would gather and weep. Was there no comfort for them? Like them, I was filled with a sense of hopelessness. So I asked mom and dad where the little girl was now. Dad drew me close and told me about two places. "Many choose to follow Satan and, when they die, they follow him to a place of hopelessness called hell. But Jesus is preparing a place in heaven for His children who belong to Him. To be His child, you need to be sorry for the wrong things you have done and ask Jesus to forgive you. Then you can ask Jesus to be the King [take control] of your life, and tell Jesus you want to follow Him always." That day I trusted Jesus as my personal Savior. Dad told me I was guaranteed eternal life with Christ, and He "will never leave you or let you be alone" (Hebrews 13:5). Jesus would always be my Best Friend.

In my early teenage years, our family moved again. I started drifting away from Jesus and compromising my standards as a Christian. Church became a routine, and fellowship with other believers meant little to me. I thought it would be boring to live the rest of my life this way. After all, I was saved and didn't have to worry about going to hell. That was good enough for me! Since I was guaranteed a place in heaven anyway, why not have a little fun on earth?

I just didn't want to get too involved with God. He had probably picked out some short little bald-headed man with horn-rimmed glasses for me to marry. And what if He asked me to be a missionary in some foreign country? Forget it! No way! I tried to convince myself I was happy just knowing Jesus but not being too involved with Him. Yet deep down I had to admit I was not happy, that I was too proud to give Christ full control of my life, and I was not where God wanted me to be as a Christian.

Then my father was called back to Arizona to serve the Lord among the Navajo people. I really fought moving down there and leaving all my friends behind. It was really different in Arizona. We lived in a remote part of the reservation. That was hard enough for mom and us kids. But when I had to attend boarding school far from home, that was too much. I really struggled, for I no longer had mom and dad around to lean on. I was always trying to get home at every opportunity, but my parents encouraged me instead to look to the Lord for help. I began to think about my spiritual life, and about giving my needs to God.

I tried again to live for the Lord, but my life just seemed like one long roller-coaster ride. One day I would be happy, and the next day I would be overwhelmed with problems. Then I began to understand that Jesus not only offers salvation, but that He "came so they might have life, a great full life"

(John 10:10). Life with Jesus is not meant to be boring at all! I began taking my problems to God and soon was seeing answers to my prayers. Of course, I had to learn that sometimes God's answer is "no" or "wait." But when I finally decided to surrender my life and future completely to God, then I stepped off that roller-coaster for good.

6. Childhood Faith Goes Deeper

Key Verse - Psalm 121:1-5

"...My help comes from the Lord, who made heaven and earth..."

After going to church every Sunday, the Word of God became just a cliche in her ears. She and her mother were the only Christians on the Algonquin reservation, so she never knew any other young native believers to encourage her. The young people she did meet kept asking why she denied her heritage.

I TRUSTED CHRIST when I was eight years old, during a children's meeting at our church in Quebec. At the time I truly understood I was a sinner who needed Jesus as my Savior. But the devil was not done with me! He sent doubts by the dozens, especially in my teenage years. The phrase "Jesus Saves" became a cliche to me. It was taught to me in church, in Sunday School, in Vacation Bible School, until I became immune to the Word of God. I would sit with my ears turned off and my thoughts miles away from what was being spoken.

Although my father was not a Christian, my mother loved the Lord and tried to teach me about Jesus. We attended an Anglo-French church in town since there were no other Christians on our Algonquin reservation. I grew up without ever meeting other native Christian young people like myself, who could encourage me to keep on living for Jesus. In fact, the native young people I did meet asked why I denied my Indian heritage by believing a white man's religion.

When I was old enough, I got a job in Ontario about five hundred miles from home. The place was a small northern town on James Bay and I did not find any other Christians. A year later I was sent to a larger town and there met some young people who believed as I did. But soon after arriving, I also met some young people who spoke to me about their beliefs in the old native religion. They sounded very convincing when they said I was denying my Indian heritage. Not knowing the Bible well enough, I had no Christian answer to give them. I began to have doubts and be swayed. "What's the real reason," I asked myself, "why I believe in a white man's religion when I myself am an Indian?"

And after all, why should I? I had my whole life planned out according to what I wanted. I thought that I was living a pretty good life since I did not drink or smoke or do drugs. But even though I had not been speaking much to God, He is faithful and kept on speaking to me. Inside my heart, I knew He wanted me—and not just part of me, but a total commitment. Several times over my teenage years I had rededicated my life to the Lord and tried to follow Him, not realizing He didn't want me to just "try." God wanted me to completely give myself up and let Him help me to live a true Christian life.

For about a week after those young people said I was denying my native heritage, a terrific war raged in my heart. It was worse than a war fought with bows and arrows and rifles. But since I have always liked the plain truth in everything, I prayed and asked God to show me the answers. The Lord stepped in and showed me that, even though I was not committing open sins, no life is good enough unless Christ is at the head of it. Once I thought "Jesus Saves" was a cliche, but now I reaffirmed my belief in Him once and for all. When I did that, the "peace of God [that] is much greater than the human mind can understand" (Philippians 4:7) returned to my heart.

After this struggle, I realized that I needed to know more of God's Word. Whether I was asking the questions, or other people were asking me about Jesus, I needed to be ready with answers. The Lord has led me to attend a Bible college, but at least I have learned the most basic lesson—my future is in God's hand and He will direct me. "Where will my help come from? My help comes from the Lord, Who made heaven and earth. He will not let your feet go out from under you...[for] the Lord watches over you" (Psalm 121:1-5).

7. Doubting Heart Flooded With Peace

Key Verse - Matthew 7:21-23

"...The one who does the things My Father in heaven wants him to do will go into the holy nation of heaven..."

Because of a broken home, she found a sense of "family" by attending church youth activities. Over the years, the Christian crowd became her crowd, the people she identified with. This Cayuga woman knew all the right Christian talk and even worked in the ministry. But had she ever really trusted Jesus?

IT'S A HARD THING to want to be a Christian and live like a Christian, and still not be sure you are one. I went through girls' Bible clubs, teen church groups, and after graduation I went to work for a Christian ministry. But through all of it, because of my pride, I never faced the question of whether I had truly trusted Christ and was born again. "I must be a Christian," I kept telling myself, "since I live a good life, and tell others about Jesus and go to church." Yet even though I argued, I was not sure— and my pride held me back from telling anyone about my spiritual struggle.

I am a Cayuga Indian from southern Ontario, though I grew up in New York State near the Tuscarora reservation. Raised in a broken home, I felt left out and did not have much motivation for anything—especially school. As a result I failed one grade and barely passed two others. When I was in fourth grade, one of my Indian girlfriends invited me to her Bible club. There I heard the Gospel of Christ for the first time. I was really impressed that God loved me so much that He sent His Son Jesus to die on the cross and then raised him to life again to take away my sins.

After a year of attending Bible club and Sunday School, I went to the altar with my other Indian friends to accept the Lord. But I was not really serious about my decision. Perhaps I just went forward because my friends were doing it. Because of my family situation, the Bible club and Sunday School had become a kind of "home" where I could belong. Here was a group I could identify with. So through my school years I hung around with the Christian crowd, doing what they did so I could fit in and be accepted.

Just before I graduated from high school, my guidance counselor advised me not to go to college. Looking at my school record, he said I probably could not finish. I took his advice and looked for a job. Since I wanted to stay in a comfortable Christian crowd, I applied for secretarial work with several Christian ministries. Soon after graduation I was hired by a large ministry organization in Nebraska, partly because I told them (though I was not sure myself) I was a Christian. For the next year I worked in the office, all the time wearing a good Christian face and using the right Christian talk. My organization was involved in ministry all over the world, and I wanted to be accepted.

My pride kept me from looking inside myself. I

thought Christian workers weren't supposed to have doubts! Then after a year at the ministry, I went to Chicago for a conference that taught life principles from the Bible. By the time it was over, the Holy Spirit was dealing with my heart about whether I had ever really accepted Christ. Perhaps that trip was what I needed, a chance to do some honest thinking away from my usual environment. At home I was always surrounded by people who knew me and expected to see the Christian I claimed to be. But now the Holy Spirit had started me thinking.

About a year later I left Nebraska and went to live in Chicago. Despite the change of scenery, the Holy Spirit had not let go of me. At last I put aside my pride and went to see my youth pastor. "I am not sure if I am a Christian or not," I told him. "I asked Jesus to come into my life when I was eleven, but I have no assurance I am saved." He suggested we pray right then and settle the matter. So I did, and what a peace and joy I felt! At last I knew for sure that I had trusted Jesus Christ as my Savior and He had accepted me as His child. The doubts were completely gone.

After we prayed, the two of us went to the college-age prayer meeting held each week at our church. Then I gave my very first testimony for the Lord. And I discovered that all my pride, which had kept me from dealing with my doubts sooner, was really for nothing! Of course, the other young people were surprised to learn I had just been saved, since they too thought I was a Christian. But their outpouring of love was tremendous, because they were rejoicing right along with me.

Some months later I enrolled at a Bible school in Chicago, where I majored in home missions. That summer I even had the chance to work with an Indian mission. When I came back to school for my second year, that fall semester we had a missionary conference on campus. On the last night of the conference, I felt God calling me to go and serve Him among my own people. Then the speaker invited students to stand up and make their commitments public. But my pride was stubborn, and I would not go forward and say I was willing to be a missionary.

Later that night, when I was back in my room, the Holy Spirit kept prompting me to make a decision. Would I accept God's call to missions or not? Finally, laying awake in bed, I told the Lord I was willing to serve Him in Indian missions. And God took me at my word. After graduation I was accepted by a native missionary fellowship in Canada, working at first on my home reservation in Ontario and then later in the area of Indian gospel literature. As I look back over my life, I am glad for God's Holy Spirit. If He had not kept speaking to me, I might still be wondering if I was really accepted by God.

Today because of Him, I can share the Gospel with my people. Since I found the answer, I know they can too. I feel a great urgency in this task. For I am afraid that on the final day of judgment some of my people will stand before Jesus and, as I once did, expect their good works to be enough. But Jesus says, "Not everyone who says to Me, `Lord, Lord,' will go into the holy nation of heaven...Many people will say to Me on that day, `Lord, Lord, did we not preach in Your Name?'... Then I will say to them in plain words, `I never knew you. Go away from Me'" (Matthew 7:21-23). I had to settle the issue of either trusting or rejecting Jesus as my Savior, and so must you.

THINGS TO THINK ABOUT

1. A Comfortable Life But No Joy

The native woman in this story said, "When I drifted away from God and stopped living for Him, I had to live with the results of my disobedience—an empty life and marriage, despite all the nice things I had. And I became dead, as far as doing anything for God. Only when I turned my life back to the Lord could He use me and bless me." Read James 2:14-19. Do you perform good works to "be" saved, or because you "are" saved? Why?

2. My Sister's Prayers Changed Me

This story teaches good principles for coping with a strained marriage and an unbelieving spouse (see the explanations for 1 Peter 3:1-2 and 1 Corinthians 7:13-14). But apathy toward God often starts when you join yourself to those who reject Jesus. Read 2 Corinthians 6:14-18. By what standard should you, as a Christian, evaluate your relationships? What should you do in a wrong relationship? When you join the wrong crowd, how does that affect your Christian life?

3. Christmas Was Almost a Disaster

When things are going good, don't you always want a little bit more? Read 1 Timothy 6:9-10, then go back and read verses 6-8. According to verses 9-10, at least five things happen to people who put money ahead of everything. What are they? And what is the remedy suggested in verses 6-8?

4. I Placed My Dream on Hold

After giving everything else to God, perhaps the thing that gives you trouble is giving Him your career. That is hard, because the future includes your own hopes and dreams. Read Jeremiah 29:11-13. Why can you trust God and His plans? What are the benefits of following His plan and drawing closer to Him?

5. A Boring Roller-Coaster Ride

Are you reluctant to be active for God because it may seem to involve sacrifice? The native woman in this story was afraid God might force her to marry a "nerdy" man or go to a foreign country. Read John 10:1-15. Why is Jesus alone able to offer you a "great full life"? Why is it wrong to be afraid of Him?

6. Childhood Faith Goes Deeper

What happens when you have no Christian friends? If you are alone, with nobody to give you encouragement, you may become afraid to take a stand for God. Read Psalm 121:1-8. Because of the way native people live, perhaps you may have difficulty finding other native Christians who can be your friends. In what specific ways can God be the help you need? Why is God able to make this promise?

7. Doubting Heart Flooded With Peace

The woman in this story shows you can go along with a religious crowd, but cannot serve God until you personally decide to trust Jesus as Savior. Read Matthew 7:21-23. If you practice native religion, what does verse 22 say to you? Will such claims be enough to gain heaven? In "doing the things God wants" (verse 21), doesn't that begin with trusting Jesus? If you reject Christ, does anything else you do matter to God?

WHAT GOD'S WORD SAYS

You can have the blessings of the Gospel if you are willing to:

REPENT: Be sorry for the wrong things you have done...sorry enough to quit them. "God did not remember these times when people did not know better. But now He tells all men everywhere to be sorry for their sins and to turn from them." Acts 17:30

CONFESS: Tell GOD that you have sinned. "If you say with your mouth that Jesus is Lord, and believe in your heart that God raised Him from the dead, you will be saved from the punishment of sin." Romans 10:9

BELIEVE: that Jesus died for you. "Put your trust in the Lord Jesus Christ and you ... will be saved from the punishment of sin." Acts 16:31

ASK: God to forgive you. "If we tell Him our sins, He is faithful and we can depend on Him to forgive us our sins. He will make our lives clean from all sin." 1 John 1:9

RECEIVE: Jesus as your Saviour. "He gave the right and the power to become children of God, to those who receive Him... to those who put their trust in His Name." John 1:12.

A PRAYER OF INVITATION

If you feel that God is speaking to you and you would like to respond to what you have just read about believing in Jesus and receiving Him into your heart, please pray the following prayer or say in your own words what is said below:

"Dear Jesus, I realize I am a sinner. I long for peace in my heart. I believe you are the Holy Son of God, that you came down and died on the cross for my sins. Thank You for doing this for me. I am sorry for my sins. Please forgive me. With Your help, I will turn my back on them. By faith, I receive You into my life as my personal Saviour and

Lord. From now on, I want to please You."

If you have followed these steps and asked Christ to take control of your life, get a copy of God's Word, the Bible, and begin reading it. Also start talking to God in prayer. Go to church regularly. Choose a church where God' message of salvatiion is taught.

TO THE READER

If you have prayed this prayer, the publishers of The Conquering Indian would like to hear from you. Please write your name on the coupon below, or if you don't want to cut up this book, just write on another sheet of paper, and mail it to:

Indian Life Books

P.O. Box 3765, RPO Redwood Centre

Winnipeg, MB Canada R2W 3R6

• •

_____ I prayed the prayer suggested in The Conquering Indian, and now I would like more information live as a Christian.

_____ Please send me some free literature on how to live as a Christian.

_____ Please write to me and tell me the name of someone who can give me personal help.

My name is _____

Address _____

Town _____

Prov/State _____ Postal/Zip_____

EMMAUS CORRESPONDENCE SCHOOL

If you would like to begin studying the Bible, Emmaus Correspondence School is offering a twelve lesson correspondence course entitled BORN TO WIN to those who are currently in prison. This course is specifically designed for prisoners.

Write to: Born to Win, Indian Life Ministries
PO Box 3765 RPO Redwood Centre
Winnipeg MB R2W 3R6 Canada

My name is _____

Address _____

Town _____

Prov/State _____ Postal/Zip_____

_ _ _ _ _ _ _ _ _ _ _ _ _ _ _ _ _ _ _ _

FREE BIBLE OFFER
For Those in Prison

Indian Life Ministries and Mr. Ray Gowan would like to send you a free Bible if you are currently in prison and are interested in what God's Word has to say to you. To receive your free Bible, write to:

Mr. Ray Gowan, c/o Indian Life Ministries
PO Box 3765 RPO Redwood Centre
Winnipeg MB R2W 3R6

My name is _____

Address _____

Town _____

Prov/State _____ Postal/Zip_____

From the publishers of
The Conquering Indian...

More Good Reading

The Grieving Indian
by Arthur H. with George McPeek

This Canadian best seller is full of real-life stories about hurting people. Like The Conquering Indian, it is also a book of encouragement, help and inspiration. Something every Indian should read. A must for everyone who works with Native people. Mass paperback. 128 pages.$4.95 each, plus GST (in Canada) and postage.

Indian Life Magazine

Indian Life Magazine is North America's largest circulation Native publication. In its colorful pages you will find positive news of Indian people and events, first-person stories, photo features, family life articles, and much more. Published six times a year. Write for a free sample copy. Find out why over 100,000 people read this paper. A one-year subscription is only $7.00 (plus GST in Canada). Quantity prices are available.